SOVEREIGN SCREENS

SOVEREIGN
SCREENS

ABORIGINAL MEDIA on the
CANADIAN WEST COAST

KRISTIN L. DOWELL

University of Nebraska Press | Lincoln and London

This book was made possible by the
generous support of a publication
subvention grant from the Office of
the Vice President for Research, Office
of the Provost, the Dean's Office of
the College of Arts and Sciences, and
the Department of Anthropology
at the University of Oklahoma.

Library of Congress
Cataloging-in-Publication Data
Dowell, Kristin L.
Sovereign screens: aboriginal
media on the Canadian West
Coast / Kristin L. Dowell.
pages cm
Includes bibliographical
references and index.
ISBN 978-0-8032-4538-9 (cloth:
alk. paper)
ISBN 978-0-8032-9696-1 (paper:
alk. paper)
1. Visual anthropology—British
Columbia—Vancouver.
2. Motion pictures in ethnology—
British Columbia—Vancouver.
3. Indigenous films—British
Columbia—Vancouver. 4. Motion
picture producers and directors—
British Columbia—Vancouver.
5. Indigenous peoples in motion
pictures. 6. Indigenous peoples—
British Columbia—Vancouver.
7. Vancouver (B.C.)—Social
life and customs. 8. Canada—
Cultural policy. I. Title.
GN347.D69 2013
301.0971133—dc23   2013022151

For Vancouver's Aboriginal filmmakers who so generously shared their time, creativity, and spirit with me on this project.

And for my family, for everything.

Contents

Illustrations

Preface

One bright spring morning, I sit with Cleo Reece (Cree), filmmaker, activist, mother, grandmother, and Indigenous Media Arts Group (IMAG) founding member, sharing coffee at the bakery around the corner from the IMAG office. Our conversation meanders from talking about her filmmaking career to her long involvement in Aboriginal[1] activism to the latest update on her grandchildren. The IMAGENAtion Aboriginal Film and Video Festival finished a few weeks ago, and our conversation turns to the festival.

"How did you come up with the name IMAGENation for the festival?" I ask, remarking, "That's a very powerful name."

Cleo responds, "Well, we wanted to do something about our image. So we came up with 'Image Nation' because we call ourselves nations rather than tribes. The image is what's important because that's what video is."

Cleo leans in close, our hands on our coffee mugs almost touching in the cramped space at the small table. Softly, but forcefully, she declares, "That's what we're trying to portray, our own image in our own way rather than somebody else's take on us. We're doing it ourselves! We're producing our own images. And *nation* is a strong word, and we're made up of nations. So why not an image nation?"

The emphasis that Cleo Reece placed on the capacity of Aboriginal media to express self-determination illustrates the central concept of this book—Aboriginal visual sovereignty.[2] As an ethnographer I was profoundly struck by this idea of an "image nation," and throughout my fieldwork I was interested in the ways in which a discourse of "reclaiming the screen" (Ginsburg 2002) was a significant aspect of the narratives of the Aboriginal filmmakers, artists, and activists with whom I worked in Vancouver.[3] *Sovereign Screens* explores the idea of Aboriginal visual sovereignty by examining the role of media production in shaping community practices and cultural identity among intertribal, urban Aboriginal filmmakers in Vancouver, Coast Salish territory, British Columbia. I use the frame of Aboriginal visual sovereignty to address the ways in which Aboriginal media makers seek to "decolonize the screen" (Columpar 2010; Singer 2001; Raheja 2011) as I analyze aspects of on-screen Aboriginal media aesthetics. However, as an anthropologist of media I focus on the off-screen, behind-the-scenes, social processes of Aboriginal media production. In this book I argue that Aboriginal media production simultaneously alters the visual landscape of Canadian media by representing Aboriginal stories on-screen and serves as a vital off-screen practice through which new forms of Aboriginal sociality and community are created and negotiated. In other words Aboriginal media are more than merely expressive of Aboriginal narratives and cultural traditions; they are also constitutive of Aboriginal social relationships.

Canada has been at the forefront of the global indigenous media movement through its pioneering legacy of state support for indigenous media production for over forty years. From the 1969 Challenge for Change Program of the National Film Board of Canada (NFB) to the 1999 launch of the groundbreaking Aboriginal Peoples Television Network (APTN), the Canadian government, in response to pressure from Aboriginal activists, has offered support for Aboriginal filmmakers through institutional funds, training programs, and access to media resources. This longevity of state support has helped to sustain a vibrant, diverse, and multigenerational group of Aboriginal filmmakers.

Vancouver is home to an Aboriginal media world that has made numerous contributions to the field of Aboriginal media production in Canada and to the global indigenous media movement. Vancouver is an incredibly productive center for the production, distribution, and circulation of Aboriginal media. There are dozens of individuals working in various capacities in the media industry, several Aboriginal-owned production companies, Canada's premier Aboriginal media training program (Capilano University Indigenous Independent Digital Filmmaking Program), an APTN production office, several APTN television shows in production each season, a National Film Board of Canada office, and artist-run centers (grunt gallery, Video In/ Video Out [VIVO], and the Western Front)—all contributing to a vibrant Aboriginal media world.

As a visual anthropologist I have had the privilege to work in this dynamic, cutting-edge media world where Aboriginal media makers create innovative media works ranging from documentaries and community media to television shows and feature films to experimental video and new media. These media makers interrogate colonial histories, articulate Aboriginal narratives, and reclaim the screen for purposes of cultural documentation, language preservation, and inventive digital storytelling. Through the stories and voices of the Vancouver filmmakers with whom I have worked, I aim to give the reader an on-the-ground ethnographic sense of the challenges and accomplishments of these filmmakers who actively invest media technology with Aboriginal cultural protocols, stories, and aesthetics, creating new cinematic visions in the process.

Researching Aboriginal Media in Vancouver

I became interested in Vancouver's Aboriginal media world after working as an intern in the Smithsonian's National Museum of the American Indian Film and Video Center while a graduate student in 2000.[4] As an intern I assisted with the cataloguing of videotape festival submissions for the 2000 Native American Film and Video Festival. While viewing these submissions, I noticed that there were a large number from Canada, a significant portion of which were submitted from Vancouver in a wide range of genres. Filmmakers in Vancouver were not just making documentaries but appeared just as likely to be creating experimental video, feature films, and short narrative films. I was intrigued by the creative output of Aboriginal filmmakers in Vancouver, and I was curious about how Vancouver became a center for Aboriginal media in Canada.

After several short "pre-fieldwork" visits to Vancouver in 2002, I learned that Vancouver was home to IMAGeNation—an annual Aboriginal Film and Video Festival—three Aboriginal media training programs, a National Film Board of Canada office, art galleries exhibiting contemporary Aboriginal art, and a nonprofit Aboriginal media resource center named the Indigenous Media Arts Group. There is an infrastructure in place for the production, exhibition, distribution, and reception of Aboriginal media in Vancouver. IMAG was a key site in this infrastructure, and it was at IMAG where I found a home base in Vancouver as a volunteer while getting to know many people in Vancouver's Aboriginal media world.

During thirteen months of fieldwork between August 2003 and September 2004, I conducted research primarily at the Indigenous Media Arts Group, the Museum of Anthropology (MOA) at the University of British Columbia (UBC), and the National Film Board of Canada. I worked most closely with IMAG and spent most days during the week hanging out at the IMAG office helping out in any way that I could. I lived in the Mount Pleasant neighborhood, a residential neighborhood with a sizeable percentage of Aboriginal artists and filmmakers as well as being home to many artist-run centers, including IMAG, the grunt gallery, and the Western Front. While working as a volunteer at IMAG, I organized their video library into a computer database, assisted students with editing their videos, made VHS dubs of videos for filmmakers to submit to film festivals, helped to organize fundraising events, assisted with publicity for IMAG screenings, and attended IMAG staff meetings.[5] During the 2004 IMAGeNation Aboriginal Film and Video Festival hosted by IMAG, I served on the programming committee and helped in the organization of the film festival as well as doing numerous behind-the-scenes tasks to keep the festival running smoothly.[6] My deep engagement with the activities of the IMAG office provides the material for chapter 1, which conveys an ethnographic portrait of daily life in this lively grassroots media organization.

Having access to the daily office activities at IMAG was invaluable because I learned firsthand the ways in which it served as a community center and a focal point for Aboriginal filmmakers in Vancouver. Numerous filmmakers, artists, and community members stopped by the IMAG office, and it was during countless hours of participant-observation through "hanging out" at IMAG that I came to know key members of Vancouver's Aboriginal media world. My relationships with filmmakers established through IMAG, particularly those with the film festival staff, became strong friendships, and I spent many hours with filmmakers in their homes sharing meals, helping to care for their children, attending family nights at the Friendship Centre, attending art openings at the grunt gallery, and sharing many conversations over endless cups of coffee. These friendships enabled me to see the ways in which the networks mobilized for media production were deeply embedded in the social fabric of the Aboriginal community in Vancouver, as explored in depth in chapter 4. In attending Aboriginal hip-hop events, activist gatherings, Redwire Native Youth Media events, powwows, poetry readings, Aboriginal performance art events, art exhibits, and music performances, I was able to see the ways in which Aboriginal media production is connected to a distinctive world of Aboriginal cultural and artistic production in Vancouver, as discussed extensively in chapters 5 and 6.

In addition to participant observation carried out in the IMAG office and at numerous sites of Aboriginal media production and exhibition in Vancouver, I have conducted in-depth audio-recorded interviews with Aboriginal filmmakers from a range of generations, tribal backgrounds, and levels of experience in the media industry.[7] I saw at least three generations of Aboriginal filmmakers working in Vancouver. I returned twice to Vancouver in 2005 and conducted additional interviews during my summer 2009 fieldwork stint: some of these were follow-up interviews, and several were interviews with new participants to my project. These interviews form the basis of chapter 3, which examines the impact of APTN and the representation of Aboriginal diversity on-screen within Aboriginal media.

During fieldwork I also conducted archival research at the National Film Board of Canada's headquarters in Montreal. This archival research provided much of the data for chapter 2 about Canadian cultural policy and NFB initiatives supporting Aboriginal filmmakers throughout the last forty years. Additionally, I had access to the archives at the grunt gallery, where I obtained documentation about every Aboriginal art exhibit and performance art event curated at the grunt gallery since it changed its mandate to include contemporary First Nations art in the early 1990s. The archival material from the NFB and grunt gallery along with filmmaker interviews, participation in screenings, oral histories with "older generation" filmmakers, and documentation of local Aboriginal community events provided a framework for understanding the emergence of Vancouver as a center for Aboriginal media production as well as the ways in which this world is embedded in the urban Aboriginal community and larger arts world in Vancouver.

IMAG officially disbanded in 2007 and now no longer exists as an active organization. However, that does not diminish its legacy or the tremendous impact it made while it was active in Vancouver. While in operation IMAG screened over 450 Aboriginal and international indigenous films and videos at eight IMAGeNation Aboriginal Film and Video Festivals. IMAG trained dozens of Aboriginal youth and adults in their beginning and advanced media training programs and hosted numerous workshops on Aboriginal media. They honored key figures in Canadian Aboriginal media industry, including Alanis Obomsawin (Abenaki), Shirley Cheechoo (Cree), Loretta Todd (Cree/ Métis), and Dana Claxton (Hunkpapa Lakota),[8] and offered video equipment and editing facilities for local Aboriginal filmmakers while participating in activist events and collaborating on Aboriginal art exhibits with various artist-run centers. There is no doubt that IMAG and its dedicated board members, staff, and volunteers made a lasting difference in raising visibility for Aboriginal media in Vancouver.

This book is, in part, an homage to the significant impact a grassroots community media organization such as IMAG can have on Aboriginal media production and on the cultural and community needs of Vancouver's urban Aboriginal community. As an anthropologist I found it disconcerting to see a key organization with which I have worked dissolve. After all, despite the postmodern turn in anthropology and the deconstruction of the culture concept whereby anthropologists have rejected the notion of culture as static, timeless, and bounded in a turn toward highlighting change, hetereogeneity, tension, and disagreement (Abu-Lughod 1991), change can still be unsettling, both for the anthropologist and for the people with whom anthropologists work. But the reality is that cultures do change, people move on, and organizations disband for a whole host of reasons. Change and flux are particularly characteristic of grassroots indigenous media and arts organizations where there are limited resources, unstable funding and a heavy reliance on a few key individuals who put in long hours often with little compensation and with the risk of burnout. The dissolution of IMAG should not be seen as a failure, but instead as an indicator of the shorter lifespan of some arts organizations that nonetheless make a significant impact while in existence.[9] That IMAG no longer exists does not mean that Aboriginal media production has ceased in Vancouver. On the contrary, as discussed in the epilogue, there are new and inventive ways in which Aboriginal filmmakers continue to make media on the Canadian West Coast.

Acknowledgments

This book has been many years in the making and represents the culmination of a long journey to get here. There are many people to thank. I extend my deepest gratitude to all the film-makers with whom I worked in Vancouver. It is a tremendous honor for me to be able to work within Vancouver's Aboriginal media world. I thank you all for your encouragement and friend-ship throughout the research process. Your dedication to telling Aboriginal stories and commitment to using this technology to build community remain an inspiration.

I extend a special thank you to those filmmakers who became like family to me as they generously welcomed me into their homes and lives. For wonderful conversation over countless dinners, trips to Granville Island, and sipping cups of tea late into the night, I thank Vera Wabegijig and her daughters Storm Standing on the Road and Grace Wabegijig, whose strength, cre-ativity, humor, and kindness continue to be a blessing in my life. I thank Leena Minifie for her generosity of spirit and friendship, Odessa Shuquaya and her daughter Nakiah Shuquaya for their friendship, support, and encouragement. I thank Cleo Reece and her family, especially her daughter Skeena, for welcoming me into their home, where I shared in delicious home-cooked meals and learned many new words while being defeated many times in our Scrabble games! I am deeply grateful to Loretta Todd, without whom this research simply would not have been possible. I thank the IMAG Board of Directors, which, at the time I did fieldwork, included Dana Claxton, Dorothy Christian, Zoe Hopkins, Cleo Reece, and Jackson Crick, for their permission and support to do research with IMAG. A special thank-you to Kevin Lee Burton and Helen Haig-Brown, who generously shared with me copies of their films and gave permission for me to screen these films in presentations and classroom settings.

I thank the Indigenous Media Arts Group, the Museum of Anthropology, and the National Film Board of Canada, which provided letters of support for this research project and served as institutional hosts. I thank Jennifer Kramer, Michael Ames, and Jill Baird for hosting me as a Fulbright Scholar with a research affiliation at the Museum of Anthropology. I thank Bernard Lutz, archivist at the National Film Board of Canada (NFB) for his help with my archival research at the NFB. I also thank George Johnson, formerly with the NFB's Pacific Centre in Vancouver, who provided letters of support for my research project. Thank you to Glenn Alteen, Daina Warren, and Aiyyana Maracle at the grunt gallery for providing access to the gallery's archives and for sharing their wealth of knowledge about the role of contemporary First Nations art in Vancouver's artist-run centers. I also thank Video Out Distributors for making videotapes available for my research and to Wanda Vanderstoop at Vtape for her support in providing access to DVDs of several films featured in this book and for her assistance with film stills for the book. I also thank Ragnhild Milewski for his assistance with film stills from the NFB films included in this book.

This research began while I was a graduate student at New York University, and I must offer my deepest thanks to my primary advisers Faye Ginsburg, Karen Blu, and Fred Myers, whose influence on this book is evident throughout. I cannot thank you enough for your mentorship and intellectual guidance as well as for the numerous research and academic opportunities you made available to me. It was a privilege to have been a graduate student in the Department of Anthropology at New York University, whose preeminent faculty provided the intellectual environment in which my research project was nurtured and from whom I have learned so much. The training and skills that I acquired through the Culture and Media Program honed my understanding of media production, strengthening the theoretical framing of my research as well as providing skills that I could contribute to Aboriginal filmmakers in Vancouver.

I am tremendously grateful for the generous financial and academic support NYU's Department of Anthropology gave me, especially the opportunity to participate in the 2004–2005 Indigenous Cosmologies Working Group in the Center for Religion and Media and as a festival assistant for the First Nations\ First Features Film Festival. Working on the First Nations\First Features Festival was invaluable in shaping my understanding of the global circulation of indigenous media as well as introducing me to important indigenous filmmaker networks while providing funding and support for my work. My research was also enriched through my work as a teaching assistant at NYU. I greatly benefited from the opportunity to be a teaching assistant for courses with Karen Blu, Fred Myers, and Tejaswini Ganti, as well as from the opportunity to work as a research assistant for Faye Ginsburg.

I am indebted to Faye Ginsburg for sharing the resource of her remarkable indigenous media collection and for the resources of NYU's Culture and Media Program. This project would not have been possible without her support and mentorship.

I am also tremendously thankful for the chance to work with Karen Blu, who was an incredible mentor to me throughout graduate school and whose scholarship enabled me to place my research within a comparative Native North American framework. I am indebted to Fred Myers, under whose guidance I learned a remarkable amount about the role of artistic production in indigenous life. I also thank Jeff Himpele and Lorna Roth for their insightful feedback about my research and writing.

It was through my work at the Film and Video Center at the Smithsonian's National Museum of the American Indian (NMAI) that I first became interested in developing a research project with Aboriginal filmmakers in Vancouver. I thank Elizabeth Weatherford, Amalia Cordova, Millie Seubert, and Michelle Svenson from the NMAI Film and Video Center for their instrumental support in helping me to develop this project.

This research has benefited from several presentation opportunities at the School for Advanced Research (SAR) Membership Lecture series on visual anthropology and at the University of Rochester Humanities Project on visual representations of Native Americans. Thank you to James Brooks, Jean Schaumberg, and Jason Ordaz at the SAR and to Eleana Kim, Janet Berlo, Rosemarie Ferreri, and Carlie Fishgold for their assistance in my travels for these lectures. The inquisitive questions and dialogue during the question and answer session after these lectures helped me to clarify my argument in this book. And it was such fun to present Aboriginal experimental media to appreciative and engaged audiences!

I have received much help and guidance from colleagues who read earlier drafts of this manuscript. I thank Susanna Rosenbaum, Eleana Kim, Aaron Glass, Danny Fisher, and Luther Elliott for their careful reading and constructive criticism in our writing group. I also thank Ayako Takamori, Lydia Boyd, April Strickland, Sabra Thorner, Rebecca Howes-Mischel, Brooke Nixon-Friedheim, and Stephanie Sadre-Orafai for their insights, helpful suggestions, and friendship. I thank my cohort including Stephanie Spehar, Nina Siulc, and Amahl Bishara for their camaraderie and friendship throughout graduate school. I also extend my deepest gratitude and admiration to Jessica Cattelino, who has been a remarkably generous mentor and dear friend throughout graduate school and beyond.

I was fortunate to have had the opportunity to be a faculty member in the Department of Folk Studies and Anthropology at Western Kentucky University and to work with extraordinary colleagues there, especially Michael Ann Williams, Erika Brady, Darlene Applegate, Kate Hudepohl, and Tim Evans. I cannot thank you enough for your support of me as a junior colleague. I learned so much while a faculty member there and could not have asked for a better departmental home.

I would like to thank the many students of my visual anthropology classes who have offered questions, critiques, and feedback about my research on Aboriginal media over the years. Being a professor is truly a blessed occupation, and there is nothing more rewarding than having the chance to work with extraordinary and intellectually rigorous students. I extend a special thank-you to Mahdis Koohestani for the opportunity to collaborate on an independent study course on Iranian media and for your feedback on this book as well as for your assistance during the final revisions. Thank you also to Cassandra Warren, Jeffrey Morning, Randi Dossey, Amanda Hardeman, Matthew Hale, Amanda Lillard, Calli Waltrip, Donna Longhorn, Jamie Gua, and Royce Freeman.

This book manuscript benefited immensely from my participation in an anthropology writing group at the University of Oklahoma. I am so thankful for my writing group colleagues: Circe Sturm (who is now at the University of Texas at Austin), Marc David, Amanda Minks, Daniel Mains, Erika Robb-Larkins, and Misha Klein, whose insightful criticism, tough questions, and editorial eyes all improved this manuscript substantially. I simply could not have done it without you, and for that I am eternally grateful. My deepest gratitude and admiration to Amanda Minks, who graciously read many drafts of the entire manuscript and who has been such a generous colleague and dear friend throughout this whole process, in particular keeping me on track during the final revisions! I also wish to extend my sincerest thanks to all of my colleagues at the University of Oklahoma, who make teaching and working here such a pleasure: in particular Daniel Swan, Mary Linn, Diane Warren, Misha Klein, Lesley Rankin-Hill, Pat Gilman, and Susan Vehik, who have provided specific feedback and support on this project, and Tassie Hirschfeld, faculty mentor extraordinaire!

My deepest thanks and highest regards to Matthew Bokovoy for his interest in and engagement with this project and for his insightful editorial eye. I am especially thankful for the editorial feedback from Joeth Zucco and my copyeditor Jane Curran, whose keen suggestions strengthened the book.

A special thank you to my undergraduate advisers, Janet Berlo and Robert Foster, at the University of Rochester, who supervised my honors thesis project and encouraged me to pursue graduate school. I thank Janet Berlo for her mentorship, encouragement, intellectual inspiration, and friendship. I thank Robert Foster for encouraging me to pursue graduate school and a career in anthropology. I would not be where I am today without the support and guidance you both provided during my years at the University of Rochester.

I am deeply indebted to my family for encouraging me to pursue my dream of receiving a PhD and providing the necessary support to see it become a reality. I thank my parents, Ed and Valerie Dowell, whose countless sacrifices to support my educational pursuits and whose love sustained me through this process. Words cannot begin to convey how much this has meant to me. I thank my brother Brian Dowell for his unceasing support and encouragement and my grandparents Brian and Marilyn Burke for instilling in me an intellectual curiosity from an early age. Thank you for your constant belief in my academic endeavors and for always reminding me how pleased Emily and John would have been to see me fulfill the academic legacy they were not able to complete. I thank my grandmother Doris Dowell for her thoughtfulness, love, and kind words. I also thank Andrea Burke-Harris, Gregg Harris, and Laurie Naglee for believing in me. My deepest thanks and highest regards to Sereta Wilson and the staff of Annie's Ruff House for taking such good care of my dog, Arlo, on all those long writing days!

A special thank you to Karl Schmidt for technical assistance with the photographs in this book and to Todd Fagin, who designed such an elegant map for the book.

My deepest gratitude and highest regard to Jeff Beekman, whom I met toward the end of completing this book but whose insightful observations during many conversations about my research and our shared interests in art and media have enriched this book and my life immeasurably.

My sincerest gratitude to the remarkable P.E.O. sisters of Chapter FA in Gahanna, Ohio, and Chapter P in New Rochelle, New York, whom I greatly admire. Their numerous hours of fundraising every year provide financial support for women in higher education, and their support, in part, made my graduate education possible.

This research has been funded by the generosity of many fellowships, including a Fulbright Fellowship to Canada, the Canadian Embassy Graduate Student Fellowship, P.E.O. Scholar Award, New York University MacCracken Fellowship, Beinecke Brothers Memorial Scholarship, the Annette Weiner Memorial Fellowship, the New York University Department of Anthropology, the Ethel-Jane Westfeldt Bunting Summer Scholar Fellowship at the School for Advanced Research, a regular faculty fellowship from Western Kentucky University, and three junior faculty summer fellowships, travel grants, faculty enrichment grants, and the Ed Cline Faculty Development Award from the University of Oklahoma.

Duane Gastant' Aucoin (Tlingit) said to me shortly before I left Vancouver, "Eegooiyax'wan. Do your best." I hope that the Aboriginal filmmakers with whom I worked feel that this book lives up to my best effort to represent their films, their lives, and their stories. The filmmakers with whom I worked in Vancouver have given me so much in their generosity of spirit, friendship, and creativity. Any proceeds generated from the sale of this book will be donated to the Vancouver Indigenous Media Arts Festival (VIMAF) as long as that organization is in existence. In the event that VIMAF is not viable in the future, then I will donate the proceeds to another organization that supports Aboriginal media production in Vancouver.

This book has been influenced by those thanked here as well as others; however, any inaccuracies or misinterpretations in the book are, as always, solely my own.

Abbreviations

AFP	Aboriginal Filmmaking Program
AFTP	Aboriginal Film and Television Program (Capilano College)
AIM	American Indian Movement
APTN	Aboriginal Peoples Television Network
BBM	Bureau of Broadcast Management
CBC	Canadian Broadcasting Corporation
CFDC	Canadian Film Development Corporation
CGMPB	Canadian Government Motion Picture Bureau
CRTC	Canadian Radio-television and Telecommunications Commission
CTV	Canadian Television
CYC	Company of Young Canadians
DIA	Department of Indian Affairs
DTES	Downtown Eastside
FNAP	First Nations Access Program
IFC	Indian Film Crew
IFTP	Indian Film Training Program
IIDFP	Independent Indigenous Digital Filmmaking Program (Capilano

	University—formerly Capilano College)
IMAG	Indigenous Media Arts Group
INAC	Department of Indian and Northern Affairs
KAYA	Knowledgeable Aboriginal Youth Advocates
MOA	Museum of Anthropology (University of British Columbia)
NARP	Native Alliance for Red Power
NFB	National Film Board of Canada
NMAI	National Museum of the American Indian
PANE	Protest Alliance Against Native Extermination
SAR	School of Advanced Research
SFU	Simon Fraser University
TRC	Truth and Reconciliation Commission
UBC	University of British Columbia
UBCIC	Union of B.C. Indian Chiefs
UNYA	Urban Native Youth Association
VIMAF	Vancouver Indigenous Media Arts Festival
VIVO	Video In/Video Out

Introduction

Vancouver's Aboriginal Media World

What does Aboriginal sovereignty look like on- and off-screen? This question has guided my decade-long research on Aboriginal media in Canada and is a significant question among Aboriginal filmmakers who define Aboriginal media practice through their work. Many scholars recognize the political dimensions of Aboriginal sovereignty through attention to land claims, treaty rights, tribal governments, and economic development within Aboriginal communities. *Visual* sovereignty is a concept pioneered by Tuscarora artist and scholar Jolene Rickard (1995) that has proven to be a salient framework expanded upon by other scholars of indigenous media (Ginsburg 2002; Lewis 2006; Raheja 2007; Singer 2001; Wilson and Stewart 2008). I use the concept of Aboriginal visual sovereignty to analyze the ways in which Aboriginal filmmakers stake a claim for Aboriginal stories in the dominant Canadian "mediascape" (Appadurai 1991) while simultaneously reimagining the screen to incorporate Aboriginal cultural protocols, languages, and aesthetics on-screen as well as off-screen.[1]

Aboriginal sovereignty represents the distinctive political status that derives from Aboriginal peoples' ties to lands prior to colonization. Sovereignty references a variety of domains in Aboriginal life from cultural to political to spiritual, and also, I would argue, to the domain of media production. I define *visual sovereignty* as the articulation of Aboriginal peoples' distinctive cultural traditions, political status, and collective identities through aesthetic and cinematic means. I locate Aboriginal visual sovereignty in the *act of production*. As Cleo Reece emphatically proclaimed in the story that opens the preface, "We're doing it ourselves! We're producing our own images." This *is* Aboriginal visual sovereignty. Like Reece, I contend that an Aboriginal filmmaker's act of creating a media work is an act of self-determination. Speaking back to the legacy of misrepresentation in dominant media is an act of cultural autonomy that reclaims the screen to tell Aboriginal stories from Aboriginal perspectives. Some scholars have explored whether there is an "indigenous aesthetic" within Aboriginal media (Leuthold 1998), often focusing on certain formal elements in indigenous cinema such as the emphasis on land or a nonlinear storytelling structure. Other scholars have focused on the transnational and intercultural dimensions of "Fourth World cinema" in search of postcolonial poetics within international indigenous films (Columpar 2010). These approaches often focus on the on-screen aesthetics of Aboriginal media and comparisons between dominant and Aboriginal cinematic aesthetics.

I agree that the on-screen aesthetics of Aboriginal media are distinctive in that Aboriginal filmmakers draw on aspects of indigeneity in the tone, structure, editing, framing, and content on-screen. However, there is no singular Aboriginal media aesthetic, but rather multiple Aboriginal aesthetics that reflect the individual artistic expression of the filmmaker and the Aboriginal nation in which he or she is a citizen. I argue that the off-screen production process itself is crucial for understanding media production as an act of sovereignty. Filmmaking is an inherently social process that often requires the labor of numerous individuals in order to complete a project. Aboriginal filmmakers often rely upon friends and family during this production process. The production process creates more than merely a set of film or video footage; it is a process through which Aboriginal social relationships can be created, negotiated, and nurtured. Translating an indigenous story to the screen is an *active* process, and it is out of these off-screen negotiations that Aboriginal social relations can be shaped and constituted. Given the history of the disruption of Aboriginal families and communities through colonial policies—the creation of reserves, the gender discrimination in the Indian Act, and the residential school system—it is an act of sovereignty to bridge these ruptures and repair Aboriginal social relationships through the process of media production.[2]

Aboriginal social ties can also be reflected in the role of the intended audience for an Aboriginal film. When an Aboriginal director is behind the camera, his or her tribal community and an Aboriginal audience are often configured as the primary audience, in stark contrast to mainstream media where Aboriginal viewers are rarely constructed as a key audience demographic. This consideration of an Aboriginal audience for Aboriginal media also expresses visual sovereignty. The filmmakers with whom I work make media that circulates nationally and globally. And yet these filmmakers articulate a sense of making films for their Aboriginal communities first and foremost, and secondly for other indigenous audiences in Canada and around the world. These various audiences as well as non-Native audiences will interpret the film differently. For example, a Tsilhqot'in audience watching Helen Haig-Brown's film *ʔEʔAnx: The Cave* (2009), a film discussed extensively in chapter 6, will be able to draw upon a shared set of cultural knowledge regarding Tsilhqot'in territory and the traditional story upon which this film is based. However, the film, with its suspense and character-driven narrative, also resonates with other Aboriginal audiences and with non-Native audiences. Having Aboriginal films, such as *The Cave*, circulate nationally and globally is also an aspect of Aboriginal visual sovereignty. The significance of having non-Native audiences recognize these media works *as Aboriginal* serves as a form of recognition of Aboriginal presence in Canada, an acknowledgment that is all too often absent within the broader politics of Canadian settler colonialism and an acknowledgment that can serve to buttress other forms of Aboriginal political action.

Aboriginal sovereignty is not only a political act but is also a cultural process taking shape in and through Aboriginal media.[3] As film scholars Pamela Wilson and Michelle Stewart assert, "In this landscape, control of media representation and of cultural self-definition asserts and signifies cultural and political sovereignty itself" (Wilson and Stewart 2008, 5). Artists and filmmakers express Aboriginal sovereignty and self-determination through the production of their art and media. For Tuscarora scholar Jolene Rickard the concept of visual sovereignty is the representation of indigenous self-determination, cultural traditions, and aesthetics through visual forms. She declares, "Today, sovereignty is taking shape in visual thought as indigenous artists negotiate cultural space" (Rickard 1995, 51). Aboriginal media can express visual sovereignty through the creation of Aboriginal film aesthetics, the ways in which cultural protocol is incorporated into media production, or the inclusion of Aboriginal media in domains, such as the broadcasting system, that have been predominantly Euro-Canadian.

Aboriginal filmmakers reclaim the screen to tell their own stories by taking the means of media production into their own hands. Sociologist and social theorist Stuart Hall addresses a similar situation with the politics of representation in black British cinema, asserting that "the cultural politics of black British filmmakers encompasses first, the question of *access* to the rights to representation by black artists and black cultural workers themselves" (Hall 1996, 164). Claiming a visual space to create their own representations is a particularly political act for Aboriginal Canadian and Native American filmmakers who have faced a long history of objectification at the hands of non-Native filmmakers.[4] Yet, Aboriginal media production

Fig. 1. Vancouver, British Columbia, city skyline. Photo by Todd A. Hayward.

is more than merely an on-screen intervention. By seizing and reconfiguring the means of production, Aboriginal filmmakers overturn unequal power dynamics to claim their right to self-representation. This is precisely the process in which filmmakers in Vancouver's Aboriginal media world are engaged to articulate visual sovereignty on- and off-screen.

Urban Aboriginal Identity in Vancouver

"I find it difficult that Vancouver has this identity now as this international cosmopolitan center that has many cultures, which it does, but there's no recognition that we're all guests on Coast Salish land." exclaimed Kamala Todd (Cree/Métis)—an urban geographer, activist, filmmaker, and daughter of Loretta Todd, a key leader in Vancouver's Aboriginal media world—one morning over breakfast at a local diner. Todd worked as Aboriginal social planner for the city of Vancouver between 2000 and 2006 and was the creator of *Our City, Our Voices*, an Aboriginal oral history collaborative media project between the National Film Board of Canada and four Aboriginal communities in Vancouver. Cultural protocol on the West Coast dictates that one acknowledges the Aboriginal nation on whose traditional territory one is a guest.

Like many other Aboriginal Vancouver residents Todd expresses frustration that Vancouver marks itself as a multicultural cosmopolitan city while frequently ignoring the Aboriginal people on whose territory the city rests. It is important then, that I acknowledge that Vancouver is built on traditional Coast Salish territory and that during my fieldwork I was a guest upon Coast Salish land.

Vancouver is home to Canada's third largest urban Aboriginal population, behind Winnipeg and Edmonton, with approximately 40,000 people representing a range of tribal backgrounds and degrees of affiliation with urban and reserve life.[5] The metro Vancouver area is also home to First Nations reserves including the Musqueam First Nation, the Squamish First Nation, and the Tsleil-Waututh First Nation. All of these First Nations are indigenous to this area. Given this diversity, Aboriginal organizations, such as the Indigenous Media Arts Group, serve as social sites that bring people together from distinct backgrounds, ages, and incomes to create a sense of shared social ties. Aboriginal people maintain a relationship with the Canadian government through the formal political structures of band councils and national organizations such as the Assembly of First Nations and Métis National Council. Urban Aboriginal populations coming from various tribal affiliations and cultural backgrounds lack a collective political structure through which to negotiate and maintain their rights vis-à-vis the provincial and federal governments. This lack of access to political representation and social services encourages urban Aboriginal people to create organizations to meet their social, cultural, and spiritual needs. Intertribal organizations, such as Aboriginal Friendship Centres, provide a venue for social events and cultural activities—powwows, family nights, community dinners, elder-youth activities, and ceremonial activities—that gather urban Aboriginal people together, shaping a shared sense of identity and community.[6]

Urban life is a social reality for the majority of Aboriginal people in Canada today, with 60 percent of Canada's Aboriginal

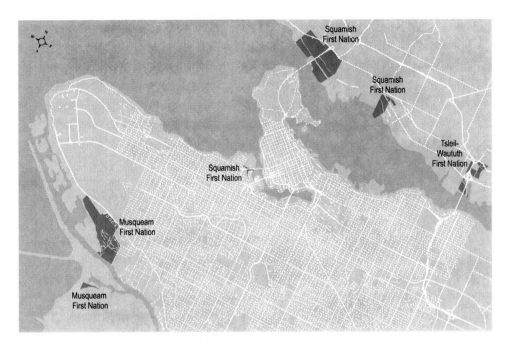

First Nations reserves in the city of Vancouver, North Vancouver, and West Vancouver. These reserves are tiny fractions of the traditional territories of the Squamish, Musqueam, and Tsleil-Waututh First Nations, whose traditional territory covers the entire extent of the metro Vancouver area. There are ongoing treaty negotiations and land claims regarding this area. Map designed by Todd Fagin.

population living off-reserve.[7] In Canada the migration to urban areas is historically connected to the Indian Act legislation under which Indian women who married non-Indian men (and non-status Indian men) lost their Indian status and the right to live on reserves (Lawrence 2004; Simpson 2007). This gendered discrimination within the Indian Act pushed generations of Indian women and their children off reserve and into urban areas. Likewise, many Métis communities were dispossessed of traditional territory and lacked formal reserves, leaving many Métis individuals to migrate to urban areas seeking housing and employment. Once off-reserve, Aboriginal people lost access to social services—that is, healthcare, education, housing—and access to cultural events and seasonal activities was sometimes difficult. Although large numbers of people relocated to urban areas during this period, it is important to remember that many people made frequent trips back to reserves to participate in social, cultural, ceremonial, and kinship obligations. This fluid movement back and forth between cities and reserves remains characteristic of urban Aboriginal communities today.

Vancouver Is an "Indigenous City"

The aim of many of the filmmakers featured in this book is to raise visibility for Aboriginal stories and experiences through their films. Kamala Todd's work emphasizes the role of media in articulating Aboriginal visual sovereignty and representing Vancouver as an "Indigenous City"—a phrase she coined in 2006 at the World Urban Forum in Vancouver to call attention to the indigenousness of Vancouver and all Canadian cities. Todd is a cultural geographer, urban planner, community activist, and filmmaker whose life's work has been dedicated to honoring the Coast Salish peoples and the diversity of Aboriginal experiences in Vancouver. She writes, "As a Métis-Cree community planner born and raised in this Coast Salish land, I am determined to see the story of Vancouver rewritten to reflect what it really is—an Indigenous City" (K. Todd 2011a, 2). As a cultural geographer and as someone who worked as the Aboriginal social planner for the city of Vancouver, Todd knows firsthand the ramifications of dominant colonial narratives that erase Aboriginal people from the land, particularly in urban areas like Vancouver. The dominant narrative of Vancouver typically focuses on "frontier tales of brave loggers, right-minded political leaders and valiant businessmen who 'tamed' a wild empty land into a civilized order of right angles and level surfaces" (1). This myth of *terra nullius* ignores the long-standing presence of the Coast Salish peoples upon whose traditional territory Vancouver resides. As Todd argues, this is "place making by erasure" (K. Todd 2011a). How then, as Todd asks, "do we increase the presence of Aboriginal perspectives and aesthetics on the land? How do we build a more inclusive city in which Aboriginal people have a significant role in shaping how we live?" (K. Todd 2011b, 2).

Throughout this book I contend that Aboriginal media is a crucial venue through which Aboriginal experiences are made visible. Todd's projects *Our City, Our Voices*, mentioned above, and *Storyscapes* embody her efforts to use media to articulate Aboriginal sovereignty and presence throughout Vancouver. Todd created the collaborative community-based multimedia *Storyscapes* in 2003 to help place Aboriginal public art in highly visited areas throughout the city as a way to inscribe Aboriginal presence on the urban landscape in Vancouver.[8] *Storyscapes* installed three sculptures entitled *People among the People*, designed by renowned Musqueam artist Susan Point, at Brockton Point in Stanley Park, a significant Coast Salish village site prior to the development of Vancouver and one of the most visited tourist sites in British Columbia. This area in Stanley Park has many totem poles made by artists from other First Nations from further north up the West Coast; however, Point's *People among the People* represents the first poles from the local Musqueam First Nation in Vancouver. This is significant because the land at Stanley Park is Coast Salish territory and following cultural protocol it is important to have poles from Coast Salish First Nations—such as the Musqueam First Nation represented at this place. These sculptures welcome visitors to the traditional lands of the Musqueam and Coast Salish people. Likewise, throughout three key neighborhoods—Gastown, Chinatown, and Kitsilano—*Storyscapes* hired local youth to gather stories from Aboriginal residents about these neighborhoods and make videos documenting their experiences in the city. This incredibly vibrant multimedia project not only engaged local Aboriginal youth in the production process, but it also worked to raise visibility for Aboriginal stories in Vancouver, thus enacting Aboriginal visual sovereignty. Todd declares, "Seeing oneself reflected in the landscape helps create a stronger sense of place and belonging to one's environment. Changing the urban landscape itself to more accurately reflect Aboriginal history and culture will contribute to Vancouver's development as a truly diverse and livable city for all."[9]

A History of Vancouver's Aboriginal Media World

Vancouver's Aboriginal "media world" (Ginsburg, Abu-Lughod, and Larkin 2002) emerged out of a particular set of historical circumstances, social movements, and Aboriginal activism. Drawing on oral histories conducted with founding filmmakers in Vancouver, I highlight several key historical events that converged to create the foundation of Vancouver's Aboriginal media world.[10] The roots of Vancouver's Aboriginal media world can be traced back to the presence of Aboriginal political activism in British Columbia and in Vancouver in the late 1960s and 1970s. In 1969 Aboriginal activists in Vancouver galvanized in reaction to the White Paper policy proposed by Jean Chrétien, the minister of the Department of Indian Affairs (DIA), and Prime Minister Pierre Trudeau. The White Paper policy sought to eliminate the financial responsibility of the federal government to First Nations while assimilating Aboriginal people into dominant Canadian society.[11] The Union of B.C. Indian Chiefs (UBCIC) was formed in response to the 1969 White Paper, actively protesting this policy by responding with "A Declaration of Indian Rights: The BC Indian Position Paper" in 1971, which became known as the "Brown Paper," advocating for Aboriginal self-determination and self-government. Throughout the 1970s and 1980s the activism of the UBCIC in Vancouver generated numerous political actions, including protests, blockades, demonstrations, and occupations of government offices. The UBCIC often used media to document and publicize their activities, integrating Aboriginal media and activism at an early stage.[12]

In the midst of this activist environment Vancouver developed an active avant-garde arts scene that included artists' collectives such as Video In/Video Out (VIVO), Vancouver Co-Op

Radio, and the Western Front. These artists' collectives supported community media projects and created an environment of alternative video, fostering a commitment to the idea that media could be participatory and locally produced instead of passively consumed. Throughout the 1970s and 1980s these collectives created opportunities for intercultural collaboration as they offered workshops for Aboriginal filmmakers and often made their equipment accessible for Aboriginal community media projects. Filmmaker and scholar Dana Claxton notes, "promoting a policy of access to the necessary tools of this emerging art form, and by encouraging an environment supporting their concerns, Aboriginal artists became increasingly associated with Video In" (Claxton 2005, 18). These programs and institutional resources are key to understanding the emergence of the distinctive avant-garde and experimental media art traditions that flourish in Vancouver's Aboriginal media world, as discussed in chapters 5 and 6.

The 1980s saw the development of two early media initiatives: the Spirit Song Native Theatre School and the Chief Dan George Media Training Program. The Spirit Song Native Theatre School was opened in the early 1980s with Margo Kane (Cree/Saulteaux/Métis) as the first Aboriginal artistic director. Many Aboriginal artists who later became filmmakers gained experience with acting, drama, dance, and scriptwriting through this program, which sought to translate Aboriginal traditional stories to the stage. In the late 1980s Loretta Todd, along with Leonard George, son of the late Chief Dan George, created the Chief Dan George Media Training Program at Capilano College.[13] This was an employment program that provided education in basic media production skills and offered opportunities for hands-on production experience, generating a number of graduates who began making documentaries, community media, experimental video, and short narratives. Several prominent Aboriginal filmmakers, including Barb Cranmer, Tracey Bonneau, Ruby Dennis, and Lenny Fisher, were trained under this program, and all continue to be involved in media in some capacity. While this first initiative was short-lived, it later inspired the development of the Capilano College Aboriginal Film and Television Program (AFTP) in 2000, now named the Capilano University Indigenous Independent Digital Filmmaking Program (IIDFP), offering basic and advanced production two-year certificate degree programs.[14]

The decade of the 1990s began with the pivotal "Oka Crisis" in the summer of 1990, a seventy-eight-day standoff between Mohawk warriors, Quebec provincial police, and the Canadian army that forcefully questioned Canadian settler colonialism.[15] The misrepresentation of the events at Oka in the mainstream media sparked a desire for many people in Vancouver to create media from Aboriginal perspectives. The Oka crisis also galvanized Aboriginal activists and artists across Canada. Archer Pechawis (Plains Cree), a performance artist, experimental media artist, and longtime activist and participant in Vancouver's arts scene, explained: "Oka changed everything. Oka really solidified the Aboriginal art community politically, socially, and artistically. But it also solidified us with other communities of color in the country which proved to be very important." The early 1990s saw the emergence of a critical discourse around representation and inclusion within Canadian cultural institutions. Aboriginal artists in Vancouver joined with other artists of color to advocate for increased visibility within museums and galleries. These conversations were precipitated by a film festival in late 1989 called "In Visible Colors," a film festival for women of color and Aboriginal women. In the context of these debates about representation, voice, and inclusion, artist-run centers such as the grunt gallery and Video In took steps to become more inclusive of Aboriginal art and media. The grunt gallery officially changed its mandate to prioritize the exhibition of contemporary First Nations art and media while Video In organized the First Nations Access Program between 1992 and 1995 to provide training and media resources to Aboriginal filmmakers in Vancouver.

In 1998 a seminal moment occurred with the establishment of

the Indigenous Media Arts Group (IMAG) and the first IMAGeNation Aboriginal Film and Video Festival, Vancouver's only annual Aboriginal film festival. IMAG provided a vital community space for Aboriginal filmmakers, hosting the annual IMAGeNation Film Festival, conducting Aboriginal media training programs, and providing media equipment and resources for local Aboriginal filmmakers. In 1999 Vancouver's Aboriginal media world, like other Aboriginal media centers in Canada, was dramatically impacted by the launch of the Aboriginal Peoples Television Network. APTN is the world's first national indigenous television channel and is available on all basic cable service in Canada. Broadcasting all genres of television programming—nightly news programs, children's programming, cooking shows, original drama series, documentary films, feature films, and current events shows—in English and French as well as thirteen different indigenous languages, APTN has revolutionized the development of an infrastructure for Aboriginal media production across Canada and impacted indigenous media production globally, as is examined in chapter 3.

Vancouver emerged as a center for Aboriginal media because of a number of factors, including: 1) the strong presence of Aboriginal activism, 2) the vibrant avant-garde arts scene in Vancouver, 3) the presence of a media infrastructure, and 4) the presence of Aboriginal media training programs. These factors—in addition to Vancouver's beautiful landscape and favorable weather—draw people to Vancouver to pursue filmmaking, but it is the intergenerational network of filmmakers, the strong role of mentorship, and the community support of Vancouver's Aboriginal media world that encourage people to remain. Filmmaker and actor Odessa Shuquaya (Kluane First Nation) noted the importance of community support in Vancouver's Aboriginal media world, which she described as a "web of people that gives you strength." The framework that sustains and strengthens Vancouver's Aboriginal media world is a matrix of off-screen relationships nurtured through the media production process.

Visual Sovereignty On- and Off-Screen:
Indigenous Plant Diva and *Writing the Land*

With a better understanding of the political, cultural, and historical contexts of Aboriginal media making, we can now return to
the question: "What does Aboriginal sovereignty look like on-
and off-screen?" Kevin Lee Burton's *Writing the Land* (2007) and
Kamala Todd's *Indigenous Plant Diva* (2008) beautifully illustrate
the idea of visual sovereignty. Both of these films were conceived
as part of the *Our City, Our Voices* project and are connected to
Kamala Todd's philosophy of using media to "write Aboriginal
presence onto the land." Both *Indigenous Plant Diva* and *Writing the Land* strive to represent Aboriginal experiences within
Vancouver, to articulate Vancouver as an Indigenous City, and to
acknowledge the Coast Salish people upon whose traditional territory Vancouver rests. Both films are experimental documentaries
that rely on innovative cinematography, split screen, and text
inscribed on-screen to represent Aboriginal stories, knowledge,
language, and land. Both films share the same cinematographer,
Helen Haig-Brown, and her fluid camera work and unique framing is evident in both films. Kamala Todd's *Indigenous Plant Diva*
is a lyrical portrait of 'T'Uy'Tanat' Cease Wyss (Squamish), a
healer and carrier of traditional plant knowledge whose Squamish name translates to "woman who travels by canoe to gather
medicines for all people." Cease Wyss is a leader in Vancouver's
urban Aboriginal community and is also a filmmaker and one
of the founders of the Indigenous Media Arts Group. This nine-
minute film opens with striking images of plants growing in
cracks alongside buildings in Vancouver and juxtaposes images of
plants with the city skyline. The viewer hears Wyss give a greet-
ing in Squamish as we see a close-up profile shot of Wyss that
fades into a wide shot of Vancouver's skyline and then a medium
shot of Wyss standing in an urban alley with graffiti on the wall.

As the film cuts from a shot of a flowing stream with text
explaining Wyss's Squamish name, the viewer hears Wyss

Fig. 2. Cease Wyss at a community garden in Vancouver. Photo by Jeff Vinnick.
© 2008 National Film Board of Canada. All rights reserved. Image courtesy of
National Film Board of Canada.

articulate Squamish philosophy in a voiceover declaring: "The
language of plants is so extensive. It carries on beyond our abilities as humans to even imagine because they are the second
oldest beings on the planet and they are our teachers. And without them we wouldn't even have air to breathe. I feel so humble
at times and little even when I'm picking the littlest plants. I
think you've existed longer than I can ever imagine existing."
Paying homage to Wyss's extensive knowledge of plants, the film
utilizes split screen and innovative use of text to imprint traditional ecological knowledge regarding plants on-screen. Using

shots of plants growing throughout the city, Todd deftly identifies each plant and then explains the symptoms and illnesses that these plants can be used to heal. This recenters Vancouver as an Aboriginal city and as a space where Squamish knowledge about the land is still a central part of everyday life for resident Cease Wyss. Wyss proclaims: "Everywhere I go in this city I find plant life. I find it growing up through the cracks of the sidewalk. I see it growing out of the sides of buildings. I see it in the community gardens and throughout the whole landscape of the city." The film fulfills Todd's mission to raise visibility for the Coast Salish peoples as well as to represent how traditional plant knowledge resonates with and is relevant to urban Aboriginal people.

The film shifts from representations of specific plants and their medicinal uses to a split screen image of a close-up shot of Wyss with the Vancouver skyline in the background as she declares: "I always know in my heart and in my mind that I am connected to this land for many centuries. And I feel really good about that." This asserts visual sovereignty by articulating the long-standing connection that Coast Salish people have with the land in Vancouver and by repositioning Vancouver as an Aboriginal city. This poignant film ends with a powerful discussion about the transmission of this knowledge as the camera follows Wyss showing plants to her twelve-year-old daughter, Senaqwila, and talking about how important it was to her to pass this knowledge down to her daughter. "Through her whole life I've taken her with me gathering . . . I didn't ever force this knowledge on her but by bringing her out and teaching her this on a daily basis through her whole life I have filtered this knowledge through her. She'll *always* have this teaching . . . I've given her a big gift and I hope she carries it her whole life." The film ends with a medium shot of Wyss with her daughter standing in the forest smiling and holding plants they've gathered. This emphasis on the intergenerational transmission of knowledge is a key aspect of the off-screen impact of visual sovereignty and a component of Todd's work with *Storyscapes* and *Our City, Our Voices*.

Fig. 3. Filmmaker Kevin Lee Burton with Larry Grant on set of *Writing the Land* (2007). *Writing the Land* © 2007 National Film Board of Canada. All rights reserved. Image courtesy of the National Film Board of Canada.

Kevin Lee Burton (Swampy Cree), whose films are discussed extensively in chapter 5, was trained at Capilano College and IMAG and was a resident of Vancouver throughout my fieldwork. He directed *Writing the Land* (2007), a profile of Musqueam elder Larry Grant that lyrically explores the connection between land, language, and identity. The film opens with Larry Grant stating, "Vancouver is truly within the sacred land of Musqueam territory." The opening sequence shows Grant on traditional Musqueam territory, but the camera focuses on details such as Grant's hands or his shoes standing in a field of long grasses along the shore, the grasses from which the Musqueam people get their name. Tacking back and forth between shots of Grant on traditional Musqueam territory and the urban landscape of Vancouver's city streets, we hear about Grant's life growing up in both of these spaces, about the displacement of Musqueam people and the impact of urban development on their lands, as well as about pressures he felt to stop speaking his native language—hənq̓əminəm̓.[16] At the end of the film Grant encourages Aboriginal youth to learn their languages by describing his experience enrolling in the Musqueam Language Program at the University of British Columbia as an adult and feeling the hənq̓əminəm̓ words "rise up from him."

Stylistically this film is innovative in its cinematography as there are no traditional talking head interviews—instead Grant is always filmed outside on the land and the camera is fluid, constantly moving around to situate Grant within the landscape. Additionally, the inventive use of text on-screen also reinforces Aboriginal visual sovereignty as the hənq̓əminəm̓ words for various places and objects are imprinted onto the visual track—from plants used for traditional medicines to the name for Vancouver's neighborhoods of Downtown Eastside and Strathcona. Similar to the use of text on-screen in *Indigenous Plant Diva*, this visual effect in *Writing the Land* literally inscribes the urban Vancouver landscape, with a Musqueam presence asserting Aboriginal political sovereignty in a uniquely cinematic way. The presence of Larry Grant telling his life history to the filmmaker within the visibly urban Vancouver cityscape—the tall glass-fronted high-rise buildings so distinctive of Vancouver's skyline—claims the urban Vancouver space *as an Aboriginal space* emphasizing the urban Aboriginal presence in Vancouver, and the long-standing ties that Coast Salish peoples have to this place.

A medium shot of the filmmaker interviewing Grant standing outside with the city skyline behind them shows the filmmaker listening attentively to Grant's story and brings a reflexivity to the film through the acknowledgment of the filmmaker's presence. This also demonstrates the off-screen dynamic of Aboriginal media production and the way in which it can generate Aboriginal social relationships, particularly intergenerational ties, which is analyzed in greater depth in chapter 4. Burton, a fluent Cree speaker and a fierce advocate for maintaining and revitalizing Aboriginal languages, welcomed the opportunity to connect with Larry Grant through this media project. The film concludes with Grant looking directly into the camera and declaring, "My name is *Sʔayəɬəq*. I am from Musqueam." The visual track then shifts to scenes of the grasses grazing the shoreline of the water on Musqueam traditional territory while his voiceover continues: "As my ancestors *qiyeplenəxʷ* and *xʷəlciməltxʷ* we have been here forever. We are the original people here on this territory." This powerful short film provides more than merely a profile of one Musqueam elder; through innovative cinematography and editing techniques it inscribes the urban space of Vancouver as Musqueam space, just as *Indigenous Plant Diva* profiled Cease Wyss and inscribed Vancouver as a Coast Salish space, a clear articulation of Aboriginal visual sovereignty.

Conclusion

I believe that it is crucial to understand Aboriginal media within a framework of visual sovereignty to link this practice to broader Aboriginal political movements. The impact of this work moves beyond merely an artistic expression to enact a form of cultural autonomy that articulates Aboriginal aesthetics, cosmologies, cultural practices, and self-determination in visual and cultural realms. Dana Claxton explained, "I think that Aboriginal media is really about self-determination and in other ways I think it's also about self-government." Given the history of the administration of Aboriginal lives through bureaucratic regimes—the reserve system, residential schools, and the Indian Act—Aboriginal media can speak back to this legacy by reclaiming the screen through acts of Aboriginal visual sovereignty. For some filmmakers the mere presence of Aboriginal faces and voices on screen is itself a revolutionary act of self-determination.

My perspective on Aboriginal media as visual sovereignty has been impacted by the work of Loretta Todd, who posed a set of provocative questions in a 2005 essay:

> Have we truly decolonized our imaginations when it comes to how we represent ourselves in media—both in the aesthetics and content of our stories? Have we internalized the images made of us, the idea of "us" by the colonizer—from the camera angles to the editing to the music? Are we their tour guides or even recruiters into their world view? Or is it with subversive intentions, as acts of sovereignty, that we take up the camera and signal forth our presence and our stories? (L. Todd 2005, 107)

The media made by the Aboriginal filmmakers introduced in this book, such as Kevin Lee Burton's *Writing the Land* and Kamala Todd's *Indigenous Plant Diva* discussed above, take up Loretta Todd's challenge to make films in a way that redefines cinema in the service of Aboriginal visual sovereignty. The media practice of Aboriginal filmmakers in Vancouver reflects visions informed by their individual artistic perspectives yet deeply rooted in their cultural ties to Aboriginal nations and the intertribal urban Aboriginal community in Vancouver.

CHAPTER ONE

The Indigenous Media Arts Group

On a crisp, sunny October afternoon the Indigenous Media Arts Group (IMAG) office bustles with activity. Cleo Reece, IMAG director, talks on the phone with a funding agency about a grant, her daughter Honey stops by with her two children, Ohkuu and Musky, Leonard edits a student video about his drum group, and Mary drops in to make copies of her video, a clip of which will be aired on *The New Canoe*, a local Aboriginal arts television show. The noise level rises as Musky plays a computer game on Cleo's computer with its electronic sci-fi audio effects, punctuating the sounds of the powwow drum from the computer where Leonard sits editing. Honey leaves to run a few errands, so I offer to hold the baby, Ohkuu, while trying to help Mary figure out how to make a mini-DV copy of her video. Musky, frustrated with the computer game, calls out, "Kookum!¹ Kookum! How do you get this game to work?" Meanwhile the high-pitched refrain of powwow singing permeates the office from Leonard's computer as he looks at the same clip over and over to choose where to make his edit. I'm searching for the cable we need to hook the video camera up to the monitor while trying to manage Ohkuu as he plays with my hair. "I'm not sure this cable will work," I say to Mary while trying an A/V cable in various combinations between the camera and the monitor. Within this buzz of activity in the office, I realize for the first time that IMAG functions as more than a media resource center. Beyond the media produced in the social space of IMAG, invaluable kinship, community, and cultural ties are forged here as well.

Introduction

While Aboriginal media have made an impact on-screen within the Canadian mediascape, they have also made a tremendous off-screen impact in the social life of Aboriginal communities. For anthropologists of media, the social life behind media production is a testament to the power of media to alter and strengthen social ties. Drawing upon my access to the "behind the scenes" life of media production as an IMAG volunteer, I highlight how a sense of community is shaped, contested, and negotiated among urban Aboriginal filmmakers within the social spaces of media production. I locate Aboriginal visual sovereignty in the acts of media production; therefore, a site like IMAG is especially significant for analyzing the social spaces in which Aboriginal media is produced. What are the conditions of production for Aboriginal media makers working at IMAG? How do Aboriginal filmmakers mobilize resources and labor to produce their media? How does media production alter Aboriginal social relationships, cultural practices, and intergenerational ties? Within the diverse, intertribal urban Aboriginal community in Vancouver, how does media production affect practices and discourses of "community"?

I depict daily life in the social space of IMAG, an important gathering place that helped build social relationships within Vancouver's urban Aboriginal community. My ethnography of IMAG reveals the important ways in which Aboriginal sociality and discourses of "community" are produced through media production, as well as the off-screen impact of this grassroots organization in the social life of Vancouver's Aboriginal community. Additionally, this chapter focuses on the 2004 IMAGeNation Aboriginal Film and Video Festival, a film festival that was held annually by IMAG between 1998 and 2006. The IMAGeNation Festival provided a key screening venue that raised visibility for Aboriginal media, particularly in showcasing the work of emerging filmmakers. IMAGeNation was a central annual Aboriginal cultural event that brought the community together and created an Aboriginal social space in which to tell Aboriginal stories to Aboriginal audiences, while reflecting Aboriginal cultural values through its programming, planning, and enactment.

The Avant-Garde Origins of the Indigenous Media Arts Group

The Indigenous Media Arts Group was founded in 1998 as a collective of Aboriginal media artists that aimed to increase access to media equipment and Aboriginal representation in artist-run centers in Vancouver. Artist-run centers emerged in Canada in the 1970s as an alternative exhibition venue for artists seeking to exhibit their work in a noncommercial venue.[2] Vancouver has been a hub for artist-run centers in Canada for over forty years, with numerous exhibitions of independent artists whose work has pushed the boundaries of media arts, new media, performance art, and video installation (J. Abbott 2000).[3]

IMAG had roots within this avant-garde and independent art world as it initially grew out of the First Nations Access Program (FNAP) at Video In (now known as Video In/Video Out [VIVO] Media Arts Centre), a leader in experimental video and media arts in Vancouver since the early 1970s.[4] (FNAP was founded in 1992 by Margo Kane and was created to "fill a gap in video productions by First Nations producers." The primary objective was to "assist in the development and creation of new video work by training First Nations people in all aspects of video production" (J. Abbott 2000, 178). The program operated between 1992 and 1995, after which time the Indigenous Media Arts Group was created.[5]

IMAG never received an operating grant, so funding was pieced together from various government agencies including the Department of Canadian Heritage, Canada Council for the Arts, the First Peoples Cultural Foundation, the Urban Aboriginal Strategy, and the city of Vancouver. Functioning from grant to grant created an unstable funding environment for the organization, an experience that many grassroots arts and cultural organizations face. IMAG had a board of directors, usually consisting of four or five Aboriginal filmmakers who volunteered their time at IMAG. During my fieldwork in 2003 to 2004, when I worked as a volunteer at IMAG, there was one full-time staff person managing the office administration, a grant writer, a bookkeeper, and a training program coordinator. During the planning of the 2004 IMAGeNation Film Festival additional staff members were hired, including a festival coordinator, a publicist, a graphic designer, a volunteer coordinator, and a festival programming committee consisting of four or five local Aboriginal filmmakers.

IMAG was housed in the same building complex as Video In, maintaining a strong connection with Video In that often made their equipment and screening room available for IMAG events. During 2003 to 2004 IMAG maintained an office space that consisted of one room approximately twelve feet by twenty-four feet in which operated all IMAG activities—film festival organization, daily office operation, editing suites, equipment, and training programs. IMAG was located near the intersection of Main Street and 4th Avenue in Vancouver's Mount Pleasant neighborhood, a center for the avant-garde art, performance art, and experimental video scene in Vancouver. After a temporary move to an office building on Vancouver's Downtown Eastside on Pender and Abbott Streets across from a Native housing complex, IMAG moved back into their former office space on Main Street.[6] They remained in the Main Street location for another year before disbanding as an organization in 2007.[7] All of the equipment, archives, and resources of the IMAG office were packed up and placed into storage.

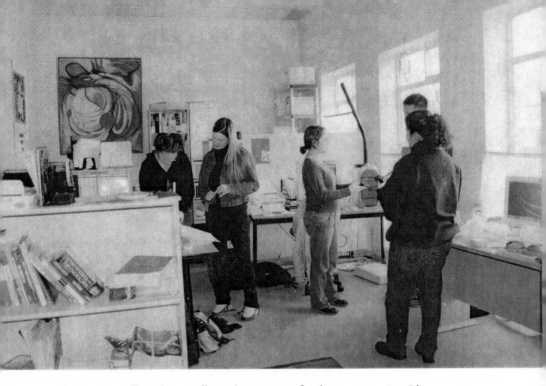

Fig. 4. IMAG office where staff members prepare for the IMAGENation Film Festival. February 2004. Photo by author.

Enacting Aboriginal Cultural Autonomy

Although Aboriginal media artists utilized the resources and training available through the First Nations Access Program at Video In, they sought to create a media organization that was operated by and for Aboriginal people rather than work under the auspices and control of Video In. Archer Pechawis has been involved in Vancouver's Aboriginal and avant-garde art worlds for almost thirty years with an arts career that ranges from professional street juggling to acting to performance art to spoken word and new media. Although he has received support from non-Aboriginal artist-run centers, like the grunt gallery, he feels that organizations like IMAG, run by and for Aboriginal artists, have made an important contribution to building a sense of Aboriginal community in Vancouver. During an interview he acknowledged that "a lot of the other artist-run centers in town have been very supportive of Aboriginal work. I think that the important thing is the Aboriginal organizations themselves. IMAG, for example, that's where the important work really happens is when Aboriginals work for Aboriginals." He paused before noting, "That's not to disparage the work that artist-run centers have been doing, but it's just important that we as Aboriginals take responsibility for our own community." It is this philosophy of Aboriginal cultural autonomy that contributed to the decision to separate from Video In.

The founding members of IMAG wanted to create an organization that would use media as a tool for community organizing. In the early morning quiet of the IMAG office, Cleo Reece explained, "Aboriginal media definitely does bring people together. When there's a production being made people are interested and they want to be involved in some way. They want to be involved in something that tells a story that's real about themselves or about their own people." Reece contends that Aboriginal people desire to see Aboriginal faces reflected on-screen, but she emphasizes the way in which Aboriginal media production can become a catalyst off-screen around which the community gets collectively involved in the production process.[8] Instead of serving as passive audiences, Aboriginal people find in IMAG an environment to become *active* participants in media production. Reece exclaims: "There's media everywhere and rather than be passive consumers of what's being offered, to be able to make their own media gives them a lot more power. It's empowering and it's also creative and it's strengthening for our people to make their own media." This emphasis on IMAG as a site of cultural autonomy reinforces my location of Aboriginal visual sovereignty in the acts of media production and in control over the tools of media production.

According to its 2002 promotional brochure, IMAG was founded as a collective of Aboriginal artists and filmmakers with a mandate to "encourage and facilitate the promotion, development, and dissemination of First Peoples media arts, arts and culture through our annual media festivals in Vancouver and rural communities throughout B.C." Its initial purpose was to organize an annual Aboriginal film and video festival to provide a screening venue for Aboriginal media that was absent from other film festivals and mainstream media venues in Vancouver. In an interview for the APTN television series *Storytellers in Motion*, Dana Claxton recalled the story behind the creation of IMAG and the IMAGeNation film festival. She explains:

> One of the significant moments was when Shelley Niro (Mohawk) made her film *Honey Moccasin* (1998). She self produced it, she wrote it, she directed it, and she shot it in 16mm film, and I thought it was an extraordinary feat. And she had been sending it around to film festivals and nobody would program it, cause it's this very kooky experimental film, but it still warranted being screened. And I thought, they're not going to let us in! They [dominant society] don't understand our narratives, they perhaps don't want to hear our narratives, they could be afraid of our narratives, because our narratives make them have to think about who they are in relationship to us. So with the invitation of Cleo Reece and some other people we got together and had a meeting and decided to put on a film festival here in Vancouver. It was a reaction to being excluded. (*Storytellers in Motion*, 2006)

In addition to hosting the annual Aboriginal Film and Video Festival, IMAG remained committed to supporting media training programs as well as operating a resource center offering video equipment for rental to members of the community at a low cost or free if they volunteered their time at IMAG.

IMAG held its first media training program in 2000 and in the summer of 2003 hosted a youth program and a professional development program to provide advanced technical training. During the winter of 2004 they received funding from the Greater Vancouver Urban Aboriginal Strategy to run "Healing Hands: Voices of Resistance," a healing-themed training program for at-risk Aboriginal youth. Throughout the fall and winter of 2004–2005 IMAG once again held a training program for youth

Fig. 5. IMAG promotional brochure, 2004. Logo designed by Gord Hill. Image courtesy of Cleo Reece and Gord Hill.

and a professional development program. These training programs provided a service by offering access to technical training and artistic development for Aboriginal community members. For many young Aboriginal people interested in learning about video production, but unsure whether they wanted to commit to the two-year certificate program at Capilano's Indigenous Independent Digital Filmmaking Program (IIDFP), IMAG's training programs offered an introduction to basic media skills.

In contrast to the IIDFP program that is geared toward training Aboriginal filmmakers for involvement in the film and television industries, IMAG was a *media arts* organization and approached Aboriginal media from an artistic perspective.[9] Leena Minifie (Gitxaala) completed both the Capilano College AFTP program and professional development programs at IMAG. We sat in her Eastside apartment one night discussing the differences between the various Aboriginal media training programs in Vancouver. She noted that IMAG was important because it provided an entry point for Aboriginal filmmakers to learn about new media.[10] She asserted, "IMAG focuses on new media art which is something that I think is really important for us to get into and understand and use." Cleo Reece pointed out that IMAG seeks to develop their students as artists and encourages them to approach video production as merely one aspect of their creative development, stating: "Most of our programs have really focused on it [media] as an art form. The goal is to have people develop their skills as artists and enhance their creativity to make these videos."

"INDIAN BUZZERS" AND UNRELIABLE EQUIPMENT—AUGUST 2003

Walking north on Main Street through the Mount Pleasant neighborhood, you walk past numerous coffee shops, apartment buildings, residential side streets, a Dairy Queen, the local IGA, a bingo hall, a Salvation Army thrift shop, a Filipino grocery store, an organic food shop, art galleries, and a hardware store. Pass the intersection of Broadway and Main to continue several more blocks downhill, and you'll reach Main Street and 4th Avenue where, on your left, just past the turquoise and pink motel, there is a one-story industrial building with a sign advertising storage space and Video In, the artist-run center specializing in experimental video and media arts. There is no sign indicating that this building houses IMAG, just a wide bank of windows facing the street and a locked front door. Arriving at IMAG to begin fieldwork, I stood outside this door pressing the buzzer to no avail. I waited outside the building while cars whizzed by on this busy thoroughfare, wondering if I was at the wrong building, until finally someone came out and let me in. Cleo Reece welcomed me into the office, laughing as she explained that the buzzer had been broken for quite some time. "Just knock on the window when you get here, then someone will come out and let you in. That's our "Indian buzzer"!"

While this broken buzzer might seem insignificant or trivial, it is in fact symbolic of the material conditions and financial constraints structuring the space and activities within the IMAG office. Without an operating grant and with unstable and sporadic funding, it was often difficult enough to stretch what little financial resources IMAG had to cover the cost of payroll, rent, and training programs, much less find the money to fix the buzzer when a simple knock on the window worked just as effectively. This IMAG "Indian buzzer" was the subject of much joking within the IMAG office, particularly because it elicited frustrated and perplexed reactions from non-Native people such as delivery men, postal workers, or ethnographers, who kept pressing the broken buzzer to no avail. Although this "Indian buzzer" was reflective of limited material conditions with which IMAG staff members had to work, it served as a "gatekeeping" device in that through word of mouth and experience at IMAG, Aboriginal community members learned of the signal of the "Indian buzzer," enabling IMAG to remain an Aboriginal space rarely disrupted by people from outside the community.

The lack of a stable financial base for IMAG daily operations was reflected not only in the difficulty of paying staff members

Fig. 6. The building where the IMAG office was located from 1998 to 2004. The door to IMAG is located inside the vestibule on the left. IMAG's office space is the room behind the second bank of windows on the left. Photo by author.

regularly, but also in the state of the equipment at the IMAG office. The office housed three computers, one for administrative purposes and two for editing. The administrative computer was sometimes unusable because of computer viruses, while the software on the editing computer sporadically malfunctioned so that a student trying to edit often could view the images but not hear the audio on the footage. As a volunteer I gradually learned how classroom instruction, daily office operations, and media production persevered through limited material conditions and an often unreliable technological environment. IMAG maintained a small video collection and resource library with various Native newspapers, magazines, books, and information about grants and funding. There were two Sony PD150 digital cameras, sound equipment, tripod, and lighting kit that could be rented or loaned to Aboriginal filmmakers. Additionally, there was a TV monitor, VCR, and DVD player used to screen footage or watch videos from the collection.

From the "Indian buzzer" to the duct-taped batteries in the remote control to the cramped office space that hosted numerous office activities to the frustration of dealing with computer equipment frequently malfunctioning, the conditions of production within IMAG required staff members and filmmakers to make the best of the limited circumstances and available equipment.[11] The fact that projects were produced with less than state-of-the-art equipment and inside an often chaotic office space with people checking email, editing videos, attending media training classes, and organizing a festival, not to mention discussing the latest community news and upcoming events, speaks to the dedication of Aboriginal filmmakers to their media practice and also to the dynamic social space of IMAG in which these activities occurred. These conditions of production suggest the ways in which Aboriginal media production at IMAG was deeply embedded in the cultural, spiritual, political, and social activities of Vancouver's urban Aboriginal community.

Accessing Resources and the Role of Mentorship

Although IMAG started as an organization to host an annual Aboriginal film festival, the long-term aim was to provide access to media resources for local Aboriginal filmmakers. IMAG became a crucial site where emerging filmmakers with little funding could access equipment and training to produce their work. While sitting in my small basement apartment one morning with Vera Wabegijig (Anishnaabe), a former IMAG training program coordinator, we discussed the impact that IMAG had on emerging Aboriginal filmmakers. She observed: "Cameras and edit suites are two of the main things that are really expensive

Fig. 7. Vera Wabegijig editing at IMAG. February 2004. Photo by author.

for people if they're just starting out. They don't have the money to go rent the equipment. But IMAG rents things out for free if they know that someone's just starting out." This clarification that IMAG rents equipment for free highlights the way in which IMAG strives to get this equipment into the hands of low-income filmmakers who would not otherwise have access to equipment. Yet, as Wabegijig notes, IMAG does expect something in return for loaning out equipment. Instead of a rental fee, Wabegijig continued: "IMAG expects time back into IMAG. They just want people to become involved in the organizing and keeping IMAG afloat and trying to keep it organized." This flexible loaning policy made the equipment available to a wide range of community members but also drew those members into an ongoing relationship with IMAG activities by requiring people to volunteer their time in lieu of a rental fee. The policy of equipment loans in exchange for volunteer time draws more filmmakers into the "web of people" generated within IMAG activities that serves to create a sense of "community" among Aboriginal filmmakers.

Ryan Mitchell-Morrison (Mi'gmaq), an emerging filmmaker, artist, and DJ, illustrated the fluid incorporation of individuals into a "network of relations" at IMAG as he walked off the street into the fold of IMAG's media community. At a local organic coffee shop on a rather sultry June afternoon he sounded amazed when recalling the ease with which IMAG staff members welcomed him, explaining: "I was really broke and depressed and I was kind of in a rut. I was walking by IMAG one day and I literally just walked in and said, 'Hey, this is me, this is what I do. What are you guys doing? Is there some way I can be a part of it?'" Mitchell-Morrison credits IMAG with developing his technical skills and motivating him to continue making his eclectic media art in which he mixes media and found 16mm footage while creating live electronic soundtracks. "Since then it's like they've taken me under their wing. I was able to take advantage of all the facilities and grow in confidence towards making stuff on Final Cut Pro. Now I just love it and I can't stop!" His eyes light up as he laughs. "So yeah, thanks to IMAG actually for doing these things for me. It's been totally invaluable, it's changed everything." For Mitchell-Morrison, IMAG not only welcomed him but also provided access to equipment, the training to use it, and a community of filmmakers that took him "under their wing."

The social space of IMAG extends the "network of relations" created through IMAG's media activities by nurturing intergenerational ties through mentorship as prominent local Aboriginal filmmakers such as Dana Claxton, Loretta Todd, Greg Coyes, and Zoe Hopkins serve as instructors for IMAG's training programs and as IMAG board members. Claxton connected with Mitchell-Morrison as an instructor in the 2003 professional development training program. She spoke fondly of Mitchell-Morrison, noting that "to me he's happening and he's someone to watch. I'm curious to see what he'll do. I'm also very excited about the next generation because they're just doing things differently." Both Mitchell-Morrison and Wabegijig found important mentoring relationships and training at IMAG and remained involved with ongoing activities of the group. Wabegijig served as the youth training program coordinator for two years, and Mitchell-Morrison served as an instructor, technical assistant, and mentor to the youth in IMAG's training programs. Their involvement as instructors and staff continues to strengthen the "network of relations" that sustains the work at IMAG and provides an important link between their own mentors and the next generation of filmmakers in the Aboriginal youth attending IMAG's training programs.

"Community Is Not a Place, but a Network of Relations"

Anthropologist Susan Lobo characterizes urban Indian communities as "fluid networks based on relationships," noting that while urban Indian residence is dispersed, there are "nodes on the community network that include the many American Indian organizations found in urban areas, seasonal or intermittent events or activities, and sites that hold connotations of special significance" (Lobo 2003, 505). Like Lobo's notion of the "node," Renya Ramirez articulates a concept of "the hub" in her ethnography on urban Indian identity in Silicon Valley. The "node" and the "hub" are salient frameworks for understanding the place of IMAG within Vancouver's urban Aboriginal community. Ramirez describes "the hub" as "a geographical concept. Hubs can represent actual places. Gathering sites or hubs can include cultural events, such as powwows and sweat lodge ceremonies, as well as social and political activities, such as meetings and family gatherings" (Ramirez 2007, 3). She goes on to explain that "the hub suggests how landless Native Americans maintain a sense of connection to their tribal homelands and urban spaces through participation in cultural circuits and maintenance of social networks, as well as shared activity with other Native Americans in the city and on the reservation" (3).

IMAG functioned as an important "node on the community network" and "hub" in Vancouver. It is but one of many Aboriginal organizations—including the Aboriginal Friendship

Fig. 8. Aboriginal Friendship Centre, Vancouver, July 2004. Photo by author.

Centre, Knowledgeable Aboriginal Youth Advocates (KAYA), Urban Native Youth Association (UNYA), *Redwire Native Youth Magazine,* and the Aboriginal Front Door—that serve the needs of Vancouver's Aboriginal community. IMAG provided one site of stability within the fluidity that characterizes urban Aboriginal life and served as an important community center as well as media production center.

Wilma Mankiller (Cherokee) describes the urban Indian community as not "a place, but rather a network of relatedness, of people linked to one another because of family, tribe, shared experiences and shared understandings about those experiences" (Mankiller 2002, xix). Unlike other characterizations of "community" as geographically bounded, urban Aboriginal communities are built on networks of relationships and organizations, such as IMAG, that serve as "nodes" on that network to provide a crucial social space in which the community gathers together to nurture, create, and sustain these relationships.

Odessa Shuquaya emphasized the importance of organizations like IMAG in the urban context where Native people aren't "living traditionally anymore." Late one spring evening, after putting her daughter to bed, we sat at her dining room table speaking about the role of media production in Aboriginal social life in Vancouver. She emphatically proclaimed, "Being in an urban setting we're not living traditionally. We're not living in smaller groups. We're not living with our extended families anymore. Those days are over for a lot of us here in the big city. So I think that just having that web of people [at IMAG] encourages you and gives you strength." Shuquaya explicitly framed the relationships produced at IMAG as providing key "webs of people" that reconfigure "traditional" Aboriginal kinship and sociality to meet the demands of urban life.

IMAG was intimately connected with other Aboriginal organizations and "hubs"—such as the Aboriginal Friendship Centre, the First Nations Longhouse at the University of British Columbia, and the Native Education Centre—that form a landscape of urban Aboriginal spaces within Vancouver. Yet the urban Aboriginal community is not geographically bounded by these spaces but is constituted out of the "networks of relationships" (Lobo 2003) that are produced *within* these spaces. Aboriginal filmmakers draw upon these "webs of people" to provide support, assistance, and labor on media projects. The relationships produced in the social space of daily activities and annual events at IMAG generate a discourse of "Aboriginal community" and Aboriginal sociality that move beyond the space of the actual media production.

Discourses of "Community"

Aboriginal filmmakers describe Vancouver as having a "community" of Aboriginal filmmakers.[12] This represents a perception of Vancouver's Aboriginal media world as "community oriented." Odessa Shuquaya explains, "I think what makes it Aboriginal is the community feel and I think that's the biggest thing for me." Likewise, Vera Wabegijig locates the difference between mainstream media and Aboriginal media in ties to community, stating: "All the Aboriginal productions that I know they're not into being mainstream at all, they're more community based. They want to bring their stories back to their community. They're representing their community." Barb Cranmer describes her filmmaking as rooted in a sense of responsibility to her community. She explained: "I have been involved in film and video for over twenty-five years. The inspiration for my work has come from our people's rich history and stories that are very important. They are stories that most often go unheard. I am the messenger of these stories and our communities have entrusted me with these stories to bring to the wider public."

This articulation of Aboriginal media as community oriented locates this practice as deeply enmeshed in the social networks and cultural life of Aboriginal communities. Media production is a social activity that requires the mobilization of many skills, resources, and hands to see a project through from start to finish. The Aboriginal media world in Vancouver, while large in comparison to other Aboriginal media worlds in Canada, is nonetheless small enough for people to know and to rely on each other for employment, social support, and labor on their own projects.

The Boundaries of "Community"

In 2004 the IMAG staff decided to include a Métis program in the IMAGeNation Film Festival as a way to extend the "network of relations" to the Métis community, with the hope of increasing Métis audience attendance and establishing collaborative partnerships with local Métis cultural organizations.[13] The decision to include a Métis program prompted discussion around the politics of "who is and who isn't Indian," reflecting a negotiation around the boundaries of the "Aboriginal community" and "Aboriginality."

On a cold and wet January afternoon the IMAG office bustles with activity as the opening night for the 2004 IMAGENation Aboriginal Film and Video Festival is only three weeks away. The festival staff including Cleo Reece, festival director, Leena Minifie, festival publicist, Odessa Shuquaya, festival coordinator, Vera Wabegijig, training program coordinator, and myself sit around the table in the IMAG office discussing the latest programming decisions.

A young Aboriginal woman stops by the office to use the computer to work on a school project, and as our conversation turns toward the inclusion of a Métis film program, this woman, who had previously worked on the IMAGENation programming committee, exclaims, "Geez, I leave this organization and when I come back you're programming Métis!"

Leena replies, "What's wrong with Métis?"

The other woman responds, "Nothing. They're just not Aboriginal."[14] The air in the office grows a bit tense.

The woman then chuckles and self-effacingly declares, "What do I know about being Aboriginal anyway? I don't even know what that term *Aboriginal* is!"

Cleo chimes in, "*Aboriginal* is an okay term to use, it just means original people." Cleo, an elder, diffuses the tension by reminding us of the shared indigeneity of Aboriginal people as "original people," regardless of the designation Métis, status, or nonstatus.

The designation of Métis people as "not Aboriginal" is reflective not only of one aspect of a local discourse on Aboriginality in Vancouver, but also of legal divisions entrenched in Canada's 1982 Constitution in which the Canadian government recognized three legal categories of Aboriginal peoples: status Indians (First Nations), Métis, and Inuit. Scholar Bonita Lawrence attributes these legal distinctions to the colonial apparatus that naturalized divisions between "Indian" and "Métis," when, in fact, these are social constructions created in Canadian policy. She states that when Canada created these legal categories in the 1982

Constitution, "this recognition has indelibly separated "Métis" from "Indian" as coherent and distinctly separate entities in the minds of the public (and many indigenous people), as if there had always been, forever, hard and fast physical and cultural distinctions between all Indians and all Métis" (Lawrence 2004, 95). The impact of colonial legal regimes has exacerbated and deepened these divisions between Métis and Aboriginal.[15]

In describing the Vancouver Aboriginal media world as a "community" I am not asserting that there is agreement between all members, nor do I want to leave the reader with the impression that this is a taken-for-granted category by Aboriginal filmmakers. As seen in the vignette above, there are divisions within this community, as within all communities, but it is through their shared dialogue—about who is included as a member, what constitutes "Aboriginal media," the social obligations of filmmakers, the role of family and kinship within these practices, what kinds of stories filmmakers should tell—that the boundaries of this community are produced. Filmmakers in Vancouver are working in a diverse, urban setting with Aboriginal people from numerous tribal backgrounds, generations, and socioeconomic backgrounds. One of the ways that Aboriginal filmmakers respond to the demands of urban life is to use media production as a practice around which an Aboriginal "community"—or social group with shared practices, discourses, and goals—can be shaped and negotiated.

Aboriginal filmmakers can be thought of as a "community of practice" (Lave and Wenger 1991) that exists within the broader urban Aboriginal community. A community of practice is "an aggregate of people who come together around mutual engagement in an endeavor. Ways of doing things, ways of talking, beliefs, values, power relations—in short practices—emerge" (Eckert and McConnell-Ginet 1992, 463). Aboriginal filmmakers come together to form a community of practice through their mutual engagement in the practices of media production. They use the term *community* to refer both to the larger Vancouver

Aboriginal community and to the community of Aboriginal film-makers. While I initially tried to analytically separate these two social groups, Archer Pechawis chided me for trying to make this distinction. It is important to keep in mind, as he reminded me, that "it's a very Western idea to even have this conversation about the 'Native media community' as if it is somehow different from the Native community. Because it's not, there is no difference." He emphatically asserted: "We *are* the Native community. We're Indians. We're part of the community. Media and art are just what we do." Throughout this book I use the term *community*, as do the filmmakers with whom I worked, to refer both to the community of practice of Aboriginal filmmaking and the larger urban Aboriginal community.

It is no accident that Vancouver's Aboriginal media world is perceived to be "community-oriented" and that IMAG members articulate a discourse of "community building" through the organization's activities and events. Vancouver's established filmmakers such as Archer Pechawis, Cleo Reece, Dana Claxton, Loretta Todd, Donald Morin, and Dorothy Christian are all activists who consciously work to use artistic practice and media production as a tool for grassroots community building. Some individuals of this generation suffered through residential schools and the foster care system or had family members impacted by these colonial policies. Some were not raised on reserves or had limited contact with their Native families and cultural communities. Through their life histories and lived experiences some individuals knew firsthand the consequences of *not* having an Aboriginal community. They fought for access to training and resources for Aboriginal media production and used their projects to recuperate Aboriginal histories, cultural traditions, and social practices to create a foundation for the emergent Aboriginal media world in Vancouver that generated a sense of shared "community." Younger filmmakers such as Odessa Shuquaya, Leena Minifie, Vera Wabegijig, Kevin Lee Burton, and Helen Haig-Brown identify "responsibility to community," as nurtured by these founders, as a key cultural value within Aboriginal media.

Odessa Shuquaya sees the production of community ties as one of the most important functions of IMAG, explaining, "IMAG is just a great support system. I think it's more than just networking because I believe that you actually *are* creating relationships with people and you do become part of the community." She highlighted the importance of "having a Native community" in an urban setting, stating, "I think that's very important, especially for urban Natives because many people are displaced from their communities." She also emphasized the "reciprocity" of these networks, declaring: "If you need someone to help you with something they can be there for you or you can help your community by employing them in the future or they'll employ you. It's a really reciprocal thing." Leena Minifie identified IMAG as a hub of information where individuals involved in various domains of the Aboriginal media world (e.g., independent production, television production, National Film Board of Canada projects, experimental video) can learn about each other's projects and the latest community news. She describes IMAG as a "focal point," saying: "I don't think we would have as vibrant or supportive of a community if we didn't have groups that tie people together. A lot of the producers don't talk to each other, people don't know who's working on what. People wouldn't be able to meet up and bump into each other if there wasn't a focal point. I think IMAG *is* that focal point in Vancouver."

CONSTRUCTING ABORIGINAL SPACE IN VANCOUVER—JANUARY 2004

"What if we have part of the opening night events at an art gallery?" Leena Minifie, festival publicist, proposes to the programming committee.

"We always have the opening night events at the Friendship Centre. Everyone in the community comes out for opening night." Cleo Reece, the festival director responds.

"Yeah, but this year we're having video installations as part of opening night. We can't put those in the gym at the Friendship Centre. The lighting is terrible and there isn't any space," Leena points out.

Odessa Shuquaya, festival coordinator, cautions, "But will people really go to an art gallery for opening night?"

Vera Wabegijig, festival assistant, quips, "Yeah, Indians don't go to galleries!"[16]

Everyone in the IMAG office laughs along with Vera, who can always be counted on for a good joke.

"What if we had the film screenings and food at the Friendship Centre and then moved part of the evening's events to an art gallery like the grunt gallery or Western Front?" Leena asks tentatively.[17]

"No one has cars to get from the Friendship Centre to the grunt." Odessa highlights the logistical problems of splitting the opening night events between two locations. "And most people don't have money for the bus either!"

"We wouldn't want to divide the community on opening night between those that would want to go to a gallery and those that wouldn't," Vera adds.

"This festival is for the people. It's for the community. That's why we have all the food on opening night and we don't charge an admission fee. We want as many of our people as possible to be there. We're not moving the opening night from the Friendship Centre." Cleo gently reminds the younger staff members.

"I definitely agree. I wouldn't want to cause any divisions. I just thought it would be nice to have a gallery space for these video installations. It would be nice for the community to see this kind of work too," Leena replies.

"How about we try to get the Simon Baker Room at the Friendship Centre? That way we could have video installations in there and people could go back and forth from there to the gym," Cleo offers as a compromise.[18]

"That sounds good. I like that idea," Vera responds, and Leena nods in agreement. They are the artists whose video installations will be exhibited during opening night.

"I think the Métis fiddlers have that room booked already, but I'll give them a call and see if I can get them to let us use the room," Odessa adds.

The location for opening night is settled. It will remain at the Friendship Centre, an Aboriginal social space that is accessible to the community and in which community members feel comfortable. Everyone at IMAG agrees that the best part about IMAGeNation on opening night is seeing so many community members come out to see their own stories on-screen.

Screening IMAGeNation: Creating
Visibility for Aboriginal Media

The IMAGeNation Festival provided an important screening venue to show Aboriginal media to the Aboriginal community who are considered the primary festival audience. In an interview for an IMAG student video project Cleo Reece proclaimed: "To us this festival is something really exciting. It's unique in this part of the world. We are showing stories of people that would not be shown. It's a validation of the work of the artists. It's something to be really proud of and to celebrate. This is what we try to do every year."

By "showing stories of people that would not be shown" the festival claims a space for Aboriginal voices and stories and enacts visual sovereignty. Just as Aboriginal filmmakers work to ensure that Aboriginal people see themselves reflected on-screen, IMAGeNation was a key venue through which this media is reflected back to Aboriginal audiences. Zoe Hopkins (Heiltsuk/Mohawk), an IMAG board member and a filmmaker, echoed Reece, saying, "I think the IMAGeNation festival is a really great venue to show work that wouldn't normally get seen in mainstream festivals. People like screening with other Native filmmakers so it's a really nice venue to do that."

Aboriginal media projects are collaborative undertakings, and several filmmakers explained that the most satisfying thing about

Fig. 9. Opening night of the 2004 IMAGeNation Aboriginal Film and Video Festival held at the Aboriginal Friendship Centre. February 26, 2004. Photo by author.

being an Aboriginal filmmaker is watching Aboriginal audiences respond to their seeing their own faces on-screen. Aboriginal film festivals like IMAGeNation are increasingly becoming the most accessible venue to reach a broad Aboriginal audience.[19] Dorothy Christian (Secwepemc/Syilx), a member of the 2004 IMAGeNation Programming Committee, reinforced this sentiment, noting, "The thing that I love to see are people's faces when they see themselves or their community or their family on screen. To me it's like, yeah, it was worth all the hassles that we went through to get this done. To me that's the best part." Christian reminded me that Aboriginal media is inscribed with social relationships and family ties that are resonant for Aboriginal audiences.

Other filmmakers highlight the potential of IMAGeNation to elevate recognition for Aboriginal media by the larger Vancouver society. One February afternoon while sitting around in the IMAG office several staff members and volunteers discussed possible future directions of IMAG. One filmmaker viewed IMAG as a space that could garner increased recognition for Aboriginal media, explaining: "We're producing a lot of really great work here and it's not getting the level of recognition that it could. I see IMAG as having the potential to be more than just this office. It has a chance, through events like the festival, to broaden out the recognition and impact of Aboriginal media."[20] While the activities of IMAG extend the "network of relations" to build a stronger sense of community among Aboriginal filmmakers, IMAGeNation broadened visibility for Aboriginal media and to claim recognition for this work within Vancouver.

Gathering the Community

The IMAGeNation Festival physically brought the Vancouver Aboriginal community together in a shared social space over the course of four days of screenings and cultural events. The community focus of the festival was evident in every aspect of the festival organization from the program schedule to the screening venue to pay-what-you-can ticket prices for community members to the opening night celebration held at the Friendship Centre. IMAGeNation was an important annual community event that reinforced and strengthened the "network of relations," including invaluable intergenerational ties. Cleo Reece situated IMAGeNation within this matrix of Aboriginal social relations, writing in the 2004 IMAGeNation Festival program, "Elders and children, teenagers and adults converge at events throughout the year and IMAGeNation is one of them, creating a unity of purpose and celebration in times of hardship and stress" (Reece 2004, 23). Elder Bob George (Tsleil-Waututh) echoed this sentiment during his welcoming prayer at the opening night of the 2004 IMAGeNa-tion Festival. He praised the work of the festival for "gathering us all here today" and repeatedly remarked how happy he was to see everyone together. He recalled that his elders told him that it is "important for us to come together like this," while he called for more events like IMAGeNation, stating that "we need to have more gatherings like this for our people here in the city."

Dana Claxton described the "ripple effects" of IMAGeNation, explaining that "if you put it [IMAGeNation Festival] on the people will come. I think it's a very important festival because it just brings the work out and people come and see the work." She noted: "the spinoff effects of that are, young people going, 'Hey, I can do this.' I think it has huge rippling effects on the Aboriginal community as a whole in terms of self-identification and self-analysis." The idea that if you "put the festival on, the people will come" motivated festival staff during the intensive labor required to organize IMAGeNation each year as they saw the positive impact on the community and sought to ensure that there remained a venue where Aboriginal people could see their own stories on-screen at an event that also strengthened social ties and cultural identity.

Conclusion

IMAG performed myriad roles and social functions within the Aboriginal media world and the larger urban Aboriginal com-munity. By offering media training workshops, providing social support, serving as a makeshift childcare center for the family of IMAG staff and students, always having a pot of coffee and food around, or burning sage to smudge the office, IMAG functioned as a vibrant community center and a crucial "hub" in Vancou-ver's Aboriginal community. These community practices and social relationships produced at IMAG are as equally vital as the actual media production activity that occurred within and outside the walls of the IMAG office. Cleo Reece, in particular, played a prominent role in daily activities of the organization as an "auntie" to the students and filmmakers who came through IMAG's door. As an "auntie" and an activist who consciously used what little resources and funds IMAG had in the service of building community ties and responding to the needs of Aboriginal media artists, Reece provided a welcoming presence to those who visited IMAG. The daily activities of the office—the social life behind media production—illustrate that Aboriginal media move beyond just an on-screen intervention in the Canadian mediascape but also serve as a catalyst off-screen around which Aboriginal social life, community ties, and cultural practices are enacted, created, and negotiated.

In 2007, due to a series of cascading events, IMAG disbanded largely because of financial reasons and generational differences between board members. In 2006 Cleo Reece, who was so central to the operation of IMAG, decided to move back to her traditional territory near Fort McMurray in northern Alberta. Her daughter, Skeena Reece (Cree/Tsimshian/Gitksan), ran IMAG for a while before leaving to concentrate on her own art and media practice. With no grant money coming in, and fewer individuals willing to shoulder the burden of keeping IMAG going, the organization ultimately fell apart. IMAG no longer exists as an active organization: however, that does not diminish its legacy or the tremendous impact it made while it was active in Vancouver. IMAG was in operation for nine years, and like many arts and Aboriginal cultural organizations, it was largely underfunded and forced to operate from grant to grant. During this time period IMAG began the first (and for a long time the only) Aboriginal media festival on the Canadian West Coast, trained dozens of Aboriginal filmmakers, hosted conferences on Aboriginal media, collaborated on art and media exhibitions with the grunt gallery and Video In/Video Out (VIVO), functioned as a media production center, offered video equipment for use by Aboriginal filmmakers and community members, participated in demonstrations and protests supporting Aboriginal rights, and served as a vital community center and gathering place for Aboriginal filmmakers and members of Vancouver's urban Aboriginal community. All of these accomplishments are a tribute to the tremendous dedication of the IMAG staff and volunteers. There is much frustration about the dissolution of IMAG and sadness at the hole this has created in Vancouver's Aboriginal media world and in the urban Aboriginal community at large. When I returned to Vancouver in 2009 several filmmakers lamented, "Now that we don't have IMAG, we don't get together anymore like we used to." While IMAG no longer exists, there are other venues and media arts events that continue to gather the community together. In 2011 three Aboriginal filmmakers organized the first annual Vancouver Indigenous Media Arts Festival (VIMAF), which is a new venue that has taken up the mantle where IMAG left off. As discussed in the epilogue, I look forward to seeing the new directions that this festival will take Aboriginal media in Vancouver.

CHAPTER TWO

Canadian Cultural Policy and Aboriginal Media

ONE FILMMAKER'S TAKE ON THE NATIONAL FILM
BOARD OF CANADA—FEBRUARY 2004

It's 2:30 in the morning, and Odessa and I have just returned from the closing gala of the 2004 IMAGENation Film Festival. We sit in the rental van on a darkened street in front of her apartment eating ice cream and talking about the festival. We chat about audience attendance, ticket sales, our thoughts about specific films, and the excitement of the closing party with its featured guest, War Party, a Native hip-hop group that traveled from Hobbema, Alberta, for the event. We are exhausted after four days of film screenings, events, and workshops. Our conversation turns to the National Film Board of Canada (NFB), which for the first time was involved with IMAGENation as a sponsor. Odessa's position as festival coordinator was funded as an internship through the NFB, and while she expresses gratitude for the opportunities that this internship has afforded her, she expresses hesitation about the NFB as a cultural institution. She turns to me and emphatically declares: "I have some trepidations with my political views on a government agency, such as the NFB, which is totally government funded, giving money to Aboriginal filmmakers to make films and then the NFB owns those films. They own the distribution rights—they own them! And isn't that just another form of colonialism?"

Introduction

This exchange with Odessa Shuquaya articulates a key paradoxical characteristic of Aboriginal visual sovereignty; namely, that much of the Aboriginal media produced in Canada is funded by Canadian cultural institutions. These cultural institutions—the National Film Board of Canada, Canada Council for the Arts, Telefilm Canada—provide funding for Aboriginal media under their mandate to support *Canadian* cultural sovereignty, particularly vis-à-vis American media. What implications does this embrace of Aboriginal media by Canadian cultural institutions have for Aboriginal visual sovereignty? Can Aboriginal filmmakers express cultural autonomy when they are funded by the very same Canadian government that they often critique? How does visual sovereignty mediate or intensify tensions between Canadian cultural sovereignty and Aboriginal sovereignty?

This chapter explores the complexities and paradoxes of Aboriginal visual sovereignty by analyzing the emergence of Aboriginal media production in Canada, situating it within the broader framework of Canadian cultural policy. I emphasize the role of Aboriginal activists who pushed for access to national cultural institutions throughout the 1960s and 1970s. I provide an in-depth analysis of Canada's National Film Board as a case study of a Canadian government institution that has implemented programs for Aboriginal media for over forty years. Drawing upon research in the National Film Board archives as well as interviews with Aboriginal filmmakers who have worked with the NFB, I examine both the constraints and support that the NFB has created for Aboriginal filmmakers. The NFB provides an excellent case study for examining the role of government cultural institutions in allocating resources and funding for Aboriginal media, as well as to explore the tensions that are sometimes raised during the intercultural interactions that occur when Aboriginal filmmakers work with the NFB.

Early History of the National Film Board of Canada

The early history of Canadian film production was characterized by Canadian government agencies that sought to use this technology to promote projects of nation-building (Armatage et al. 1999; Dorland 1996; Gasher 2002; Holmes 1992; R. Morris 1994).[1] Throughout the early twentieth century the Canadian state sporadically supported film production designed to meet specific political objectives—immigration, tourism, foreign investment, and the war effort—which attested to their view of film as an effective medium for education, propaganda, and nation-building (Magder 1993).[2] In 1939 the National Film Board of Canada was created under the leadership of John Grierson with the mission to "produce and promote the distribution of films designed to interpret Canada to Canadian and other nations" (G. Evans 1991, 4). The National Film Board sought to unify the disparate provincial, cultural, and ethnic experiences of Canadians by providing a national cinema that would promote a national Canadian identity. The NFB worked to "reproduce the nation as subjects who form a community of belonging to a specific imagining of the Canadian nation" (Gittings 2002, 20).

The development of the National Film Board with John Grierson at the helm entrenched documentary cinema as the quintessential Canadian film genre. Grierson viewed feature films as a form of low popular culture and envisioned a more erudite, instructional Canadian national cinema. For Grierson, "film was a medium suited to education and to the development of a more informed and democratic public opinion" (Magder 1993, 53). By 1945 the NFB had twelve production units and close to eight hundred employees, and it had become a considerable force in film production, garnering much national public support, particularly through its development of various film councils around Canada. Another unique aspect of the NFB was its development of an alternative nontheatrical distribution system. By developing "rural traveling cinema circuits" the NFB brought films to small communities across the country. Ninety-two rural cinema circuits reached approximately a quarter of a million people a month by 1945 (G. Evans 1991).[3] The NFB also made films available to the public by establishing twenty different regional film libraries. The development of alternative exhibition sites for NFB films helped to garner public support and create broader audiences for NFB productions, attempting to forge national identity through a shared spectatorship (Gittings 2002).

In the 1960s the NFB underwent a shift in ideological and production structure as it decentralized and began a process of regionalization that reconfigured the earlier emphasis on national identity to focus on the diversity of Canadian regional experiences (G. Evans 1991; Gittings 2002; Magder 1993). In the late 1960s the NFB established the Challenge for Change Program to use media production for social activism among minority and disadvantaged groups around the country (G. Evans 1991). Technological developments enabled this shift as the NFB's in-house laboratory was at the forefront of the development of lightweight, portable filmmaking equipment enabling community-based filmmaking and low-budget feature films (Feldman 1996). The move away from the universalizing pan-Canadianism of earlier NFB works extended to gender difference in 1974 when the NFB established Studio D, the world's first publicly funded women's production unit (Armatage et al. 1999).[4] This ideological shift in the NFB's structure encouraged the production of films that produced alternative narratives of Canadian history, experiences, and identity. Thus, while the NFB was initially created as an institution to promote nationalist visions of Canadian identity, its programs providing access to filmmakers from marginalized communities ultimately led the NFB to support films, such as Alanis Obomsawin's *Kanehsatake: 270 Years of Resistance* (1993), that interrogate and challenge dominant Canadian national narratives (Gittings 2002).

Canadian Film Policy in "Hollywood North"

A Canadian feature film industry did not develop in the early twentieth century largely as a result of the dominance of Hollywood film production and the lack of Canadian state support for feature films.[5] In 1967 the Canadian government invested $10 million dollars in Canadian feature film production through the creation of the Canadian Film Development Corporation (CFDC). However, the American monopoly on theatrical distribution in Canada kept the Canadian public from seeing Canadian features (Pendakur 1990).[6] Although Canadian feature films have won international critical acclaim, it is estimated that a scant 2 percent of Canadian cinema screens reflect Canadian images back to their audiences (Gittings 2002). Canada remains a large market for American films, and American distributors continue to include Canada as part of their "domestic market."[7]

In this climate Canadian producers work to ensure that Canadian content, experiences, and narratives are not completely eclipsed by the overwhelming presence of American media. Under the 1991 Broadcasting Act, the Canadian government defined broadcasting as a "public service essential to national and cultural sovereignty." To enact this policy Canada's broadcasting regulator, the Canadian Radio-television and Telecommunications Commission (CRTC), established a system of "quotas" to regulate the amount of Canadian program content broadcast in Canada. The resulting Canadian content rules, which came to be known as "CanCon," were devised to stimulate Canada's cultural production by ensuring greater exposure for Canadian artists in Canada's marketplaces. CanCon rules apply to radio, television, and specialty broadcasting, but not to cinema.[8]

Sarah Polley, a Canadian actor who has actively supported independent Canadian film and television production, urged the Canadian government to enforce the Broadcasting Act to provide more support for Canadian cinema. Speaking before Parliament in April 2005 she proclaimed, "It's time our government fixed its film policy that has sold our screens to another country." She proposed that the government force theaters to show more Canadian films and their screen trailers. "I think it should be part of broadcasters' licensing requirements that they show trailers for Canadian films," she declared in an interview on *Canada A M* that aired prior to her appearance before the committee. "Otherwise, I don't know how we're supposed to, with the deluge of American films and their $100-million marketing budgets, how we're ever supposed to have the opportunity to choose what we want to see."[9]

Aboriginal media fit prominently into this concern for Canadian cinematic content, and some of the international film success that Canadian films have received in the last few years is the result of Aboriginal films. Aboriginal film continues to play a strong role in the presence of Canadian film in film festivals around the world, as demonstrated by the 2004 Sundance Film Festival where eighteen Canadian films were represented, seven of which were by Aboriginal directors. Additionally, during the 2011 Native American Film and Video Festival held by the Smithsonian's National Museum of the American Indian in New York, the press release indicates that forty out of the eighty films screened were produced in Canada.[10] The strong government support for Aboriginal media in Canada is part of a larger effort by the Canadian government to maintain Canadian content on-screen and to strengthen the Canadian media industry. This support has subsequently heightened the predominance of Aboriginal Canadian media in international indigenous film festivals and global circuits.

Canadian State Support for Aboriginal Media

Embraced as part of the national project of preserving Canadian content on Canadian screens, the Canadian government has implemented funding, training, and production resources for Aboriginal filmmakers since the 1970s. Aboriginal filmmakers contend that access to and control over the production of images of their lives, communities, and experiences are central to Aboriginal self-determination. Tlingit filmmaker Carol Geddes asserts that "as First Nations people move into an era of greater self-determination, one of the important aspects of that self-determination is to interpret our own realities in media . . . and we must take the means of production of our images into our own hands as a way of taking our place as distinct cultures in Canada" (Geddes qtd. in de Rosa 2002). Aboriginal media production is intimately connected to political activism as much as cultural practices of storytelling, as Aboriginal filmmakers strive to represent the experiences of their communities (Chaat Smith 1994; Kalafatic 1999; Silverman 2002; Singer 2001).

To examine the emergence of Aboriginal media production as a vibrant "field of cultural production" (Bourdieu 1993), one must look at the ways in which the Canadian state, responding to pressure from Aboriginal filmmakers and activists, has supported the development of funding, training, production facilities, broadcasting, and distribution for Aboriginal media. Gains for Aboriginal media, whether in the form of changes in broadcast policy or the allocation of funding, are the direct result of many decades of hard work, lobbying, and activism by Aboriginal media producers and their non-Aboriginal supporters within these institutions. It is important to acknowledge the role of non-Aboriginal producers and activists at the National Film Board such as George Stoney, Colin Low, Dorothy Hénaut, and Bonnie Klein, who provided support for Aboriginal media programs, as well as Lorna Roth, who helped with efforts to develop Northern Native broadcasting, and Norman Cohn, who has been a collaborator with Zacharias Kunuk and Igloolik Isuma Productions for several decades.

In the following section I trace the emergence of Aboriginal media in Canada from the earliest initiatives at the National Film Board to the development of the Aboriginal Filmmaking Program. The NFB serves as a case study for examining the uneasy embrace of Aboriginal media within broader efforts to support

Canadian cultural sovereignty on-screen that raises tensions for Aboriginal visual sovereignty. Interviews with Aboriginal filmmakers who have worked with the NFB are interwoven with archival materials to provide a history of the impact of Canadian cultural policy on Aboriginal media practices.

Early Initiatives at the National Film Board

> Challenge for Change attempts to implicate the communications media in the process of social change. The training of an Indian Film Crew is based on the belief that people should speak for themselves instead of being spoken for.
> DOROTHY TODD HÉNAUT AND BONNIE KLEIN,
> "In the Hands of Citizens: A Video Report"

One of the first venues of Canadian state support for Aboriginal media production began in 1969 with the inauguration of the National Film Board's Challenge for Change program.[11] This program was designed to use filmmaking for social activism, providing the tools of media production to disadvantaged communities so that they could document their experiences (G. Evans 1991). The aim of the Challenge for Change program was to "improve communications, create greater understanding, promote new ideas and provoke social change" (Hénaut and Klein 1969, 1). New film and video technologies in the late 1960s and early 1970s made equipment portable, accessible, inexpensive, and a central feature of social activism. One of the remarkable innovations of this program was the involvement of NFB staff in training local film crews to document their stories and struggles from their own perspectives.[12] Many of the Challenge for Change film projects worked with urban and rural poor communities in an effort to raise awareness of their situation and improve access to government resources and aid for these communities.[13]

Dorothy Todd Hénaut, Challenge for Change staff member and editor of the *Challenge for Change Newsletters*, described the goal of this program: "Our main role is to experiment with a certain approach to film and other media, putting the media into the hands of the voiceless, developing films that will be useful tools for them, reversing the classic role of the filmmaker as subjective—or objective—observer, to that of the filmmaker as social catalyst—and a new kind of social worker" (Hénaut 1970, 2). The Challenge for Change program developed a theory of film as an effective medium for social change to create a wider representation of Canadian experiences and raise awareness about social issues in Canadian society.[14]

The Challenge for Change program was active until 1980 and produced over 140 films during that time (Waugh, Baker, and Winton 2010). Although the program officially ended in 1980, the spirit of using film and video to "give voice to the voiceless" carried over into many other initiatives within the NFB, including Studio One and the Aboriginal Filmmaking Program, which are discussed below.[15]

Indian Film Crew

By the late 1960s the National Film Board had made many films concerning Aboriginal issues, but there had not yet been a film produced by an Aboriginal filmmaker. When American documentary filmmaker and activist George Stoney became the head of the Challenge for Change program in 1969, he sought to use this program to help Indian political activists document their struggles and community experiences. Created in 1968, the Indian Film Crew (IFC) was a joint project between the Company of Young Canadians (CYC), a government-sponsored youth volunteer organization, the National Film Board, and the Department of Indian and Northern Affairs Canada (INAC).[16] Under the initial arrangement the NFB provided training, equipment, and facilities while the Company of Young Canadians covered minimal living expenses in Montreal and on location.[17] The Indian Film Crew operated between 1968 and 1970, training six Aboriginal men and one Aboriginal woman in basic film production skills, beginning with a six-week general cinema course and additional months of specialized training in certain film trades (e.g., editing, cinematography, sound) before starting on their projects in the field. The aim of the IFC was to "promote social change by stimulating dialogue among the various Indian nations living on reserves" (Carriere 1990, 5). The Challenge for Change staff sought to reflect Aboriginal diversity by choosing participants from various reserves across Canada.[18]

Although the Indian Film Crew program did provide basic training for several Aboriginal filmmakers, it did not serve as a long-term commitment to Aboriginal film production. The NFB recognized this and, in 1971, developed the Indian Film Training Program (IFTP) to provide more advanced training and offer additional filmmaking opportunities for Aboriginal filmmakers. Working with INAC, the NFB chose six Indians from various tribes and communities to participate in the Indian Film Training Program in Montreal from 1971 to 1973.

INAC was eager to support the IFTP as an opportunity to create employment and job skills training for Aboriginal youth. In a 1970 letter to the NFB, Assistant Deputy Minister for Indian and Northern Affairs J. B. Bergevin stated that the INAC was "happy to support training Indians in filmmaking with the acquisition of skills in film-making leading to the Indians employment in the industry will be the main criterion in our joint training program, and the production of Indian content films will be of secondary consideration, as there can be no guarantee that films of Indian content will be produced."[19] INAC administrators saw the Indian Film Training Program at the National Film Board as a way to provide job training and employment for Aboriginal youth to integrate them within the job force of the Canadian nation-state.[20]

The early films produced under both the Indian Film Crew and the Indian Film Training Program reflected a dedication and commitment to Aboriginal political activism.[21] The first film completed by the Indian Film Crew was *The Ballad of Crowfoot* (1968) produced by Willie Dunn (Mi'kmaq), which used archival photographs and an original score to create a scathing indictment of Canada's historical and contemporary treatment of Aboriginal peoples. Another powerful film produced under this program was *You Are on Indian Land* (1969), directed by George Stoney and made at the request of Mike Mitchell, a Mohawk activist who was part of the Indian Film Crew. This film documented Mohawk activists blocking an international bridge to protest the Canadian government charging duties on goods brought into Canada from the United States, in violation of the 1794 Jay Treaty under which Aboriginal people are guaranteed free passage across the U.S.-Canadian border. This film was screened in many different reserve communities and helped to encourage other Native activists to use film to document their activism. *You Are on Indian Land* traveled to the United States and was screened at the American Indian Movement (AIM) 1969–1971 occupation of Alcatraz, building solidarity between Native political activists across the U.S.-Canadian border.[22] Although participants expressed concern about insufficient funding and the lack of long-term commitment, the Challenge for Change program was instrumental in providing an early forum through the IFC and IFTP for Indian activists to learn the technical skills for film production, opening up a space within the NFB for Indian-produced work documenting Indian perspectives (Ginsburg 1999).

To address a longer-term commitment to Aboriginal filmmaking, IFC and IFTP participants proposed that the NFB establish an "Indian studio" similar to the NFB's English and French production studios. Mike Mitchell's (Mohawk) 1973 proposal argues:

These young men [through IFC and IFTP] have developed skills and techniques which, to this time, have been almost non-existent and which should be utilized for the benefit of Indian communities. This however, creates a *problem*: the contract will expire at the end of May, so there will be no money for them to make films. Also, within the NFB there exist two productions; one English, one French. The Indians do not fit in either. Anyway, the Film Board budget is usually spent a year ahead, so the solution right now would be for the Indians to have their own Indian Film Production.[23]

This proposal also raised a larger issue: while cultural institutions, such as the NFB, were willing to fund basic training programs for Aboriginal people, the lack of full-time employment opportunities or advanced training ultimately did not dismantle structural discrimination facing Aboriginal filmmakers in the media industry. Although the IFC and IFTP participants pointed out this issue in the early 1970s, it remains a central concern of Aboriginal filmmakers today. Cultural institutions including the NFB, Canada Council, CBC, or Telefilm often do not alter their institutional structure by hiring full-time Aboriginal staff members.

Studio One: An NFB Aboriginal Production Unit

Although it took many years to make Mike Mitchell's dream of an Indian studio a reality, an Aboriginal production studio, named Studio One, was created at the NFB in 1991.[24] Several social and political factors influenced the development of Studio One in the early 1990s. In the late 1980s and early 1990s debates about the politics of representation were prominent as Aboriginal activists pushed for attention to land claims, resource rights, and treaty rights in Canada, while Aboriginal artists, writers, and filmmakers brought attention to the long history of appropriation of Aboriginal stories by non-Aboriginal people. Several non-Aboriginal filmmakers at the NFB sustained careers producing films about Aboriginal stories, and Aboriginal filmmakers pushed for the NFB to ensure that Aboriginal people told Aboriginal stories. The NFB consulted with filmmakers and organizations at the Aboriginal Film and Video Makers Symposium held in Edmonton in 1991 and consequently decided to move forward with plans to develop an Aboriginal studio. An important political factor in the timing of the development of Studio One was undoubtedly the Oka crisis in 1990—a seventy-eight-day armed standoff between Mohawk warriors of Kanehsatake and Kahn-awake, Quebec provincial police, and Canadian soldiers—that remained fresh in the minds of the NFB staff as well as in the national Canadian consciousness.[25] The Oka crisis prompted the Canadian government to reevaluate its relationship with Aboriginal communities and in 1992 led to an investigation for the Royal Commission on Aboriginal Peoples.[26]

In the post-Oka era, Aboriginal activists and filmmakers sought to ensure that Aboriginal filmmakers were given access to the resources, equipment, and training necessary to produce Aboriginal media *by and for* Aboriginal people. The NFB's decision to support the development of Studio One was one aspect of the Canadian government's response to Oka and an attempt to implement programming, access to training, and funding as a move toward reconciliation. In addition to providing training for Aboriginal filmmakers to tell their own stories, Studio One was positioned as a resource for improving communication and understanding between Aboriginal and non-Aboriginal communities, thus situating it within the NFB's mandate to "interpret Canada to Canadians." A proposal for Studio One later states: "While our political structures are familiar with the issues at hand, the Canadian public has only seen a non-native media's interpretation of those issues. This cannot satisfy the aboriginal communities and, in the end, denies all Canadians an important reflection of a part of our national reality."[27] While the NFB envisioned Studio One as a place to create media that would educate the broader Canadian audience about Aboriginal issues from Aboriginal perspectives, Aboriginal filmmakers saw Studio One as a chance to create media for Aboriginal audiences and to strengthen training and production skills in the emerging field of Aboriginal media.

Studio One was located in Edmonton, Alberta, with an initial budget of $250,000 devoted exclusively to training and technical support for Aboriginal filmmakers. Edmonton was chosen because of its "proximity to a large concentration of First

Peoples" and because the NFB's Northwest Centre, also located in Edmonton, agreed to provide infrastructure to administer and coordinate the studio to lessen costs. Studio One staff initially hoped to raise a $1.4 million budget for the Studio but were only able to raise $250,000 for the first year. At this time Studio One had the lowest budget of all NFB studios, and in 1991 the total budget of $250,000 was roughly equal to the average cost of one documentary.[28] Issues of underfunding plagued Studio One, and many Aboriginal filmmakers interpreted limited funds as a lack of commitment by the NFB to Aboriginal filmmaking.

As discussed in the opening vignette of this chapter, the copyright of Aboriginal projects produced at the NFB is held by the NFB, and these projects are required to have an NFB executive producer overseeing the production. This is the case for all films produced with NFB. Odessa Shuquaya raised the question about whether this is another form of colonialism to have the NFB owning the copyright over Aboriginal films. However, Alanis Obomsawin, a filmmaker and executive producer who has worked for the NFB for over four decades, spoke highly of the NFB in an interview with scholar Randolph Lewis. She declared: "That is the incredible part of this country. There is a freedom that doesn't exist anywhere else. Even in the NFB, which is a government institution, the politicians cannot dictate what films are being made here, which is very beautiful. At the same time, the government—not only the rest of the people in the country—learn about what is wrong and what is right and what they are doing. So it is a very healthy place to be" (Lewis 2003, 5). With the exception of Obomsawin, there are few Aboriginal people as executive producers at the NFB. This forces Aboriginal filmmakers to work with non-Aboriginal NFB executive producers who exercise considerable creative control and authority over productions.[29] The financial and institutional realities of Aboriginal media production mean that many of these productions are intercultural projects with financing and oversight by non-Aboriginal producers.

Restructuring Studio One:
The Aboriginal Filmmaking Program

In 1996 Studio One transitioned from a physical location to a "virtual studio" as the NFB's Aboriginal Filmmaking Program (AFP), which decentralized the Aboriginal studio and enabled Aboriginal filmmakers to gain access to equipment, training, and resources at any of the NFB's regional offices in Montreal, Vancouver, Edmonton, Halifax, Toronto, and Winnipeg (de Rosa 2002; Gittings 2002). This shift responded to Aboriginal filmmakers who wanted to make films in their respective regions instead of having to relocate to Edmonton. The development of the AFP also earmarked additional funds from the NFB, creating a $1 million annual budget to be used exclusively for productions and coproductions with Aboriginal filmmakers across the Canada.[30] The NFB implemented an evaluation study of Studio One before developing plans to restructure the studio, ultimately concluding that the importance of Studio One lay in its symbolic support for Aboriginal filmmakers, but that the Studio One model had not been effective in meeting the needs of Aboriginal filmmakers (de Rosa 1995).[31]

Aboriginal filmmakers argue that given the historic disparities in funding and access to filmmaking, the NFB has an obligation to increase levels of funding for Aboriginal media. Some Aboriginal filmmakers believe that the NFB does not prioritize Aboriginal media because of the relatively small percentage of money allocated to Aboriginal filmmaking.[32] When the Aboriginal filmmakers interviewed for the Studio One evaluative report were asked to list what their filmmaking needs were, virtually every response indicated a need for funding as well as equipment, resources, and a means to distribute Aboriginal media. One Métis filmmaker and writer succinctly stated in the evaluation report: "The concept of a 'virtual studio' with producer and director is okay, provided there isn't 'virtual monies' to make it a reality. I think the NFB has to bite the bullet and commit real-hard-to-part-with-cash to see Studio One a reality. Studio One's 'virtual studio' must also have the power to make its own decisions apart from any other NFB body" (Dumont qtd. in de Rosa 1995, 15).

Aboriginal filmmakers apply to their NFB regional office, and if their project is chosen, they work with NFB producers in their regional office to produce their film or video. There is a panel of judges—consisting of NFB staff and Aboriginal filmmakers invited by NFB staff—that determines which Aboriginal projects will get funded each year. Additionally, each project funded under the AFP is required to have at least two training positions to facilitate training and mentorship of emerging Aboriginal filmmakers by providing hands-on production experience.[33]

In 2006 Stephen Harper was elected prime minister of Canada, the first person elected to this position from the reconstituted Conservative Party. This ushered in an era of cutbacks to public funding of arts and cultural organizations, including to the NFB. As part of these funding cuts at the NFB, the Aboriginal Film-making Program was eliminated as a separate funding stream.[34] However, the NFB continues to maintain a commitment to supporting Aboriginal media production, particularly to developing support for emerging Aboriginal filmmakers. Aboriginal films continue to be produced under the NFB; however, the funding of these films comes out of the general production budgets for the English and French Studios. The NFB has produced over one thousand films by Aboriginal directors, and many of these films are central to the NFB's ongoing project of digitizing their entire catalog of thirteen thousand films and eventually making all these films available online.

Controlling the Cultural Purse

In 1996, as the NFB dismantled Studio One to create the Aboriginal Filmmaking Program, Telefilm Canada initiated an Aboriginal Production Fund designed to support Aboriginal cultural programming and languages in Canadian television.

Although cultural institutions such as Telefilm Canada, the National Film Board, and the Canada Council all have pockets of funding available for Aboriginal media production, the budgets allocated to these funds are low compared to the overall budgets. According to Jeff Bear's report *At the Crossroads*, in 2004 it was estimated there was approximately $12 million available for Aboriginal media production in Canada distributed among the NFB, Canada Council for the Arts, APTN, and Telefilm Canada (Bear 2004, 29). However, compared to the 2004 budgets of Telefilm, at approximately $270 million, or the CBC at $600 million, this is a relatively low level of funding.[35] Some Aboriginal filmmakers call for a larger percentage of the overall budgets of these institutions to be allocated for Aboriginal media, perhaps to at least reflect Aboriginal peoples' 4 percent of the total Canadian population. Filmmakers have also suggested consolidating all of the Aboriginal funding streams from these various organizations into one budget to ensure easier access to these resources. Activists would also like to see increased Aboriginal involvement as board members and staff at these organizations and to have greater control over decision making about the management of the cultural resources for Aboriginal media (Bear 2004). Dana Claxton pointed out, "If we think of the public cultural purse that the government has, a minimal amount of that goes to Indian people compared to other communities. We certainly aren't getting a larger share, it's actually quite a minute share of the cultural purse compared to the ballet or the symphony. So I mean there is some funding there. Should there be more? I think of course." While Aboriginal filmmakers appreciate the funding opportunities that *are* available, there is a concern that Aboriginal media receives relatively little of the overall Canadian cultural purse.

Aboriginal filmmakers are not limited to applying for funding only through the Aboriginal programs at these organizations but can apply in the general categories as well. However, the difficulties faced by Zacharias Kunuk (Inuk) seeking funds from the general Telefilm Feature Film Fund for his feature film *Atanarjuat* is just one example of the resistance Aboriginal projects can face in receiving equal consideration in the general category at these cultural institutions. In 1998 the Telefilm Aboriginal Production Fund capped all requests at $200,000, a figure far below that needed to complete a feature film. In 1998, when Zacharias Kunuk and Igloolik Isuma Productions sought funding to complete *Atanarjuat,* they wanted to be considered in the general production category in order to be eligible for larger funds. Scholar Faye Ginsburg argues: "Never imagining that Aboriginal funds might be needed for a feature film that would exceed all expectations, these well-intended policies supportive of indigenous 'culture-making' thus smuggled in limitations that also threaten to confine Aboriginal producers to under-resourced 'media reservations'" (Ginsburg 2003, 828). After Telefilm Canada denied their request to be considered in the general category, the *Atanarjuat* filmmakers took their case to the press, emphasizing the unequal access Aboriginal filmmakers experience within Canadian cultural institutions. As the filmmakers pointed out, they face barriers beyond financial ones. There are a host of cultural, geographic, and socioeconomic barriers that filmmakers in Igloolik, and Aboriginal producers across Canada, face in accessing mainstream Canadian cultural institutions. Kunuk explicitly addressed these barriers in a newspaper interview, declaring:

> From Igloolik, we cannot easily have lunch with Telefilm, or make personal contacts that smooth funding systems along. Our key Inuit producers and creative personnel express themselves much better in Inuktitut, a language none of your staff speaks. . . . In the last ten years of professional filmmaking with our programs shown in 16 different countries . . . no executive from Telefilm. . . . or any other participant in the national broadcasting system has ever visited Igloolik to see where, how, and why we work as we do, to see for themselves

our daily reality, our different way of working, of storytelling, of Inuit corporate culture. This is our disadvantage: southern ignorance, not northern inability. (Radz 1998, D3)

Igloolik Isuma Productions and the directors of *Atanarjuat* eventually received reconsideration in the Telefilm general feature film category and were awarded $537,000, but only after the National Film Board signed on as a coproducer.

The question of funding and resources for Aboriginal media in Canada highlights myriad questions about inclusion and exclusion of Aboriginal people within the cultural and national public spheres in Canada. Ultimately, as Faye Ginsburg notes, "the issue is one of cultural citizenship and whose cultural practices are configured within the national public arena in Canada" (Ginsburg 2003, 829). Aboriginal filmmakers fight for greater access to resources from the Canadian cultural purse because of the historical exclusion of Aboriginal participation in these arenas, but also because of the distinctive place of Aboriginal peoples in Canadian society. Over the course of many conversations about Aboriginal media and funding I heard many filmmakers articulate a desire to connect Aboriginal media to broader political activism to gain recognition for Aboriginal rights. Several filmmakers expressed a desire to see their own Aboriginal funding institution so that Aboriginal filmmakers wouldn't have to be tied to funding from Canadian cultural institutions. The funding of Aboriginal media and the relationship that Aboriginal filmmakers and artists have with mainstream Canadian cultural institutions speaks to the larger political and social concerns of Aboriginal people with regard to their relationship with Canadian government and society. Aboriginal filmmakers do not see this funding as merely a generous handout from these Canadian institutions but view these funds as connected to Aboriginal rights and a moral responsibility on the part of the Canadian government, given the history of its relationship with Aboriginal peoples, to fund and sustain an Aboriginal media world that will tell Aboriginal stories from Aboriginal perspectives, narratives that are indigenous to the land and central to Canadian society. The ability to be self-sustaining and to have access to adequate funding is deeply connected to Aboriginal visual sovereignty. The ability to finance and produce Aboriginal media is now largely dependent on grants and funding from dominant Canadian cultural institutions, raising tensions between Canadian cultural sovereignty and Aboriginal efforts to articulate their stories on-screen.

The issue of funding and monetary resources for Aboriginal media is a crucial one and deserves more in-depth analysis. I raise this point here to emphasize that although Canadian cultural institutions such as the NFB, Telefilm Canada, and the Canada Council have been instrumental in helping to support and fund Aboriginal media production, Aboriginal activists continue to push for increased access to equitable funds and resources in order to build capacity and develop the emerging field of Aboriginal media into a fully self-sustaining Aboriginal media industry. Canadian cultural institutions embrace funding for Aboriginal media as part of their broader initiatives to promote Canadian cultural sovereignty. However, Aboriginal activists and filmmakers advocate for a more equitable distribution of those resources so that the Aboriginal media industry can build toward capacity and reinforce Aboriginal sovereignty.

From the American perspective, where there are no federal funding programs devoted to Native American media production as in Canada, it is clear that these national cultural institutions and frameworks for funding *do* make a tremendous difference in the production and distribution of Aboriginal media. Between the NFB's Studio One/AFP, Telefilm Canada's Aboriginal Production Fund, and APTN, the Canadian government has created an infrastructure that supports the training, funding, production, and distribution of Aboriginal media. Aboriginal filmmakers are producing work ranging from feature films to television productions to experimental video to documentaries that have garnered critical acclaim within Canada and internationally.[36] *Atanarjuat:*

The Fast Runner (2001) received wide critical acclaim winning numerous international film awards such as the 2001 Cannes Film Festival's Camera d'Or Prize for Best First Feature Film and garnering an Academy Award nomination as Canada's selection for Best Foreign Language Film in 2002. *Atanarjuat* went on to become Canada's highest grossing film of 2002. Igloolik Isuma followed up the success of *Atanarjuat* with critically acclaimed and successful features *The Journals of Knud Rasmussen* (2006) and *Before Tomorrow* (2008).

Aboriginal Media as Visual Sovereignty

The Canadian National Film Board's involvement in programs for Aboriginal media illustrates the sometimes uneasy embrace of Aboriginal media by the Canadian government in its efforts to maintain Canadian cultural sovereignty. This embrace by Canadian cultural institutions often raises a tension between Aboriginal sovereignty and Canadian sovereignty, which is reflective of the broader relationship between Aboriginal peoples and the Canadian nation-state. I contend that Aboriginal media financed through Canadian cultural institutions are reflective of Aboriginal visual sovereignty. The idea of *visual sovereignty* builds upon the concept of Native political sovereignty that recognizes the distinctive relationship of Native peoples to the nation-state given their status as indigenous peoples. The legal and political status of Native communities—often recognized through legal and jurisdictional procedures such as the treaty process—reflects their status as the original inhabitants of the lands of the encompassing settler state. Aboriginal people in Canada and American Indians in the United States are often seen to be "citizens plus" (Cairns 2000) or "nations within" (V. Deloria and Lytle 1984) as a result of their original presence in the United States and Canada prior to colonization.

The Canadian government affirmed Aboriginal title and Aboriginal rights through the Constitution Act in 1982 (Asch 1984). These rights were upheld by the Supreme Court of Canada decisions in the 1990 *Sparrow* case supporting Aboriginal fishing rights (Coates 2000) and in the landmark 1997 *Delgamuukw* decision that defined Aboriginal title as rights to the land and not just hunting or fishing on the land (C. Roth 2002). These cases affirm a legal recognition of Aboriginal rights to land, resources, and self-determination. Aboriginal political activists and organizations, such as the Union of B.C. Indian Chiefs (UBCIC), have historically used media as vehicles through which to articulate and publicize their positions and protests.[37]

Aboriginal activism has historically been, and remains, strong in British Columbia, a province in which—with the exception of a few treaties signed on Vancouver Island in the mid-nineteenth century—there were no treaties signed with the Canadian government until 1996 when the Nisga'a signed an agreement in principle with the British Columbia provincial and federal governments.[38] The current and ongoing BC Treaty Process Agreement has provided a framework for Aboriginal political activists to seek recognition for fishing rights, land claims, Aboriginal rights, economic development, education, and self-government for Aboriginal communities. The current and ongoing treaty process stands in stark contrast to the United States, where Congress stopped negotiating treaties in 1871. Treaties signify recognition of Aboriginal sovereignty and mark the distinctive political status of Aboriginal peoples. Treaties are negotiated with other nations, but not with minority groups, further reinforcing the political status of Aboriginal peoples as nations.[39]

While these forms of activism recognize the political and legal dimensions of tribal sovereignty, legal scholars Wallace Coffey (Comanche) and Rebecca Tsosie (Yaqui) advocate rethinking tribal sovereignty beyond the scope of political and legal definitions toward a concept of "cultural sovereignty." They assert: "The concept of cultural sovereignty is valuable because it allows us, as Native people, to chart a course for the future. In that sense, cultural sovereignty may well become a tool to protect our rights to language, religion, art, tradition, and the distinctive norms and customs that guide our societies" (Coffey and Tsosie 2001, 196). Coffey and Tsosie's concept of cultural sovereignty is echoed in the work of Beverly Singer, who analyzed Native American media production as a form of cultural sovereignty (Singer 2001), in Randolph Lewis's concept of "cinema of sovereignty" (Lewis 2006), in Michelle Raheja's scholarship on visual sovereignty as a critique of dominant (mis)representations of Native Americans (Raheja 2007), and in Robert Warrior, whose scholarship has emphasized cultural and intellectual sovereignty in Native American scholarship and literature (Warrior 1994).

Visual sovereignty is a concept influenced by art historians, anthropologists, and Native legal scholars who have examined the economic, cultural, political, and spiritual aspects of indigenous sovereignty. Jessica Cattelino's insightful ethnography *High Stakes* on the "cultural currency" of Seminole casino gaming revenue analyzes the ways in which this revenue is used to promote and maintain Seminole cultural production. Cattelino found that casino gaming revenues were made distinctive through their use in Seminole cultural projects, thereby reinforcing their political sovereignty. Cattelino makes an important contribution to the theorization of indigenous sovereignty in *High Stakes*. Instead of viewing indigenous sovereignty in a binary model of autonomy or dependency, Cattelino argues that indigenous sovereignty can be characterized by relations of interdependence. Engagement with casino gaming has drawn the Seminole Tribe into relations of interdependence with other tribes, with local non-Seminole residents, with the state of Florida, and with the federal government. She contends, "Seminoles enact sovereignty in part through relations of *interdependence*, for example through economic exchange and political and legal negotiations with other sovereigns" (Cattelino 2008, 17). She argues that these relations of interdependency reinforce Seminole political distinctiveness by fostering economic development that in turn supports Seminole cultural projects. This is the "materiality of sovereignty," and these relations of interdependency help to support indigenous cultural autonomy, so aptly illustrated by Cattelino's analysis of the use of casino revenues to build Seminole housing in ways that are reflective of kinship and clan (Cattelino 2008).

Cattelino urges scholars to "attend to the sophisticated ways that indigenous groups—and, by extension other nations, assert their sovereignty in part through interactions with others" (Cattelino 2008, 190). Cattelino's theorization of sovereignty as interdependency sheds light on the structural frameworks in place that support the production, distribution, and circulation of Aboriginal media in Canada. Aboriginal media makers do not exist in a vacuum outside of engagement with dominant Canadian state institutions or mainstream society. The ability to produce and distribute their media comes in large part through their relationships with Canadian cultural institutions such as the National Film Board of Canada, the Canada Council for the Arts, and provincial arts councils. It is precisely their "relations of interdependency" with these Canadian cultural institutions that support the robust production of Aboriginal media. This could be seen as a paradoxical aspect of visual sovereignty or a "Faustian contract" (Ginsburg 1991) facing Aboriginal media makers. In order to produce their media they are drawn into these engagements with dominant Canadian cultural institutions. However, Aboriginal media carries the potential to recenter Canadian narratives to assert Aboriginal visual sovereignty through their work. Similarly, other scholars of indigenous media have examined the numerous ways in which indigenous media makers around the globe integrate media technology in culturally specific ways, thus strengthening cultural and political sovereignty (Ginsburg 2002, 1994b, 1991; Turner 1992; Singer 2001; Wilson and Stewart 2008).

The on-screen impact of Aboriginal media production is immeasurable as filmmakers reclaim the screen to tell Aboriginal stories within Canada's mediascape while promoting Aboriginal language revitalization by making media in Aboriginal languages. The off-screen impact of Aboriginal media helps to facilitate intergenerational relationships in the production process and foster new forms of social relationships by reconnecting urban filmmakers with their traditional territories and reserve communities. This is made possible in large part because of filmmaker relationships with Canadian funding organizations, broadcasters, and the support of many non-Aboriginal producers, technicians, crew members, and collaborators. This is not to say that Aboriginal filmmakers don't struggle to gain equitable representation within the Canadian national mediascape. That filmmakers often struggle to gain access to resources from dominant institutions to produce their work while maintaining their cultural autonomy is characteristic of the broader political conditions faced by Aboriginal people whose lives and sovereignty are compromised by the Canadian settler state that encompasses them. The point, however, is that these intercultural engagements and relations of interdependence in the financing of Aboriginal media can be productive in supporting Aboriginal visual sovereignty through the media projects produced under these circumstances.

Conclusion

The emergence of Aboriginal media has reshaped the politics of representation in Canada and created a new media space in which Aboriginal experiences, histories, and narratives are cinematically represented to counter dominant misrepresentations of Aboriginal life. In Canada, Aboriginal producers have played a strong role in negotiating with the federal government to create cultural policies that make funds, resources, broadcasting, and institutions available for Aboriginal media production. Access to media production as an expression of self-representation and self-determination has become a powerful arena of Native political activism (Weatherford 1996) and cultural citizenship (Ginsburg 2003).

In looking at the tremendous impact of the Canadian government on Aboriginal media, it is evident that government cultural policy can have a powerful effect on the ability of Aboriginal filmmakers to produce and distribute their work. From the founding of the National Film Board of Canada—a central Canadian film-making institution that views access to media production as integral to a shared cultural and national citizenship—Canada's cultural policy has worked to extend access to participation in media production to minority and Aboriginal communities. Despite the funding and resources that government cultural institutions have made available to Aboriginal filmmakers, they still face barriers within the media industry, and there remains a need for a more equitable distribution of Canada's cultural purse. Although funding inequities remain, I argue that relative to other settler nation-states such as the United States, Canada has been more receptive to Aboriginal concerns about media self-representation, in part because Canada is concerned to maintain Canadian content on Canadian screens in response to the onslaught of American media. As communications scholar Marc Raboy states, "From the origins of public broadcasting in the 1930s through the free trade talks of 1988, communication policy has been seen as a central bulwark of Canadian cultural and even political sovereignty vis-à-vis the United States" (Raboy 1996, 154). Canadian state support of Aboriginal media has integrated Aboriginal media production into Canadian projects of nation-building through cultural production. This can raise tensions between Aboriginal sovereignty and Canadian sovereignty, which is reflective of the broader political landscape between Aboriginal peoples and the Canadian nation-state. Aboriginal media appear to be embraced by Canadian cultural institutions as part of a broader effort to maintain Canadian content on-screen. It is clear that for Aboriginal filmmakers this is an uneasy embrace where they continue to seek equal access while endeavoring to alter the visual landscape of Canadian screens by presenting Aboriginal media that challenge dominant Canadian national narratives.

CHAPTER THREE

Aboriginal Diversity On-Screen

"SHARING OUR STORIES": THE ABORIGINAL PEOPLES TELEVISION NETWORK—AUGUST 2003

I arrive in Vancouver to begin my fieldwork, and the first thing I do is turn on the TV to channel 71, the Aboriginal Peoples Television Network (APTN). The first image that greets me is an APTN promotional spot in which a sophisticated, professionally dressed Aboriginal woman gazes into the camera declaring, "My grandfather is a traditional man with contemporary ideas. He's filled with the knowledge of stories that he has heard from the time that he was young. And it's through these stories that he's imparted our traditions to me. And although he knew I would not live a traditional life like him, I would keep our Dene stories, values, and beliefs with me wherever I am in the world." The Aboriginal Peoples Television Network logo appears on-screen with a narrator proclaiming the network's slogan, "Sharing our stories with all Canadians, APTN."

During the next five days, I am glued to the TV, eagerly watching everything from cooking shows to children's television programs to life histories of elders to global indigenous documentaries and feature films. I am completely taken in. I see Inuit elders skinning seals in the bush, programs on Native language preservation broadcast in Cree, Maori soap operas, cooking shows featuring Aboriginal cuisine, and dramas addressing urban Aboriginal life. On my first night "in the field" I am delighted to watch APTN's *National News* and see the day's news from Aboriginal perspectives. As I view the programs presented by the world's first national indigenous broadcaster, it becomes evident to me that the presence of APTN has radically altered the stage for Aboriginal media in Canada.

Introduction

The Aboriginal Peoples Television Network adds another complex layer to the discussion about Aboriginal visual sovereignty. As a national broadcaster in Canada, APTN is connected to the mainstream Canadian mediascape; at the same time it is a vital institution for representing Aboriginal stories and experiences to *all* Canadians, Aboriginal and non-Aboriginal. In fact, the majority of the APTN audience is non-Aboriginal. What are the implications for Aboriginal visual sovereignty when non-Aboriginal audiences watch APTN? Does the witnessing of Aboriginal media by non-Aboriginal audiences strengthen visual sovereignty and recognition of Aboriginal rights? What role does APTN play in Aboriginal media in Canada?

In this chapter I analyze the ways in which Aboriginal media intervene in the Canadian national mediascape to impact on-screen representations of Aboriginal people. I address this by exploring the impact of APTN on Aboriginal media production in Canada through the perspective of Aboriginal filmmakers in Vancouver. I examine the implications of having Aboriginal experiences represented within Aboriginal venues, such as APTN, while also examining filmmaker critiques about the limitations of APTN and their desire to see other broadcasters become more inclusive of Aboriginal media. One of the key aspects of Aboriginal media as visual sovereignty is that these media, in stark contrast to the one-dimensional, stereotyped representations of Aboriginal people in mainstream media, reflect the diversity of Aboriginal experiences and perspectives. To illustrate the impact of Aboriginal diversity within Aboriginal media, I explore the representation of mixed-blood and two-spirit perspectives within Aboriginal media. The articulation of the vast array of Aboriginal perspectives and experiences within Aboriginal media enacts visual sovereignty by speaking back against misrepresentation in mainstream media and opening up spaces of inclusion for Aboriginal individuals, including those who identify as mixed-blood or two-spirit, who have experienced marginalization elsewhere.

Voice and Visibility

For Aboriginal filmmakers in Vancouver there is an urgency to create images, characters, and stories to which Aboriginal audiences can relate. The desire to reflect Aboriginal faces on-screen reveals the way in which mainstream media has rendered Aboriginal people invisible through a lack of representation and perpetuation of stereotypes. Television producer Dorothy Christian explained: "It's important to give voice. It's important for Aboriginal people to see themselves reflected on the screen to give them a sense that they exist, that we're not totally invisible." Aboriginal media can offer a direct opportunity to counter the persistent mainstream stereotypes of Aboriginal people, as Barb Cranmer ('Namgis) noted when she declared: "I think there's this notion out there that we still all live in tipis and ride horses which is so stereotypical. I think Aboriginal media has given us the opportunity to share our story by our point of view. It gives us a strong voice and a presence out there in a quite crazy world that we live in."

Filmmaker Odessa Shuquaya echoed this, saying: "I want to see Natives on screen, I just want to see them! And they don't have to be rez Indians, they don't have to be alcoholics, they don't have to be prostitutes, they don't have to be anything. They're just people, they're just telling their stories." Aboriginal filmmakers do not seek to portray a single image of Aboriginal people or to speak in a single voice, but rather to contribute a diverse and rich picture of the complexity of Aboriginal life. There are a multitude of Aboriginal perspectives and stories given the different backgrounds and experiences of Aboriginal filmmakers. Jackson Crick (Tsilhqot'in), a filmmaker and teacher in Vancouver, wryly noted: "The cool thing about being Aboriginal people telling your own story is that it's your story. It doesn't have to be the Indian next door's story! It's my story and it's what I want to say."

Filmmakers see the ability to relate to the characters on-screen as having a powerful impact, particularly on the self-esteem of Aboriginal youth. One sunny spring morning in Vancouver I sat talking with Vera Wabegijig. We talked about IMAG and the differences between mainstream and Aboriginal media. Her eyes lit up as she exclaimed:

> I just think it's cool to see Indians on the big screen, no matter what they look like! We're all different shades. We're all different nations. We're all different heights and sizes and I think it's beautiful to see that on screen. In a way it's helping the communities too. When they see more Indians on TV I think it helps with their own self-esteem. It's what we've been wanting for so long is to see ourselves.

Noting that "we're all different shades, we're all different nations," Wabegijig emphasizes the importance of portraying the diverse faces, experiences, and voices of Aboriginal people in the media.

Despite a persistent lack of access to dominant media institutions, Aboriginal media do make significant on-screen interventions in the Canadian national mediascape. One of the most significant milestones in Aboriginal media history occurred with the launch of the Aboriginal Peoples Television Network in 1999. APTN has made a tremendous impact on the Canadian national mediascape by broadcasting Aboriginal media content, 28 percent of which is broadcast in Aboriginal languages. Aboriginal people face both a profound invisibility within mainstream media and a misrepresentation as the "Hollywood Indian" that, as Muskogee artist Joy Harjo declares, has rendered Native people as merely "cardboard cut-out figures, without blood, tears or laughter" (Harjo qtd. in Lippard 1992, 92).[1] Aboriginal

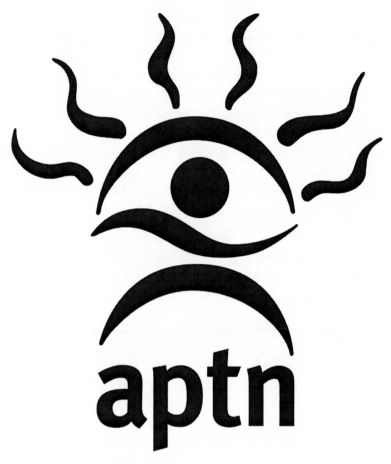

Fig. 10. APTN Logo. Courtesy of APTN.

filmmakers resist this legacy of misrepresentation by creating visibility for the diversity and complexity of Aboriginal experiences in their own work, including representations of mixed-blood and two-spirit identity.[2]

Confronting Barriers in the Mainstream Media Industry

Should I go mainstream or stay within the Aboriginal media world? Is it possible or desirable to be part of both worlds? These questions cut to the heart of the dilemma for Aboriginal filmmakers seeking to create work that maintains cultural integrity while simultaneously making an on-screen intervention into dominant media to increase visibility for their experiences. There are numerous perspectives among Aboriginal filmmakers regarding the constraints and barriers within the mainstream media industry. In a 2004 report commissioned by Telefilm Canada, television producer Jeff Bear (Maliseet) highlighted the barriers Aboriginal filmmakers face within mainstream media institutions. This report revealed a strong consensus from the report participants that there is "systemic racism when Aboriginal persons access employment opportunities in mainstream television" (Bear 2004, 14). Bear attributes this systemic racism in large part to the lack of Aboriginal people in key senior decision-making positions within the cultural and media institutions supporting Canada's mainstream media industry. The report states that "without aboriginal people in senior creative and decision-making positions, access will continue to be an impediment" and notes that "there are no aboriginal producers working at the network level in any of the conventional networks in either dramatic or documentary production" (14).[3]

Aboriginal filmmakers in Vancouver articulated a sense of marginalization from mainstream media as well as a lack of respect within these institutions for the unique storytelling styles of Aboriginal filmmakers. Kamala Todd described her frustration when working with a non-Aboriginal producer on a story she directed for *First Story*, the Aboriginal current affairs television show created by Jeff Bear that originally aired on Vancouver TV and in 2004 was broadcast on CTV.[4] In 1997 Jeff Bear had left the program and was not the producer when Kamala Todd had this frustrating experience working with a non-Aboriginal producer in the editing room. She explained: "When I was working at *First Story* I did a story about the [Aboriginal] history of Vancouver. I interviewed Chief Ian Campbell from Squamish and Leonard George from Tsleil-Waututh and they told me about some of their village sites." She paused before continuing, "These people are leaders in their community and are sharing really important knowledge. So when I put the story together, as I was taught you let people speak, you don't interrupt them, you give them that chance to tell their story. So I would take clips from them where they were describing something about their village or something about their history—they weren't long clips but I didn't like chop it up into little clips." She took a sip of coffee and continued: "I was told by the executive producer of the show who was non-Native that the clips were too long and that they needed to be sped up and more like sound-bites. I said, 'That's not how Aboriginal people tell stories! We don't cut people's words up, especially when they're leaders sharing their history with you.' So I fought them and fought them and eventually they aired it the way that I put it together which was great. But I left after that because I thought there was too much pressure to conform."

Although Todd was working on an Aboriginal television series, this show aired on a mainstream television network, creating intercultural encounters in the production and postproduction process where conflicting ideas about aesthetics and storytelling were constantly negotiated. Todd, like many Aboriginal filmmakers, expressed frustration with a mainstream television industry that seeks to mold Aboriginal stories to a mainstream media aesthetic, something with which many Aboriginal filmmakers are uncomfortable. Dorothy Christian, a television producer who worked for many years for Vision TV, a specialty multifaith network, expressed a similar frustration with her non-Aboriginal producers seeking to box her stories into a conventional media aesthetic. In an interview over coffee one Sunday afternoon she explained: "My story editor in Toronto didn't know how to manage my storytelling. She used to accuse me of using assumed knowledge. But what she didn't realize was that I was producing my segments for Native people and everybody else was a secondary audience to me." Christian articulates a key point that many mainstream television producers fail to understand: in many cases Aboriginal media are produced for Aboriginal audiences. In Aboriginal media, in stark contrast to mainstream media, Aboriginal people are configured as the primary audience from the beginning of the production through postproduction. Mainstream media networks often reject Aboriginal storytelling styles and media aesthetics because they say that it often fails to meet industry standards, but also that it doesn't speak to wider mainstream audiences (Bear 2004).

Jeff Bear articulates the fundamental struggle of Aboriginal filmmakers: "Aboriginal producers feel that they are on the outside, pushed out by a system that does not acknowledge their unique and valid styles of storytelling. Mainstream producers and commissioning editors demonstrate inflexibility in allowing for an aboriginal narrative to emerge. *Should aboriginal producers assimilate their styles in order to be accepted into the Canadian mainstream?*" (Bear 2004, 14, emphasis added). In many ways the question of how to maintain Aboriginal cultural traditions and distinctiveness in the face of pressures from dominant society reflects more than just the struggle of Aboriginal filmmakers, but it is indicative of the contemporary condition of indigenous life in the twenty-first century. How do Aboriginal people maintain Aboriginal sovereignty and cultural ways of life and at the same time create a distinctive place for Aboriginal people in Canadian society? Aboriginal people hold overlapping citizenship, as citizens in their Aboriginal nations and also as Canadian citizens. Aboriginal sovereignty does not entail a complete separation or distance from participation in Canadian life—instead Aboriginal sovereignty is about Aboriginal people being present in the national institutions and public discourses *on their own terms*, standing from a position of power to articulate their stories from their perspectives through media. Engagement with APTN or participation in mainstream broadcasting institutions does not diminish Aboriginal visual sovereignty; it in fact strengthens visual sovereignty by articulating Aboriginal stories and experiences in a way that can raise recognition of Aboriginal issues and concerns by non-Aboriginal audiences.

A question at the heart of Aboriginal media practice—whether to participate in the mainstream media industry or to remain within the Aboriginal media world—is a question that Aboriginal communities and individuals face in regard to living as contemporary Aboriginal peoples and members of Aboriginal nations encompassed by the Canadian settler state, where, as one filmmaker pointed out to me, the "colonizer lives amongst us." This question remains at the heart of contemporary Aboriginal life in Canada and plays out writ small in the debates surrounding Aboriginal media and what levels of participation Aboriginal filmmakers seek in the mainstream media industry.

Assessing the Impact of APTN

The Aboriginal Peoples Television Network has radically changed the playing field for Aboriginal media in Canada.[5] Many of the filmmakers with whom I worked in Vancouver had experience working on APTN productions, either through television series produced for APTN or having their documentaries aired on APTN. Through its visibility as a national cable channel, APTN has generated dialogue among Aboriginal filmmakers about its accomplishments, limitations, and hopes for the future.

APTN, based in Winnipeg, recently celebrated its thirteenth anniversary; it officially launched in September 1999, becoming the world's first national Aboriginal television channel.[6] APTN is available on all basic cable service within Canada and represents northern and southern Aboriginal media in the same broadcasting venue.[7] APTN is financed by a twenty-five-cent monthly cable subscriber fee, and the network also relies on advertising revenue. The mission and mandate of APTN, according to network promotional material in 2000, is to provide a "television network by Aboriginal people, about Aboriginal people and for all Canadians that provides a window into the lives and stories of Aboriginal people while seeking to assist in the development and survival of Aboriginal languages and cultures." APTN offers Aboriginal programming in English, French, and fourteen

Aboriginal languages in addition to showcasing international indigenous media. In 2003-2004 there were five Aboriginal shows in production for APTN in Vancouver: *Beyond Words, Creative Native, Art Zone, Ravens and Eagles,* and *Venturing Forth*. More recent APTN shows include *Storytellers in Motion, Tansi! Nehiyawetan: Let's Speak Cree!,* and *Raven Tales*. This production schedule had a tremendous impact on Vancouver's Aboriginal media world by providing consistent employment and generating the development of Aboriginal media training programs. The proliferation of Aboriginal television programming in Canada is largely attributed to the emergence of APTN as a national broadcaster that needs programming (Baltruschat 2004, 47).

APTN provides limited production funding and has emerged as a vital distribution venue for Aboriginal filmmakers in Canada and internationally. The network broadcasts twenty-two hours of programming per day, and scholar Kerstin Knopf notes that "there is less than 10 percent in-house production and more than 90 percent program acquisition. 86 percent of APTN's programming has Canadian content" (Knopf 2010, 89). It is important to note that not all of APTN's content is produced by Aboriginal media makers. APTN does broadcast some children's animations and feature films that showcase Aboriginal actors, even if those films have a non-Aboriginal director. Knopf questions whether APTN can truly be seen as decolonizing Canadian airwaves if it broadcasts Hollywood feature films such as *Dances with Wolves*. Knopf argues that "such movies are presented without a critical or subversive context and consequently APTN reiterates Western media practices of presenting Aboriginal culture instead of countering them" (100). I agree with Knopf's careful analysis and critique of some of APTN's programming choices with regard to feature films; however, it is important to keep in mind that some of those movie choices, particularly in the early format of the television show *Bingo and a Movie*, were highly favored by Aboriginal audiences. Knopf also highlights the ways in which APTN does reflect Aboriginal visual sovereignty in contrast to mainstream media, particularly with regard to the use of cultural protocol, the emphasis on family, the authority of elders, discursive references to the Medicine Wheel, the use of Aboriginal humor, and the representation of news coverage from an Aboriginal perspective (90–91).

Despite APTN's broadcasting of some mainstream feature films, it is an Aboriginal broadcaster that provides a crucial screening venue for independent Aboriginal media production. Communications scholar Lorna Roth points out that the presence of APTN, "at the very least, forces audiences to acknowledge that First Peoples are integral citizens of both the country and the airwaves that we all, according to the law, share" (L. Roth 2005, 208). Roth is referring to the 1991 Broadcasting Act that enshrined Aboriginal language and communication rights on a national level. Prior to 1991 broadcasting legislation in Canada specified that "all Canadians are entitled to broadcasting service in English and French as public funds become available," recognizing the "two founding nations" of Canada (Raboy 1996). The 1991 Broadcasting Act finally recognized Aboriginal communication rights as central to Canadian national broadcasting, reinforcing Aboriginal rights to represent themselves through media and the unique and significant role that Aboriginal peoples play in the Canadian nation-state.

APTN has raised the stakes for Aboriginal media in Canada by instigating the development of an infrastructure for the Aboriginal media industry. Many Aboriginal filmmakers in Vancouver want to see the Aboriginal media industry build capacity to have Aboriginal people involved at all levels in the media industry. In an interview Dana Claxton, a television producer on *ArtZone* for APTN, observed: "APTN has allowed producers and directors and writers and everybody involved—the whole production crew—to develop a work force and an Aboriginal industry so that has helped. I think APTN has been a tremendous help." Although she works primarily in media arts, Claxton articulates her work for APTN as a community responsibility, declaring, "I think there's the responsibility to do things that help your community. That's why I do these television shows knowing that it helps the children and we train people and bring people on board. It's just this whole infrastructure that we get to hire all people from our own community and teach them these skills. Then they can go off and make their own projects. It's really an obligation."

Jackson Crick, filmmaker and former director of the Aboriginal Film and Television Program at Capilano College, described the impact of APTN as encouraging Aboriginal producers to create more work because of the screening opportunities APTN provides. He explained: "APTN has made awareness for people and this Capilano College program was created because of APTN. There wouldn't be as many people in Aboriginal media if they didn't think that they had a chance of showing it on APTN someday." The Capilano program offers internships for its students on APTN productions in Vancouver, providing invaluable industry training.

APTN and Audience

APTN's viewership continues to grow, with an estimated audience share of 3 million viewers.[8] This is a respectable audience share, given the total Canadian population is approximately 33.5 million people, according to the 2011 Canadian census (APTN 2011). It has been difficult to measure the viewership of APTN in remote areas and on reserves because the Bureau of Broadcast Management (BBM) and Nielsen ratings surveys do not conduct surveys in the northern territories and in the North. Communications scholar Marian Bredin writes, "neither Aboriginal people nor reserve communities have been considered a desirable market for the advertising of consumer goods and services" (Bredin 2010, 82). This results in an underreporting of viewership for APTN and a limited ability for the network to raise advertising revenue. In 2002 APTN conducted focus groups on reserves and in the North, which found that 80 percent of the on-reserve sample reported watching APTN. In 2004, 88 percent of respondents to an APTN survey felt that it was very or somewhat important to have a station giving access to a range of Aboriginal languages (83). According to Bredin's research, the majority of APTN viewers are non-Aboriginal, based on 2003–2004 surveys, when APTN determined that "urban APTN viewers are 75 percent white, 7.4 percent Aboriginal, 5 percent black, and 12.6 percent from other ethnic backgrounds" (83). It is important to keep in mind APTN's mandate to "share Aboriginal stories with all Canadians" and that Aboriginal peoples comprise approximately 4 percent of Canada's total population. I argue that the articulation of Aboriginal stories, cultural traditions, languages, and relationships to the land to non-Aboriginal audiences is an equally important dimension of Aboriginal visual sovereignty. That APTN reaches a wide non-Aboriginal audience indicates the capacity of this media to educate the broader Canadian public about Aboriginal rights, stories, and experiences, claiming a stake for Aboriginal people within the wider Canadian public domain and mediascape.

Some filmmakers in Vancouver expressed concern that APTN is inaccessible to some Aboriginal viewers because one must have basic cable in order to view APTN, and many Aboriginal people in Vancouver often do not have cable because of the cost. Scholar Lorna Roth notes that Aboriginal viewership on reserves has been hindered because of technical limitations. She states: "Here, the major problem is not so much *maintaining* audiences but rather *figuring out* a way to reach that portion of Aboriginal reserves (mostly in the mid-North) that still does not have cable or digital satellite access. A significant portion of the approximately 35 percent of the Aboriginal populations that live on reserves is not yet receiving APTN programming" (L. Roth 2005, 212). Additionally, as scholars and critics have observed, APTN is placed high on the channel dial, which inhibits both Aboriginal and non-Aboriginal viewership because it is not a channel that viewers will randomly come across as they flip through television channels (L. Roth 2005). Yet despite concerns about the lack of access to APTN because of the associated costs of cable, the difficulty of accessing remote and reserve communities, or the high dial placement, there is a widely shared belief among Aboriginal filmmakers in Vancouver that APTN has changed the landscape for Aboriginal media, creating greater visibility and generating more jobs and production opportunities in the industry.

For Aboriginal audiences hungry to see themselves reflected on-screen, APTN represents a chance to see Aboriginal faces, stories, and experiences all day every day. Zoe Hopkins noted that in her home community of Bella Bella some young Heiltsuk children who watch APTN identify with it so much that they refer to it as the "Heiltsuk channel." In an interview she exclaimed: "More people are aware and in tune with everyone else [other Aboriginal people] in the country. When I go to Bella Bella I'll see a child on the street and they'll say, 'I saw you on the Indian channel!' And my little cousin told my mom, she said, 'I saw Zoe on the Heiltsuk channel last night!' And she so identifies with everything on the channel that she thinks it's theirs! So I think that's a beautiful thing." While Hopkins observes this popularity of the network with young children in Bella Bella, filmmaker Barb Cranmer explained that although APTN is watched in her home community of Alert Bay, it is not a favorite channel. When asked about the network in an interview she responded: "Yeah, people watch APTN. But it's not a favorite channel of people's but if they see something interesting they'll stop and watch it." She began laughing and quipped, "But we're not all sitting around at 7:00 watching *Contact!*[9] It's not brought us to do that!"

The Limits of APTN

A common refrain I heard from Vancouver filmmakers, particularly those from West Coast cultural backgrounds, was a concern about the lack of West Coast representation in APTN programming, which is perceived by some in Vancouver to be mostly focused on the North and East. Although in 2003–2004 there were five APTN productions happening in Vancouver, only one of those programs, *Ravens and Eagles*, contained exclusively West Coast Aboriginal cultural content. The other shows focused on making art from recycled materials in *ArtZone*, highlighting leaders in Aboriginal music and arts in *Beyond Words*, or emphasizing the successes of Aboriginal youth in *Venturing Forth*. Cranmer commented on this lack of West Coast representation, declaring: "It's been disappointing on a certain level with APTN. The work's here [in B.C.], there's shows out here that could be shown from B.C. and this part of the country you know. It [APTN] is very heavily on the North. I'm respectful, it's not like I'm complaining about it, but I would just like to see more from out here. Because this is part of Canada and we have strong distinct cultures out here just like anywhere else and I don't think it's been showcased enough." This lack of representation is especially striking given that Vancouver has a large Aboriginal media world and that there are many Aboriginal communities producing media throughout British Columbia.

The lack of West Coast representation is apparent in the relatively small coverage given to Aboriginal news from British Columbia on the *APTN National News* program. This is a marked absence given that Aboriginal communities in British Columbia are currently in the process of treaty negotiations generating numerous news stories, as well as protests and blockades. In 2003-2004 there was only one news correspondent for British Columbia for *APTN National News*. Todd Lamirande (Métis), who was the Vancouver news bureau correspondent for *APTN National News* at that time and who later became a national anchor for the program, echoed Cranmer's frustrations during an interview at his Vancouver office:

> The problem is B.C. is probably the most active place in North America as far as Aboriginal issues go. No treaties were ever signed in this province and that's created a lot of political activism so there's a lot to cover. It generates more news stories than I could possibly cover and I cover everything from

arts and entertainment to the hard news, the political stuff to all the protests and sports. Because of the budget we have at APTN I'm the only person out here so I can be very busy at times. But I try to cover as much as I possibly can.

Although Lamirande noted that in 2003–2004 budget restraints limited APTN from hiring more correspondents from British Columbia, he expressed a sense that *APTN National News* is making a difference as the world's only national all-Aboriginal daily news program. Lamirande has a hectic schedule but emphasized: "I enjoy doing it. I do it because for so long Aboriginal people have had no voice whatsoever in any kind of discourse whether it's political or cultural in this country. Now you have a station like APTN which has a daily news program and that's all we talk about. It's quite revolutionary when you think about it." Vancouver is now home to one of four main APTN offices and has expanded its staff.

It is clear that APTN provides an important screening venue for Aboriginal media and makes a critical intervention into the dominant Canadian mediascape by representing Aboriginal stories, cultural practices, experiences, and languages. Kamala Todd exclaimed: "Here I am watching it [APTN] and I'm seeing—this is in the early days—an Inuit grandmother cleaning a seal. Where else could you see that? That community is getting to see its people living the way they live and speaking their own language. I think that's really important for Aboriginal people to see themselves reflected, because right now they don't see themselves reflected in the media." Todd's exclamation, "Where else could you see that?" in reference to watching this Inuit grandmother skinning a seal, highlights the lack of visibility for Aboriginal programming in mainstream media. As a result APTN is viewed as the only space in Canada's national mediascape where Aboriginal people are regularly visible.

Unfortunately the presence of APTN appears to have made some broadcasters reluctant to show Aboriginal media, and filmmakers have been told by mainstream broadcasters, "You have APTN—just show it there." Dorothy Christian described her experiences with mainstream broadcasters pushing her to apply for funds only at APTN. She stated: "What I would love to see is Aboriginal work on *all* the networks. I love the fact that APTN is there, but I also think that it can be ghettoization. I'm sure that many people have run into this, where you apply for funding and it's like, 'Go to APTN.' We get dismissed because it's like well, you've got money over there." Christian's observations support the concern of media scholars that APTN could develop into a "media reservation" (Roth 2005) whereby Aboriginal media gets relegated only to APTN without other broadcasters, such as CBC or CTV, becoming more inclusive. Kamala Todd echoed this sentiment: "I think mainstream broadcasters need to make space for Aboriginal people to tell stories in their own ways. And they need to do it beyond just their one token Indian show. If you look at the mainstream broadcasters there's almost nil in Aboriginal programming so I'd say they have a lot of work to do."

Other Aboriginal filmmakers do not seek inclusion in mainstream media, asking, as did Odessa Shuquaya, "Why should we be part of the mainstream? Why don't we create our own mainstream, an Aboriginal-stream? That mainstream has shunned us or portrayed us very poorly in the past so why would we want to be a part of something that is inherently racist? If we create something that is ours then it has integrity and it speaks to not only us as an Aboriginal community in Canada, but it can inform the rest of Canada as well." As discussed earlier in the chapter, Aboriginal filmmakers negotiate this tension between working within dominant media institutions or working outside these systems to create an independent Aboriginal system. Is it possible to be *in* but not *of* the system? Can one use the funds and resources from an institution like the NFB, the Canada Council, or CBC to create an Aboriginal film or video that isn't compromised or constrained by the stipulations of working within a national cultural institution? If filmmakers strive to have their work aired on mainstream broadcasters, will the constraints of mainstream conventional aesthetics or audiences inhibit or alter their media?

Although many people would like to see APTN change—whether to air more dramatic programming, a regional studio system, or more youth-oriented programming—there is a consensus that the network has forever altered the visible landscape of Aboriginal media and opened up possibilities for Aboriginal production. Jackson Crick articulated this sentiment about APTN: "They've given a voice to a lot of people and they've also given hope that our work will get seen." Zoe Hopkins eloquently stated, "APTN has changed the level of opportunity there is in terms of filmmaking and television making, but I think that we're now ready to change APTN." Lorna Roth observes, "Over the years, First Peoples have fought for, and been granted, political opportunities to build a nationwide mediaspace to heal the historical communication ruptures within their societies and between their communities and others living in Canada" (L. Roth 2005, 213). Having celebrated its thirteenth year on air and having moved beyond the initial growing pains of a new cable channel, APTN has raised the level of visibility for Aboriginal media while increasing training, production, and distribution opportunities for Aboriginal filmmakers.

In 2008 APTN launched APTN HD and continues to expand its online viewing capabilities in Canada. However, in an age of global media flows and the importance of online streaming of content, one limitation of APTN—and other Canadian broadcasters—appears to be its strict restriction to Canada both in terms of cable/satellite access and online content. Viewers outside of Canada are still unable to view the majority of the content on APTN's website and cannot access the network via satellite television services. Isuma TV, a website run by the Inuit video collective Igloolik Isuma, appears to be ahead of APTN with regard to its support for indigenous media content circulation online. Isuma TV allows indigenous media makers from around the world to create channels and upload media content. This media content is not restricted to Canadian audiences but can be viewed in both low- and high-bandwidth versions around the world. In terms of accessibility and circulation, Isuma TV surpasses APTN in its circulation of a wide range of global indigenous media, proving that the restriction of APTN to Canadian television and online audiences may be a serious limitation. However despite these limitations, APTN does represent one example of the expression of Aboriginal visual sovereignty on-screen, a visual sovereignty that speaks to both Aboriginal and non-Aboriginal audiences, given its presence on all basic cable service in Canada.

Representing Mixed-Blood Aboriginal and Métis Experiences

As a result of its limited production capacity, APTN is constantly searching for Aboriginal programming to broadcast. APTN is a venue in which a wide array of Aboriginal experiences is reflected on-screen. In fact, the Canadian Radio-television and Telecommunications Commission (CRTC) license charges APTN with a broad mandate to represent "urban and remote, northern and southern, Aboriginal and non-Aboriginal viewers" (Bredin 2010, 70). This broad mandate can raise programming challenges for APTN to meet the needs of geographically, linguistically, and culturally distinctive Aboriginal communities. The network has drawn on the talent among independent Aboriginal media producers to create work that creatively responds to the needs of the various APTN constituents and audiences.

One way in which Aboriginal media have made an on-screen intervention is through the representation of Aboriginal diversity, particularly around the inclusion of mixed-blood Aboriginal and Métis histories and narratives.[10] There is no singular Aboriginal aesthetic: instead there is a multiplicity of Aboriginal aesthetics rooted in the tribal nations, backgrounds, and artistic expression of individual filmmakers. For some filmmakers who identify as mixed-blood or Métis, media production is part of a broader movement to reclaim their identity and cultural histories.[11]

Stereotypes of Aboriginal people in mainstream media have constructed an image that neglects the history and experiences of people with mixed-blood and Métis backgrounds. It is significant that Métis and mixed-blood experiences and narratives are being recuperated *as Aboriginal* in Aboriginal media. I examine the impact of casting politics and look at how mixed-blood Aboriginal filmmakers expand the boundaries of "Aboriginality" through their on-screen representations of mixed-blood identity within Aboriginal media, focusing on the experiences of two filmmakers based in Vancouver, Odessa Shuquaya and Lisa Jackson. If, as Anishinaabe scholar Gerald Vizenor aptly observes, "mixedbloods loosen the seams in the shrouds of identities" (Vizenor 1987, 101), then mixed-blood Aboriginal filmmakers are loosening the seams of "celluloid Indians" (Kilpatrick 1999) to open up a cinematic space that provides voice and visibility for mixed-blood identity.

The issues of skin color, passing, and family silence about Native and Métis heritage are experiences shared by many Métis and mixed-blood Aboriginal people.[12] While the issue of skin color is sensitive within Native communities, it is nevertheless a trope within mixed-blood Aboriginal and Métis media production.[13] In an interview filmmaker Odessa Shuquaya, who identifies as mixed-blood, explicitly addressed the issue of skin color, describing how as a lighter-skinned, blue-eyed mixed-blood Aboriginal woman, she has experienced discrimination from Aboriginal people thinking she's not Aboriginal until she "flashes her status card" as well as from non-Native people not believing that she is Aboriginal because she looks "white." She explained: "This is a very personal struggle for me as a very light skinned Aboriginal person. I have come into contact with racism within my own community with people not believing that I was Aboriginal. I'm like, 'No, I'm Native, honest! Look I have a status card, I promise! Just let me get a tan!'" She laughed and continued, "Then sometimes I feel uncomfortable because I don't feel that I'm dark enough to be a Native person, which is totally not true because I have a Native experience. I have Native ancestry, because of that I have a Native experience. I'm a Native that's how it goes so it doesn't really matter what I look like."

For Shuquaya, her mixed-blood ancestry and light skin inhibit her work as an actor; despite her Native ancestry she has only once been cast as a Métis character and never as an Aboriginal character. Her agent informed her that she would never be considered for Native roles because she "doesn't look Native enough" to be believable in a Native role.[14] She has not been able to play a role representing her own identity because of the legacy of stereotypical representations of Aboriginal people in mainstream media that leaves little room for the experiences and faces of mixed-blood Aboriginal people. She indignantly exclaimed:

> When I was with my agent she told me I could never be cast as a Native person because I'm not dark enough. I would only be cast as an Irish/English/Swedish, possibly Russian person, as far as ethnicities go. I just thought that was garbage because that isn't true! I *am* a Native person! But she is right, people would not buy it, but on the other hand, why can't we start pushing the envelope? Why can't we start casting people in roles in which they are? Just because they don't look like what you think a Native person looks like doesn't mean that they're not or that they can't play that role well.

The lack of roles for her as a mixed-blood Aboriginal woman and the lack of on-screen visibility for those experiences have motivated her to become a filmmaker. Her primary hope is to eventually direct feature films where she can create roles that represent that spectrum of Aboriginal faces and experiences, opening a space for the visibility of mixed-blood Aboriginal experiences.

Lisa Jackson explores her conflicted relationship with her mother and Native identity in her award-winning experimental documentary *Suckerfish* (2004), which was produced with the

Fig. 11. Film still from *Suckerfish* (2004). Courtesy of Lisa Jackson.

National Film Board of Canada, screened in many film festivals, and broadcast on APTN. In this short film Jackson contemplates her connection to her Native heritage while providing a narration that examines her childhood memories of her mother's depression and addictions. In an interview with the APTN program *Storytellers in Motion,* Jackson explained that she made *Suckerfish* to "take a stand for people who didn't grow up on reserve and who maybe feel alienated because of that. And to say this is my experience and this is the way I come to being an Aboriginal person" (*Storytellers in Motion,* 2007). *Suckerfish* opens with images of Jackson as a child as animated pictures of "Indian knick knacks" rotate around her picture. Her voiceover declares:

> The first time I suspected I was a part Native was around 8 years old when once again I got some knick knacky gift with a picture of a squaw on it. I added it to my collection of leather purses and dolls with shiny black braids. One day my mother told me our family's Native name was "Nahmabin". When I

asked her what it meant she replied, "sucker". Years later I found out she'd meant suckerfish though I was relieved to find out my ancestors were named after a fish rather than a pushover. It's not the kind of Indian name you brag about at school. (*Suckerfish*, 2004)

Born to an Anglo-Canadian father and Anishinaabe mother, Jackson recalls a childhood filled with the turbulent impact of her mother's alcoholism, addictions, and depression. In the narration she states, "My mom had a rough life. Residential school stole her childhood and Native culture. Depression, drinking, and prescription drug abuse robbed her of the rest. Growing up with her and my father I often wished that I was invisible, to hide from her tantrums, drug induced stupors and visits from the paramedics. My father tried to protect me but in grade 4 despite my love for him I decided to leave my parents" (*Suckerfish,* 2004). As a child she moved to Vancouver to live with an older half sister, whom she hardly knew. During this time her mother wrote her letters, seeking to reconnect with her young daughter. These scenes are poignantly depicted through dramatized reenactments of images of her mother going about daily life without her daughter, while an actor, Cleo Reece, reads from her mother's letters. Jackson recalls, "From across the country my mother tried hard to make amends with letters, gifts and phone calls. I had little interest in a relationship. I had enough memories of her to last a lifetime" (*Suckerfish*, 2004).

The anguish of a young child unable to relate to or connect with her mother is palpable throughout the video, and just as she was deciding to reconcile with her mother, her mother suddenly died from cancer. Jackson's mother was a residential school survivor, and the video attributes the depression and addictions that dominated her adult life to her traumatic residential school experience. The film concludes with a close-up of Jackson standing in front of a mirror, pulling her hair back as the voiceover questions: "Reading my mother's words now I wonder what parts

Fig. 12. Lisa Jackson with her mother. Film still from *Suckerfish* (2004). Courtesy of Lisa Jackson.

of me come from her. My hands look more like hers all the time and sometimes I catch her piercing stare looking back at me from the mirror" (*Suckerfish*, 2004). Jackson's reflection in the mirror is superimposed with images of powwow dancing and singing as she continues: "And lately I wonder how Native I am. Is my mother's pain and suffering my only connection to her heritage? Or is there something inherently Aboriginal about the blood in my veins?" (*Suckerfish*, 2004). This question encapsulates her struggle to claim a Native identity when she wasn't raised within a Native cultural environment. Although throughout much of the video she hesitates to claim a Native identity, she concludes the video with the same refrain about her Native name that opens the video, except this time she confidently declares, "My Indian name is Nahmabin. My mother told me it means Suckerfish" (*Suckerfish*, 2004). The final image of the film is the close-up of Jackson's reflection in the mirror that dissolves into a photograph of her mother when she was young. This confident declaration in which Jackson claims her Native identity by stating her "Indian name" ultimately connects her to her mother and to her Native identity as a mixed-blood Native person.

Jackson's experience growing up with a distant and estranged connection to her Native family and cultural traditions is shared by many Métis, mixed-blood Aboriginal people, and Aboriginal children adopted out from their Aboriginal families. The hesitation to fully claim an Aboriginal identity is often expressed by Aboriginal people who for various reasons linked to the bureaucratic regimes of assimilation—such as residential school, the removal of Aboriginal children by the state to be raised in non-Aboriginal homes, the legacy of poverty, unemployment, and substance abuse as residual effects of systemic racism—were not raised in an Aboriginal community. This struggle to come to terms with one's Aboriginal identity is a frequent subject of the cultural production by mixed-blood Aboriginal and Métis filmmakers and artists.[15] The capacity of media to circulate widely has enabled mixed-blood and Métis filmmakers to link their individual experiences to a broader shared cultural experience. These media representations assert these mixed-blood stories and experiences *as Aboriginal*, thus reflecting the diversity of Aboriginal face, stories, and voices on screen.

Honoring Two-Spirit Identity

Another way in which Aboriginal media reflects Aboriginal diversity is in the growing body of work that represents two-spirit identity and stories. This work is increasingly prominent in urban Aboriginal media communities as many two-spirit people move to urban areas as a result of discrimination or oppression they feel if they live as openly gay on their reserve or in rural areas. The urban Aboriginal community in Vancouver has a sizable two-spirit community. Several filmmakers with whom I spoke in Vancouver articulate a sense of belonging there because of the urban Aboriginal community and also because of Vancouver's lesbian, gay, bisexual, and transgendered (LGBT) community. Vancouver prides itself as being a city that supports the LGBT community with legislation that favors gay marriage, television shows that are queer oriented, a large annual LGBT film festival, and many LGBT community organizations. For some two-spirit individuals life in an urban area such as Vancouver represents the first time they have become involved in a LGBT community and can comfortably live as openly gay. Many two-spirit activists argue that the presence of homophobia on reserves is a legacy of colonization, whereby Euro-Canadian ideologies about gender and sexuality forcibly replaced traditional Aboriginal multiple-gender categories and cultural or spiritual roles that two-spirit individuals played historically within Aboriginal community life.[16] Two-spirit Aboriginal activists are reclaiming these earlier Aboriginal values to challenge discrimination and acknowledge the links between colonization and the emergence of homophobia in Aboriginal communities.[17]

The desire to honor two-spirit individuals and reclaim the traditional roles of two-spirit people is reflected in media work by two-spirit filmmakers in Vancouver.[18] A multimedia project, *Children of the Rainbow (Kichx Anagaat Yatx'i)* (2003) by Tlingit filmmaker Duane Gastant' Aucoin, combined an interactive live performance with video vignettes about two-spirit identity and social issues facing the two-spirit community. In an interview one summer afternoon Aucoin described his goal for *Children of the Rainbow*:

> I wanted the whole show to be a combination of live per-
> formance and video and a celebration of the two-spirited
> history in a chronological journey from before contact how

our two-spirited people were an accepted part of First Nations society and then after contact how that destruction totally ruined the harmony. And it was just to celebrate being proud of who you are no matter what your background or orientation.

At the heart of the live show in *Children of the Rainbow* is a piece called "Sunbox," a performance of the traditional Tlingit story of how Raven stole the sun and brought light to the world. Aucoin's retelling of this story through live performance, music, and media recontextualizes this traditional Raven tale in a way that celebrates two-spirit identity by highlighting how "coming out" brings light to the world. Aucoin is a Wolf/Yanyedi member of the Teslin Tlingit Council who lived in Vancouver for a number of years before returning to Teslin in the Yukon Territory to work for his clan and First Nation government. He was trained by his elders as lead singer, drummer, and dancer for the Deslin Khwan Dancers, a traditional Tlingit dance group, and he combined his experience in storytelling, drumming, singing, theater, and media to create *Children of the Rainbow*, which won the Audience Favorite Award for Best Feature at Vancouver's Out on Screen Film Festival 2003. Out on Screen is a LGBT community organization that has collaborated with the Aboriginal community to consistently showcase two-spirit films and that served as a cosponsor for several IMAGeNation film programs that featured two-spirit films.

Aucoin's commitment to *Children of the Rainbow* was rooted in a desire to impact both the Aboriginal and LGBT communities in Vancouver and stemmed from his desire to have media reflect Aboriginal two-spirit experiences, a significant absence in the media representations he saw while growing up. He declared: "I wanted this show to make a difference in people's lives because I wish I had something like this to look to or to assist me when I was growing up. When I was younger I was ashamed being Native and ashamed being two-spirited. I wanted to take from everything that I had learned and that I had to suffer through and help to share that and I think that comes through in *Children of the Rainbow*." Media production opens up a space for previously marginalized two-spirit voices and recenters those voices within both the LGBT community and the Aboriginal community.

The 2004 IMAGeNation Aboriginal Film and Video Festival also sought to represent the two-spirit Aboriginal community by creating the first festival program dedicated to showcasing media by two-spirit filmmakers. This program, called *Bare Skins,* was curated by Leena Minifie, who saw a need for the film festival to be inclusive of Vancouver's two-spirit community. The *Bare Skins* program featured *Children of the Rainbow* (2003), as well as *Thorn Grass* (2002), a haunting tribute to sixteen-year-old Fred C. Martinez Jr., a two-spirit Diné youth who was killed in a hate crime in Cortez, Colorado, in June 2001. The program also included two shorts by local Vancouver artists: *Brain Plus World* (2001) by James Diamond, a meditation on sexual identity exploring the role of genetics versus lifestyle choices, and *My Life in the Gay Mafia* (2003) by Dusty Hagerüd (Ktunaxa), a short narrative caper in which two lovers and agents in the "Gay Mafia" are compelled to escape and begin again somewhere else. The program concluded with *13 Minutes* by Adam Garnet Jones (Métis), a short narrative about negotiating mistakes in relationships. The *Bare Skins* program was extremely successful, with a large attendance from Vancouver's Aboriginal community as well as Vancouver's LGBT community. In discussing the success of the *Bare Skins* program Minifie exclaimed:

> The *Bare Skins* program ended up being one of our most successful programs which was really crazy because it was the first time that it was done and I hope it set a precedent for the next years to come. Out on Screen loved the idea of us switching off co-presentations for their film festival which is a huge community connection to make. We have a lot of two-spirited people in Vancouver, a lot of people migrate to the city to have that community.

The presence of a two-spirit program in the 2004 IMAGeNation Aboriginal Film and Video Festival represented a conscious decision on the part of the festival staff to create a space within the festival to recognize the diversity within the Aboriginal community, to strengthen relationships with Vancouver's LGBT community and its two-spirit Aboriginal community, and to celebrate two-spirit identity in a respectful way within an Aboriginal venue.

Conclusion

This chapter has explored the on-screen interventions of Aboriginal media through APTN and efforts by mixed-blood and two-spirit filmmakers to portray their experiences. Some filmmakers express frustration at the systemic barriers to participation in the mainstream media industry, while other filmmakers focus their attention on developing capacity within the Aboriginal media industry. Analyzing the development of APTN, I examined the struggle of Aboriginal filmmakers to create their work in a way that honors the cultural worlds in which these stories are rooted, while simultaneously seeking to claim a space for inclusion of Aboriginal voices in Canada's national mediascape. Aboriginal filmmakers navigate this struggle to assert Aboriginal visual sovereignty while also seeking to gain access to Canadian national cultural institutions. Visual sovereignty entails a self-determination with regard to the on-screen representation of Aboriginal experiences. However, visual sovereignty does not imply a separation from engagement with Canadian society but rather reflects the overlapping citizenship of Aboriginal people who hold citizenship in their Aboriginal nations as well as Canadian citizenship. Visual sovereignty is an articulation of Aboriginal cultural autonomy on-screen, speaking to Aboriginal audiences by reflecting their stories on-screen, and a desire to engage with non-Aboriginal audiences on their own terms. Visual sovereignty is also evident in the off-screen production practices of Aboriginal filmmakers. In the next chapter I examine the off-screen impact of Aboriginal media production as a venue through which filmmakers create social networks and kinship ties, nurture intergenerational relationships, and reconnect to their communities of origin.

CHAPTER FOUR

Building Community Off-Screen

THE DOMINO EFFECT—MARCH 2004

I sit on the couch in my friend Leena's apartment one spring evening talking about her work as a media artist, her involvement with IMAG, and her journey to Vancouver. Leena is a dynamic and energetic media artist and dancer who is keen to ensure that Aboriginal media is reflective of the diversity of Aboriginal voices and experiences. We talk about her childhood growing up as a mixed-blood Aboriginal person and the discrimination that she experienced. The conversation shifts to the impact that her involvement in Aboriginal media has had on her family, and her voice becomes heavy with emotion as she recalls: "Getting into Aboriginal media and getting back into learning who I am has started a domino effect in my family which is probably the best thing I could ever ask for. It was a side effect I never knew would occur." Her intensely dark brown eyes meet my gaze. "My mom is now starting to learn more about herself and is proud of being Native. Now there is a sense of pride that is there and in other members of my family." Leena's honor in helping trigger this renewed sense of pride in her family's Gitxaala identity is palpable. This exchange makes it clear to me the tremendous off-screen impact that Aboriginal media can have within Aboriginal families and communities.

Introduction

While chapter 3 focuses on the on-screen impact of Aboriginal media, particularly with regard to the role of APTN and media by mixed-blood, Métis, and two-spirit filmmakers, this chapter examines the powerful way in which media production is an activity around which Aboriginal kinship and social relationships are nurtured and maintained. Throughout this chapter I analyze how urban Aboriginal filmmakers in Vancouver use media production to reintroduce themselves to their communities of origin, strengthen urban and reserve social networks, and reimagine kinship ties to help bridge the ruptures that colonial policies have wrought on Aboriginal family and community structures. I examine how Aboriginal kinship is connected to media production, focusing on the social kinship ties developed among networks of filmmakers, the maintenance of intergenerational ties, and the use of media to bridge urban and reserve spaces. The centrality of kinship to Aboriginal media, and indigenous media globally, is evident both on- and off-screen.

The social relationships and kinship ties produced through Aboriginal media are a significant aspect of my understanding of Aboriginal media as visual sovereignty. As discussed in the introduction, I locate Aboriginal visual sovereignty in the acts of media production. As shown in this chapter, Aboriginal media projects often involve the mobilization of family and community ties in the production process. One of the key markers of sovereignty is the ability to determine membership and citizenship within that nation. The legislation and regulation of Native identity by the U.S. and Canadian governments are primary ways in which these federal governments undermined Native sovereignty by replacing indigenous forms of identity, membership, and belonging with government legislation based on Euro-Canadian and Euro-American ideologies of blood and descent. These colonial policies disenfranchised some Native people from legal recognition as Indians and provided the mechanism through which they were disconnected from their communities. The U.S. system of blood quantum for tribal enrollment and the gender discrimination in the Indian status system in Canada drastically altered Aboriginal kinship, family, and community.[1] These government policies created the conditions under which many Aboriginal people were disconnected from their families, homes, reserves, and communities. It is precisely these colonial ruptures to family and kinship that Aboriginal filmmakers seek to bridge through their media work while creatively reconstituting kinship relationships in both urban and reserve settings. These are acts of sovereignty when Aboriginal filmmakers speak back to this history through their media and when they repair these kinship ties through practices of media production. In this way Aboriginal filmmakers produce more than just media: they actively produce Aboriginal social relationships as well.

"WE'VE ALL GOT THE 'POST–RESIDENTIAL SCHOOL BLUES'"—JULY 2004

It is a bright and sunny July afternoon when I meet Archer Pechawis, a well-known performance artist and filmmaker, for coffee at Soma Café on the corner of Main and Broadway. We sit at a table outside the café and take in the gorgeous mountain landscape that forms the backdrop of Vancouver's city skyline. Pechawis, a long-time activist, anarchist, and artist who has lived and worked in Vancouver's Aboriginal art world for several decades, wears his black and red National Aboriginal Day shirt in protest that today is Canada Day, a national Canadian holiday celebrating confederation held annually on July 1. Our conversation turns from Aboriginal art to politics as Pechawis explains the intergenerational impact of the Aboriginal experience of colonization. He emphatically proclaims: "As Aboriginals we've all got the 'post–residential school blues'! My mother went to residential school. You get so tired of hearing that phrase "residential school," but it really is such a quick and handy way to just identify a whole series of cultural problems that we face around child raising, child apprehension, substance issues, acculturation. As Aboriginal

artists we are Aboriginal people so we struggle with those things."
He pauses a moment. "I struggle with those things. I struggle with
my addiction problems, I struggle with my family situation and so
that has to get in the way of your art. At the same time in a huge
way it informs and it propels my work. So it's a mixed blessing."

Mediating the Residential School Experience

The long history of disruption to Aboriginal family structures
by Canadian colonial policies wrought a devastating multigenerational impact on Aboriginal families and communities.
Perhaps the most drastic rupture to Aboriginal families was
the residential school system that removed children from their
homes and communities and placed them in state- and church-
run residential schools where many experienced abuse at the
hands of teachers, priests, and nuns. The Canadian Indian Act
was amended in 1920, mandating that Indian children attend
residential school, and Native parents who refused to send their
children could be punished with legal penalties including denial
of food rations (Neizen 2000, 73). Between the late nineteenth
century and 1996, when the last residential school was closed,
150,000 Aboriginal, Métis, and Inuit children were forced to
attend one of the 130 residential schools in operation in every
Canadian province and territory, except Newfoundland, New
Brunswick, and Prince Edward Island.[2]

Although exact numbers are difficult to obtain, many children
who attended residential schools speak of the abuse they suffered
there. In his research with residential school survivors and social
workers, scholar Geoffrey York estimates that "as many as 80
percent of Indian children in Canada's mission-operated residential schools were sexually abused" (York 1989, 30). Although this
number may seem high, even the government-sponsored *Report
of the Royal Commission on Aboriginal Peoples* acknowledges,
"In the vision of residential education, discipline was curricu-
lum and punishment was an essential pedagogical technique"

(Government of Canada 1996, 366). It is important to acknowledge that not every student's experience of residential school was negative, and as adults some Native people have expressed gratitude for the education they received there. However, many others remained traumatized by the experience resulting from their separation from their families, and the abuse that many Native children faced was, horrifyingly, an all-too-common aspect of the residential school experience.

Residential schools had a tremendous negative impact on the ability of Aboriginal people to maintain kinship ties, Aboriginal languages, and cultural and ceremonial practices.[3] Residential schools created a system in which Aboriginal communities lost their younger generations and the ability to maintain social reproduction and cultural transmission. Many of the people with whom I worked closely in Vancouver were either residential school survivors or were the children of residential school survivors. The impact of residential schools reaches across generations, as those who were subjected to the institutionalized life of residential schools later battled addictions, alcoholism, and trauma from physical and sexual abuse, which inhibited their ability to care for their own children.[4] An example of the impact of the residential school experience with regard to addictions and parenting is discussed in chapter 3 in Lisa Jackson's film *Suckerfish* (2004) about her relationship with her Anishinaabe mother, a residential school survivor. This intergenerational impact has created a difficult cycle for Aboriginal individuals, families, and communities. There is much "healing work" being done with community organizations to help survivors deal with their grief and trauma from these experiences.

The Canadian government recognized the damage inflicted on Aboriginal families and communities by the residential school system when Prime Minister Stephen Harper issued a long-awaited apology on June 11, 2008. Surrounded by five Aboriginal political leaders and six residential school survivors on the Parliament floor, Prime Minister Harper declared, "Mr. Speaker, I stand before you today to offer an apology to former students of Indian residential schools. The treatment of children in Indian residential schools is a sad chapter in our history." He then continued, outlining the history of the residential school policy in Canada and explaining, "The government now recognizes that the consequences of the Indian residential schools policy were profoundly negative and that this policy has had a lasting and damaging impact on Aboriginal culture, heritage, and language. . . . The government of Canada sincerely apologizes and asks the forgiveness of the Aboriginal peoples of this country for failing them so profoundly. We are sorry."[5]

On the surface an apology may appear as an empty gesture incapable of ever fully compensating for the intergenerational abuse and damage caused by the residential school system. Certainly for some residential school survivors and Aboriginal activists, this was too little too late. However, the Canadian government has established the Truth and Reconciliation Commission (TRC), which will take testimonies from residential school survivors as well as conduct public events to educate Canadian society about the impact of residential schools. The mandate of the TRC "is to inform all Canadians about what happened in Indian Residential Schools (IRS). The Commission will document the truth of survivors, families, communities and anyone personally affected by the IRS experience" with the hope to "guide and inspire Aboriginal peoples and Canadians in a process of reconciliation and renewed relationships that are based on mutual understanding and respect."[6] Prior to this public apology, in 2007 the Canadian government created a $1.9 billion compensation package for those who were forced to attend residential schools.[7] As of April 2010, $1.55 billion had been paid, representing 75,800 cases.[8] There is no doubt that money can never fully compensate someone for their residential school experience; some residential school survivors have chosen not to accept the common experience payments. The Truth and Reconciliation Commission and the compensation funds are small steps toward attempting to acknowledge this painful history and the legacy it leaves for Aboriginal communities and to move toward building a better relationship between Aboriginal peoples and the Canadian government.

The residential school experience is a central topic in many of the videos produced by Aboriginal filmmakers. Two filmmakers with whom I worked in Vancouver—Duane Gastant' Aucoin and Lisa Jackson—have made films that address the intergenerational legacy of the residential school experience. Both Jackson and Aucoin are the children of residential school survivors. Jackson's Genie Award–winning short residential school musical, *Savage* (2009), critiques the residential school experience through a historical narrative set in the 1950s.[9] The short film opens with a Cree woman, played by actor Skeena Reece, singing a lullaby to her daughter, who has just been taken away to residential school. The audio track of the woman's gentle lullaby turns to howls of anger and anguish as the audience sees the daughter undergo a physical transformation: her hair is cut, and she is outfitted in a drab school uniform before being marched off to a classroom. There she joins a line of similarly dressed Aboriginal children whose hair obscures their faces as they gaze down at their desks while copying their lessons from the board. When the teacher leaves for a short break, the film abruptly shifts mood; the students look up, and it becomes clear to the audience they are zombies—a gesture to the pop culture influence of Michael Jackson's *Thriller* (1983) music video on Lisa Jackson. The students break out into an energetic, synchronized hip-hop dance number before sitting back down when the teacher returns to the classroom. Jackson uses zombies as a metaphor for the traumatic transformation that many Aboriginal children experienced in residential schools, and she uses the title *Savage* to reference the Canadian government policy that established residential schools. These critiques draw on Jackson's own history given that her mother was a residential school survivor. Jackson explained that she used the zombie dance sequence to represent their deadened

Fig. 13. Photo from the set of *Savage* (2009). Photo by Kris Krüg. Courtesy of Lisa Jackson.

state as the result of residential school. However, she also used this dance sequence as a way to express the resistance of the children and their spirit of survival in the face of oppression. In an email to the author on April 21, 2012, Jackson explained that she sees dance as a form of creative rebellion and resilience that offers hope for renewal and healing.

Duane G̱astant' Aucoin, a Tlingit filmmaker whose multimedia work *Children of the Rainbow* (2003) was discussed in chapter 3, created the documentary *My Own Private Lower Post* (2008) about his experience as the son of a residential school survivor and about his mother's experience at a residential school in Lower

Fig. 14. Vicky Bob and her son, Duane Ġastant' Aucoin, visit the abandoned residential school in Lower Post, British Columbia, that she attended in the early 1960s. Courtesy of Duane Ġastant' Aucoin.

Post, British Columbia, near the Yukon border. In this powerful film he documents the first time that he and his mother, Vicky Bob, have a conversation about her residential school experiences and the abuse that she and other children experienced at that school. It is a powerful and painful testimony to the horrors of the residential school experience to watch as Bob recalls being driven away with other Aboriginal children in a cattle car from her Tlingit home in Teslin, and as she describes the regimented way of life at the school and the physical abuse they experienced for speaking their language. These experiences eventually led to Bob's abusive marriage to Aucoin's father, whom she met while he was working as a boys' dorm supervisor at the residential school. The film documents this mother and son's experiences but also certainly speaks to the larger set of intergenerational issues created for Aboriginal families and communities by the residential school experience. *My Own Private Lower Post* is structured as a testimonial in the healing genre, as Aucoin and his mother return to the now abandoned school site in Lower Post to talk about his mother's experiences on camera as a way to heal from this past and move beyond it into a brighter future.

Both *Savage* and *My Own Private Lower Post* have screened as part of the national events of the Truth and Reconciliation Commission, with *Savage* screening as part of the first event held in Winnipeg in June 2010 and *My Own Private Lower Post* screening at the Inuvik national event in June 2011. Both films are deeply connected to the personal experiences of the filmmakers, but as media works that are circulated nationally and internationally, they raise awareness of the history and legacy of residential schools in Canada. They also connect these media projects to larger Aboriginal activist efforts to redress these issues through cultural and political efforts locally in Aboriginal communities and nationally through organizations such as the Truth and Reconciliation Commission.

Residential schools, the reserve system, and gender discrimination in the Indian Act—in which Aboriginal women who married non-Aboriginal (and nonstatus Aboriginal) men lost their Indian status and with it the right to live on reserve—all contributed to ruptures in Aboriginal family and community structures. Losing status forced many women and their children to leave reserves—and their family members and extended kin networks—often ending up in urban areas where they were disconnected from traditional kinship networks and reinvented these relationships in the new urban setting. In many cases the loss of status also created tensions between family members, further fostering fractures within Aboriginal kin networks and communities.[10] Given the legacy of these historical policies that disrupted Aboriginal families, many Aboriginal people feel a need to reconnect with their own family to bridge these ruptures. Through the collaborative nature of the filmmaking process, the engagement of family members in the production process, and the creation of stories about relatives and ancestors, Aboriginal media practices have become a vital way to recuperate Aboriginal kinship ties.

Reconnecting through Media: Identity and Community

Aboriginal media production can provide a powerful venue through which people regain and strengthen social connections to community, family, and extended kin networks. Many individuals in Vancouver become involved in Aboriginal media production with the intention of offering these skills to their communities of origin in order to reconnect with their own family and community. Odessa Shuquaya was mostly raised by her British mother in a predominantly white town of Nelson, British Columbia.[11] When she moved to Vancouver to attend the University of British Columbia to study acting, she became interested in getting involved in Vancouver's Aboriginal arts community:

> I'm from the Kluane First Nation on my dad's side up in the Yukon territory and I'm half British on my mother's side. I was raised by my mother in a white family, not by my father and had very little contact with my Aboriginal side. After I finished my university degree I wanted to get in contact with my roots and so I enrolled in the Aboriginal Film and Television Program at Capilano College in North Vancouver. It was fantastic because I got to meet a lot of the young members of the Native arts community in the Lower Mainland and from across Canada. There were a lot of other students from across Canada, there was a student from Nunavut and there were students from Ontario and from Alberta so it was pretty amazing. So that was a good cultural awakening for me!

She described wanting to get involved in Aboriginal media as part of her process of strengthening her cultural identity, but she also wanted to use media as "her voice." She declared: "A lot of the reason why I wanted to be involved in Aboriginal media is because it's a way to get information out and it can be a tool, it can be a voice. But it's also nice to be part of an artistic community which I think is really burgeoning in this time, it's just beginning. I believe that the people are finding our voice and

Aboriginal media is allowing us to use that medium as a story-telling device. So that's what has drawn me towards that, the political aspects as well as the way to express oneself."

Shuquaya's decision to enroll in the Capilano College program in order to become more involved with the Aboriginal community and to strengthen her cultural identity is a common refrain that Jackson Crick—former director of the Capilano College program—heard when interviewing students for the program. He found that students see media production as a way to gain a valuable skill that can serve as a means of reintroduction to their home communities or as a way for them to be connected with Vancouver's urban Aboriginal community. He explained: "It's a good tool to use because it gets you connected to your community again if you want to. You can go to your community and volunteer to do something for them, to film something for them or to teach their youth or something like that. It's a great way to reintroduce yourself to them again." However, Crick emphasizes that there are a range of desires and motivations behind students' involvement in Aboriginal media. He declared:

> I mean some people are specifically coming there because it's a cultural preservation tool. They want to take it back to their community and they want to get their own little setup of equipment and tape all their community events and inter-view their elders and use it as a language preservation tool. Maybe they have some dreams to make a documentary about their people. But then there are other people that want to be the Quentin Tarantino of the Aboriginal film world! It varies, some people that is their dream and other people they just want to have those tools and go back home.

While those that dream of becoming "the Quentin Tarantino of the Aboriginal film world" may have different ambitions, the relationships forged by using media within their community are a powerful driving force for many filmmakers. The strengthening of their cultural identity and community ties is often an unexpected but tremendously rewarding side effect of their involvement in Aboriginal media production.

This was the case for Leena Minifie, who was raised in a predominantly white town in northern British Columbia and had little contact with her extended Aboriginal family.[12] Minifie's grandmother attended residential school and later moved to an urban area where Minifie's mother was raised with relatively little contact with her Gitxaala community. As a result of the discrimination that she experienced, Minifie's mother lived most of her life silencing her Aboriginal identity. Consequently Minifie—who was urban raised and spent little time in her family's traditional territory—did not have much contact with or understanding of her Aboriginal heritage and identity. This pattern of silence throughout Minifie's childhood about her Aboriginal cultural traditions and identity is a common legacy of the impact of colonial policies on Aboriginal families across Canada. As discussed in the opening vignette, an important impact of Minifie's involvement in Aboriginal media has been the unexpected side effect of her mother becoming more interested in and proud of her Aboriginal heritage and identity. Given the history of Canadian policies such as the residential school system that physically removed Aboriginal children from their families and sought to erase Aboriginal identity and cultural practices, Aboriginal media can provide a powerful vehicle through which Aboriginal individuals can bridge cultural and familial gaps created by the ruptures of assimilation to claim a space for younger generations to learn cultural knowledge, often inspiring their parents, siblings, aunties, and uncles to do the same. This represents a powerful form of resistance and a keen articulation of Aboriginal visual sovereignty by filmmakers in the face of the legacies of Canadian colonial policies. These filmmakers choose to use media production to strengthen Aboriginal kinship and family ties, providing vital social and creative networks for Aboriginal filmmakers.

Filmmaking in the Family

While some filmmakers use media production as an opportunity to reconnect with their families and communities of origin, Vancouver's Aboriginal media world also has a striking number of members of the same family involved in media production.[13] There are several pairs of mothers and daughters, siblings, and cousins who actively participate in Vancouver's Aboriginal media world. These family ties are nurtured and sustained in part through participation in the Aboriginal media and arts community in Vancouver. Kamala Todd spoke proudly of the impact of her mother, Loretta Todd:

> When I was a teenager my mom started in film school and I would go to some of her classes up at SFU [Simon Fraser University] and she really kind of sparked me into the craft of it. It's not something that I had thought I would ever do, but I appreciated her passion for the craft of filmmaking. At that time it wasn't like it is now where everyone's a filmmaker! So I was very inspired by her. She lent a lot of her skills to Aboriginal groups that wouldn't normally have that, supporting social justice and so that inspired me about how media can support people to make change and tell their story.

Loretta Todd not only inspired her daughter to become a filmmaker, but as the first Aboriginal woman to attend Simon Fraser University's film school, she provided a role model for many people in the Aboriginal community to see that it was possible as an Aboriginal person to pursue a career in filmmaking. Dana Claxton fondly recalled:

> Loretta Todd was a big influence on people. She was the first Aboriginal woman making films here in Vancouver. Loretta was so consistent and certainly was the first Indian woman to attend the film department at SFU. And so just the fact that she was making a film, I remember the rippling effects,

that "oh my god if she could do it" then we could do it. So if anybody was an influence it was her.

Loretta Todd has remained an inspiration and mentor for young Aboriginal filmmakers whom she taught at IMAG and at the Capilano College Indigenous Independent Digital Filmmaking Program. Daughter Kamala Todd, who developed the *Our City, Our Voices* (2005) project with the National Film Board and the city of Vancouver, has made two documentaries, *Indigenous Plant Diva* (2008), discussed in the introduction, and *My Urban Eyes* (in postproduction) and has collaborated with her mother on the Cree children's APTN program, *Tansi! Nehiyawetan: Let's Speak Cree!*

Many Aboriginal filmmakers have family members who are artists if not filmmakers, and they are often influenced by the creative visions and artistic practice of these relatives in their own film work. Loretta Todd's sister Barbara Hager produces an Aboriginal television show, *The New Canoe*, and her brother is an accomplished artist and painter. Cleo Reece's sister is a talented painter, and several of her children, including Skeena Reece, Nitanis Desjarlais, and Simon Reece, are artists, performers, and singers in addition to being filmmakers. Dana Claxton collaborated with her sister Kim Goodtrack on two television shows, *Wakanheja (Sacred One)* and *ArtZone*. *Wakanheja* was fifty-two episodes for preschool-age children that contained a Lakota language component and also involved the collaboration of their aunt anthropologist, Dr. Bea Medicine. Claxton and Goodtrack then produced thirty-two episodes of *ArtZone* for Aboriginal teens that were broadcast on APTN. Rose Spahan (Coast Salish) a filmmaker, curator, and artist, often draws inspiration from the artwork of her cousin Lawrence Paul Yuxweluptun (Coast Salish). Experimental filmmaker Thirza Cuthand (Plains Cree/Scots) is the daughter of prominent artist Ruth Cuthand (Cree). Danaan Dallas (Cowichan/Scottish), an emerging filmmaker and actor, is the son of experimental filmmaker and performance artist

Fig. 15. Vera Wabegijig teaches her daughter, Storm Standing on the Road, how to use a video camera. August 2004. Photo by author.

Dolores Dallas (Cowichan). Jerilyn Webster (Nuxalk/Mohawk) and her sister Vanessa Webster (Nuxalk/Mohawk) have both participated in media training programs and are active in the Aboriginal theater and arts community. Although Leena Minifie is the first filmmaker in her family, she has an uncle who is a painter, carver, jewelry designer, and artist. Jeff Bear, a prominent leader in Aboriginal television, has a sister, Shirley Bear, who has been instrumental in maintaining traditional Aboriginal art practices such as basket weaving and beadwork. These family connections further anchor filmmakers within the broader network of the Aboriginal art world. Jackson Crick credited IMAG with providing social space in which relatives in Vancouver can meet and nurture kinship ties. Crick described how he first met his cousin Helen Haig-Brown at IMAG, declaring, "Actually the funny thing is Helen and I never met each other before. I met her through IMAG so you see how IMAG brings people together! Yeah we didn't know each other. I mean I grew up in Quesnell, she grew up in Vancouver. But her grandmother and my grandfather are brother and sister so we're second cousins."

Filmmaking is a collaborative practice that often entails mobilizing not only financial resources and equipment but also social labor to bring various skills and talents to the project. In many cases this means calling on the involvement of family members in order to complete a project. In this way Aboriginal media is more than simply expressive of Aboriginal stories; it also nurtures Aboriginal kinship and is deeply embedded in Aboriginal social life. Barb Cranmer described the way in which her filmmaking is rooted in her family and community ties, noting: "I feel fortunate to be able to live the history of our people through the films I make. I get a source of strength from my community and most importantly from my family. They have given me a strong sense of identity, knowing who I am and where I come from."

Intergenerational Relationships and Mentorship

As discussed in chapter 1, Aboriginal media production is an important practice through which intergenerational ties are nurtured in the process of mentorship between established and emerging filmmakers and connecting youth with their elders. Emerging artist Odessa Shuquaya expressed a deep sense of gratitude for support of her work by established Aboriginal filmmakers, contrasting it to her experiences within the mainstream theater community:

> When I decided to get involved in the Aboriginal artists community, I was shocked because it was more welcoming and

supportive. It was really amazing, I was really impressed. A lot of the more experienced media producers or artists they are very willing to lend me their ear to help me with any questions I had or willing to put my work up to view. For instance, Tracey Jack showed my first documentary all over the Okanagan and in with the likes of Loretta Todd and Gil Cardinal and I was so honored. That was really an honor for me and I was just amazed that they would do that.

The role of mentoring is crucial in building a sense of community and establishing intergenerational relationships in Vancouver's Aboriginal media world.

The intergenerational aspect of the Aboriginal media world in Vancouver also actively creates and reimagines kinship. As discussed above, it is a common practice for established filmmakers from the "older generation" to mentor younger filmmakers, and their roles as mentors often take on additional social responsibilities and obligations outside of the filmmaking relationship. This was particularly evident in the social networks among filmmakers who are single mothers and who provide social support for each other in the form of childcare, meals, and exchanging children's clothes, fulfilling many of the kinship roles that extended families often provide. Vera Wabegijig, Leena Minifie, and Odessa Shuquaya all maintained sister-like relationships, while Cleo Reece served as an auntie to many of the youth who came through IMAG's door. Dolores Dallas is like an aunt to Wabegijig because of Dallas's close friendship with Wabegijig's mother, and Wabegijig's daughters call Dallas "auntie." Likewise Kevin Lee Burton is like a brother to Wabegijig and often takes care of Wabegijig's daughters, to whom he is like an uncle. All of these relationships were initiated through a film project, involvement with the Aboriginal media world, or work at IMAG, but they have taken on kinship roles as these social relationships move beyond the realm of professional work relationships to provide a crucial social support system. The adoption of kinship relationships

Fig. 16. Cleo Reece and author at the IMAG office. August 2004. Photo by Vera Wabegijig. Courtesy of author.

happens intergenerationally as well as intragenerationally as individuals take on the role of aunties, uncles, sisters, brothers, and cousins in a way that helps to create an extended network of community, family, and social relationships that sustains a social support system in an urban environment.[14]

For Shuquaya and many other filmmakers in the urban setting of Vancouver the social network of Aboriginal filmmakers creates a "web of people that gives you strength." The community of Aboriginal filmmakers is articulated through an idiom of kinship whereby the social responsibilities and obligations of roles as aunties, as cousins, or as sisters becomes a tie that holds people together and also enables productive collaborative working relationships necessary to mobilize the social labor needed to complete media projects. As is discussed more extensively in chapter 6, Kevin Lee Burton and Helen Haig-Brown met and became friends while students in the Capilano College AFTP program as well as in IMAG's professional development media training program, where they became collaborators on each other's film projects. For example, Helen Haig-Brown was the cinematographer on two of Burton's films, *Writing the Land* (2007) and *Nikamowin* (2007), and was the editor on *Writing the Land* (2007). Kevin Burton often serves as a collaborator in the preproduction and production phases of Helen Haig-Brown's projects. In an interview Haig-Brown described her collaboration with Burton this way: "He's a very big part of my process. He's one of the first people that sees my rough cuts or scripts and I really trust his insights into things. I love how in depth he is and how much he thinks about it from all senses in film. He's very musical and sound driven with the visual and I think that's where we have a bit of an affinity." Both filmmakers share a similar aesthetic that leans toward the experimental genre, and both emphasize Aboriginal visual sovereignty through land, language, and identity in their films. This friendship created through film school and media training programs carries over into the social networks of these two filmmakers and has resulted in a productive media collaboration that continues even now that neither Haig-Brown nor Burton resides in Vancouver.

Aboriginal media is also used to connect elders and youth and to sustain vital intergenerational bonds needed for cultural transmission within the urban Aboriginal community. The *Our City, Our Voices* project is an example of how Aboriginal media projects that document traditional knowledge, oral histories, and life histories of elders often can become a catalyst through which Aboriginal youth initiate relationships with their elders. The first phase of the *Our City, Our Voices* project was "Storykeepers," which brought together groups of Aboriginal youth and elders from the Musqueam, Tsleil-Waututh, and Squamish reserves as well as the urban Aboriginal community in Vancouver to record the oral histories and stories of their elders. The youth were trained in video production by prominent Aboriginal filmmakers who served as mentors throughout the program. The videotaped interviews with the elders were archived with the respective groups, and the National Film Board of Canada agreed that the communities would hold the copyright to the videos and that they would have the ultimate decision about if and how to edit the footage to suit their own community needs. Through the careful program planning by Kamala Todd, the youth learned about cultural protocol, protection of indigenous knowledge, and honoring elders as well as passing on indigenous storytelling practices. In addition to the archive of elder interviews, this program resulted in the production of two short documentaries—*Our City, Our Voices: Follow the Eagle* (2005) and *Slo-Pitch* (2005)—produced in collaboration between Aboriginal filmmakers and Aboriginal residents of Vancouver's Downtown Eastside. *Follow the Eagle* profiles the Elders-in-Training Program created by the Aboriginal Front Door Society to provide guidance for the next generation of elders in Vancouver's urban Aboriginal community, while *Slo-Pitch* documents the important role that the Downtown Eastside Slo-Pitch League plays in providing family-oriented recreation for residents of the Downtown Eastside.

While a video itself is certainly no substitute for an elder, and there is no doubt that the transmission of knowledge is altered when recorded onto a video, I argue that the act of media production itself produces important Aboriginal intergenerational relationships. Kevin Lee Burton movingly declared, "the interaction with elders doesn't end once the camera stops rolling but instead opens up a space for that relationship to be maintained." Leena Minifie expressed a profound connection with Kwakawạkạ'wakw elders at Kingcome Inlet, British Columbia, as production manager on a video shoot for the television show *First Story*, an Aboriginal arts, culture, and current events show broadcast on CTV and APTN. She noted that they were given permission to film all cultural events surrounding the ceremonial big house opening—including the potlatch, songs, and dances—because the cameraman's mother was from that community. Although Minifie herself is not from that community, she was deeply moved by the experience of filming there and wanted to "honor the work they've been doing in keeping their traditions alive." She described this project as her best shooting experience and framed this video shoot as part of her "journey" by connecting with the elders there.[15] In an interview she elaborated: "I was working but I was on this journey at the same time. I was able to get close to some of the elders up there in that short period of time. To be able to really connect with the people up there and just to honor them that they did a really great job. And they're keeping it going by building the big house. They know the value of it and the kids know the value of it."

Minifie's story about her experience with elders in Kingcome Inlet, as well as the effects of the *Our City, Our Voices* project on Aboriginal youth and elders in Vancouver, speaks to the capacity of Aboriginal media to create and sustain vitally important Aboriginal kinship, social, and family relationships. Many elders embrace the technology of video production for its powerful potential to carry on their knowledge and stories, creating a lasting legacy for future generations. In an interview Barb Cranmer smiled as she remarked: "My grandmother talks about the tape recorder and the video camera being the elder now. Family potlatches are pretty well all documented [on video] now because the people see the importance of it." Aboriginal media have become new tools for intergenerational cultural transmission. By documenting cultural practices, recording elders' life histories, or recording Aboriginal languages, media technology becomes a crucial link between the generations, helping to forge kinship relationships and intergenerational ties. Odessa Shuquaya describes the need for Aboriginal documentaries that document traditional knowledge of elders:

People want to document a way of life that they feel is slipping away. Because the old ways are dying with our elders. There's a new way of being and I think a lot of people really want to capture the language and the traditional ways and preserve them. I think that's important work that needs to be done. Perhaps that's a Western way of thinking about it and perhaps that's an anthropological way of thinking about it, but if that means my grandkids can see the way my grandma tanned a moose hide, so be it. I can't show them because I don't know how to do it. The Native way is for me to pass that on to my daughter and then she passes that on to her granddaughter, but let's face it, we're urban. There are so many people that don't know how to do those things that our grandparents and our great-grandparents knew how to do.

For Shuquaya, who left the Kluane First Nation reserve and her family in the Yukon when she was a young child, the capacity of media technology to document cultural knowledge links her daughter to the elders of her community. She welcomes the possibilities opened up by media technology to maintain this knowledge for future generations. At the same time she emphasizes that media production is one of a multitude of Aboriginal adaptations to "a new way of being," particularly to the conditions facing urban Aboriginal individuals.

Bridging the Diaspora: Building Urban/Reserve Networks

Filmmakers looking to reconnect with their communities often make a video about their home community or return to shoot a film or video within their home territory or reserve. For Cleo Reece's documentary *Land Use: Mother Earth* (1993) she returned to her mother's home reserve outside Fort McMurray in northern Alberta to document environmental changes. This video was an especially important project for Reece, who had been sent as a child to a foster home when removed from her Cree reserve and family. When I asked her about this video and whether it was a way for her to reconnect with her home community and family, she replied, "Yeah, it was a way because I'd never spent any time there because I was a child when I left. So it was a way to reconnect and my brother was there [living on the reserve] and so he was the main speaker in the whole video." As mentioned in chapter 1, Cleo Reece left Vancouver to return to live in Fort McMurray, where she continues to be involved as an environmental activist speaking out against the pollution of the Tar Sands oil fields on Aboriginal lands and making documentaries about this activism. Kevin Lee Burton's video *Meskanahk (My Path)* (2005) opened up an opportunity for him to reconnect with his reserve community of Gods Lake Narrows in northern Manitoba, which he left as a teenager. This short autobiographical video was shot on his reserve and in Vancouver, and the video project became a way for Burton to reconnect with his reserve community and to resolve some of his feelings of alienation from his family and reserve community. As noted in chapter 6, Burton continues to shoot his films in Cree, on his reserve and with the involvement of his family and community.

In the short dramatic narrative film *Prayer for a Good Day* (2003), directed by Zoe Hopkins, a young girl seeks to help her father cope with his depression. Hopkins was born and raised primarily in Bella Bella in Heiltsuk territory with her mother's family, although she did spend some time as a child in her father's home community of the Six Nations reserve in Ontario. It was important to her to shoot the film on the Six Nations reserve because she wanted the beauty of the land to provide the backdrop for the story of this young girl's struggle with her father's depression. In a phone interview Hopkins described how her love for her father's traditional territory drove her filmic choices, explaining: "That's my dad's community so I felt all right to be filming there. I had always wanted to make a film there because the country's so beautiful. You can drive for miles and you're still on reserve so I just love driving around there and looking at all the big fields of corn and stuff like that. It's just so beautiful. So

I think that my love for the country there really inspired some of the way that I handled some of the shots." The centrality of land in Aboriginal media is articulated by Aboriginal filmmakers and critically analyzed by media scholars as one aspect of Aboriginal media aesthetics (Leuthold 1998; Masayesva 1995). Zoe Hopkins participated in the 2009 imagineNATIVE Festival's Embargo Collective, a group of seven international indigenous filmmakers selected by programmer Danis Goulet (Métis). Each filmmaker was given a $7,000 grant with which to make a short film. The filmmakers worked collectively over two years and gave each other sets of restrictions within which they had to work in order to push each other out of their cinematic comfort zones. Hopkins was assigned the comedy genre, and once again she returned to the Six Nations reserve, her traditional Mohawk territory, to film *Tsi tkahéhtayen (The Garden)* (2009). She worked closely with her father on the script, and he stars in the movie as a mystical gardener who harvests fruits from the earth that defy everyone's expectations. The film is in Mohawk and cleverly uses a play on pronunciation in Mohawk to create the comedy in the film as the gardener mishears what the three women in the film want him to grow for them in his garden.

Another common trope in Aboriginal media is the "going home" journey or narrative. Like other Aboriginal artists, musicians, storytellers, and writers, many Aboriginal filmmakers use media production as a tool to explore their own cultural identity, family history, and connections to their home communities, reserves, or traditional territories. For example, in *Migmaeoi Otjiosog/Mi'kmaq Family* (1994), Catherine Martin reconnects with her Mi'kmaq community, family, and cultural heritage by returning to an annual Mi'kmaq gathering on Cape Breton. *It Starts with a Whisper* (1993) is a dramatic short film in which the protagonist Shauna journeys to connect to her cultural identity with the help of three comic and tricksterish aunties. *I Want to Know Why* (1994) is an experimental video that critically explores the filmmaker's family history as her Lakota great-grandmother was forced to make the journey from South Dakota into Saskatchewan because of the brutal U.S. military policies.[16] There are also several videos—*Women in the Shadows* (1991), *Meskanahk (My Path)* (2005), and *Suckerfish* (2004)—that address Métis and mixed-blood identity in which the filmmakers return to their own home territory or community in order to reclaim their family history and cultural identity.

The use of media production to reconnect with one's home community and strengthen urban/reserve networks was also evident in IMAG programming. IMAG featured several traveling film festivals that took portions of the IMAGeNation Aboriginal Film and Video Festival program to reserves throughout British Columbia to provide an opportunity for people on reserves to see indigenous films. In 2000 the IMAG staff members took the IMAGeNation Festival on the road, screening twenty-two Aboriginal films on reserves in Duncan and Prince George, British Columbia, and in 2001 IMAG organized the Aboriginal Traveling Film Festival, which screened twenty-three films in Prince Rupert, British Columbia. In 2005 IMAG organized "Redskins Drive Home," where IMAG staff screened films at two venues in the North Okanagan, including the Splats'in reserve, one of seventeen communities of the Secwepemc Nation. In an IMAG press release in 2005 about the event Dorothy Christian stated, "I'm very excited about bringing these works to my home territory. We will be showing Aboriginal work that is not available in the neighborhood video stores and not released theatrically in the mainstream movie houses." Other examples of Aboriginal media projects connecting urban and reserve communities include the imagineNATIVE Northern Ontario Film and Video Tour, which seeks to provide access to remote and reserve communities in northern Ontario that "would not otherwise have access to independent Indigenous-made work."[17] This traveling festival presents screenings of award-winning films from that year's imagineNATIVE Film Festival, but these tours also include youth video production workshops that provide training for

Aboriginal youth. Another traveling Aboriginal media initiative is Wapikoni Mobile, a motorized mobile production studio that travels to Aboriginal communities across Quebec with the aim of training youth in media production. Since 2004 Wapikoni Mobile has produced over 375 short videos by traveling to eighteen different Aboriginal communities in Quebec and working with over 1,500 participants; this work has garnered over forty national and international awards.[18]

Activities such as the "Redskins Drive Home" film festival, imagineNATIVE's Northern Ontario Tour, and Wapikoni Mobile all create "native hubs" (Ramirez 2007) in which Aboriginal identity is strengthened through shared participation in cultural activity that invigorates social networks across and between urban areas and reserve settings. These traveling media projects, as well as individual video projects where filmmakers return to their communities of origin, serve to nurture and maintain important urban/reserve Aboriginal social networks. The process of physically returning to one's home or community to shoot a video—often about that journey itself—creates a vitally important new vehicle through which urban and reserve Aboriginal individuals strengthen social ties while creating networks that bridge the Aboriginal diaspora spanning urban settings, remote areas, and reserves.

Conclusion

In this chapter I have examined how Aboriginal media is a vital cultural practice that alters and strengthens Aboriginal kinship, often subverting Canadian colonial policies that ruptured Aboriginal families and communities to provide an arena for Aboriginal individuals to reconnect with their communities of origin, establish intergenerational relationships with elders, and creatively reimagine kinship. Aboriginal media are more than merely expressive of Aboriginal stories; they are constitutive of Aboriginal social and kinship relationships. A profound power of Aboriginal media production lies in its capacity to strengthen and alter off-screen social and family relationships. The off-screen impact of this media is evident in the way in which filmmakers in Vancouver use media not only to strengthen social networks between urban Aboriginal filmmakers but also to reconnect with their families and communities of origin. Media production requires extensive labor (e.g., cinematographers, sound engineers, editors, director, producer) and provides a venue to build social relationships between those in front of and those behind the camera during the production. Aboriginal visual sovereignty is deeply rooted in these social relationships, kinship, and family ties created through the production process. As examined in more detail in the next two chapters, these sovereign acts of production also leave marks of visual sovereignty on-screen as well.

CHAPTER FIVE

Cultural Protocol in Aboriginal Media

THE PEOPLE GO ON—OPENING NIGHT, NOVEMBER 2003

It is a brisk November evening when Loretta Todd's new film, *Kaina-yssini Imanistaisiwa: The People Go On*, opens to a packed audience at the Pacific Cinematheque. After helping all week with publicity for the screening, promoting the film across the city by distributing flyers and posters, I sit amid the standing-room-only crowd, eagerly awaiting the screening.

Loretta begins by discussing her production process and how she initially approached the Kainai elders to seek permission before beginning the film project. She continues to follow cultural protocol throughout the opening, inviting Kainai community members to speak before the screening.

Leonard Bearshirt, a young Blackfoot filmmaker from the Siksika reserve where much of the film was shot, makes his way to the front of the theater, where he plays his hand drum and sings a traditional honor song for the film's opening night. The steady beat of the drum and Leonard's high and steady voice echo across the movie theater.

Immediately after the honor song, Curtis Clearsky, a Blackfoot/Ojibwe filmmaker, hip-hop artist, and activist, performs spoken word and several hip-hop songs about his experiences growing up on the Blackfoot reserve and in Vancouver. Curtis thanks Loretta for making the film and showing the positive side of life on the rez in contrast to mainstream media that focuses on the negative aspects.

The last speaker is Beverly Hungry Wolf, a writer and elder from the Kainai community, who speaks about the impact of the film on her community. Her strong emotions regarding the film move me and other audience members as she thanks Loretta for creating such a beautiful film that "respects our land, our ancestors and their way of life."

Listening to the Kainai community members speak before the screening, I am struck by the significance of honoring social relationships and the weight of cultural protocol on Aboriginal filmmaking. This film opening vividly reveals to me the deep role of cultural protocol in Aboriginal media and the way in which visual sovereignty is enacted in myriad ways off-screen through the production process.

Introduction

The opening night of *The People Go On* was one of the first times in which I understood the extent to which Aboriginal media production makes an impact in the off-screen social relationships within Aboriginal communities. Aboriginal media nurture and constitute Aboriginal social relationships off-screen in numerous ways. That Loretta Todd, and other Aboriginal filmmakers, carefully enact cultural protocol through their production process is an act of Aboriginal visual sovereignty. Todd's documentary *The People Go On*, discussed in greater detail at the end of this chapter, is experimental in its innovation in the documentary genre and also in Todd's commitment to integrating Aboriginal cultural protocols into the production process, serving to decolonize the documentary genre on- and off-screen. In this chapter I analyze Aboriginal experimental media—a genre that is prominent within Vancouver's Aboriginal media world, given its long connection to the avant-garde art scene. I focus on the work of Dana Claxton and Loretta Todd—founders of and leaders in Vancouver's Aboriginal media world—to explore the integration of Aboriginal cultural protocols into Aboriginal media on- and off-screen. I argue that incorporation of cultural protocols into the media production process is a key aspect of Aboriginal experimental media and the "indigenization" of media technology by Aboriginal filmmakers.

Avant-garde Aboriginal Art and Experimental Media in Vancouver

Vancouver's Aboriginal media world is unique for its range of media genres including television production, feature documentaries, short narratives, experimental video, and new media. Whereas some Aboriginal media makers in other parts of Canada have been constrained by funding resources and distribution venues to primarily produce documentaries, Vancouver's Aboriginal media world has had a long history of innovative work pushing artistic boundaries and appropriating the latest technologies in the service of Aboriginal artistic expression.[1] Avant-garde art is often defined as work "characterized by unorthodox and experimental methods" (O'Pray 2003, 2). It is difficult to define experimental media or avant-garde film; however, scholars agree that it is an unconventional, highly personal, sometimes idiosyncratic, poetic, and often oppositional genre marginalized on the periphery of mainstream cinema that emphasizes the vision of the auteur filmmaker (O'Pray 20003; Verrone 2011). Film scholar Michael Verrone describes avant-garde film as "something *different*—a work that is antithetical to the mainstream, is produced outside economic and cultural channels of discourse, is (sometimes) deliberately political in nature, and is uniformly diverse in its multiple variations and forms" (Verrone 2011, 18).

I characterize Aboriginal experimental media as avant-garde both in the ways in which Aboriginal media makers experiment with on-screen aesthetics and also in the innovative and sometimes unconventional off-screen production practices. There are similarities between Aboriginal experimental media and other non-Aboriginal avant-garde films. Indeed, Aboriginal experimental media in Vancouver is often shown alongside non-Aboriginal experimental media in art gallery and artist-run center settings. There are parallels between aesthetic style — editing, framing, superimposition, montage, repetition, and split screen — between Aboriginal and non-Aboriginal avant-garde media. However, I see several key ways in which Aboriginal experimental media differ from Western, non-Aboriginal avant-garde film and video. First, Western avant-garde film places a strong emphasis on the individual director, the film auteur who creates a unique personal cinematic vision through his or her avant-garde films. This is reflective of the larger privilege in the Western art world accorded to the individual (predominantly male) artist and also reflects the Western modernist, capitalist sensibility that focuses on the autonomous individual disentangled from the weight of obligation to family and kin ties. In contrast, in Aboriginal experimental media filmmakers often position themselves as individuals enmeshed in a complex set of obligations to social relations, extended family, clan, and community ties. Their films certainly reflect their unique and individual artistic vision but also emphasize their position as individuals with ties to family, kin, community, and Aboriginal nations. Loretta Todd articulates this sense of obligation, declaring: "These stories, these films, are inherited by our children. The legacy that is in these films is inherited by other people, so everything I do I have to be very careful about why I do it, who I do it for, who's going to be hurt by this, who is going to gain from this. I have to think about the seven generations" (Todd qtd. in L. Abbott 1998, 344).[2] Honoring cultural protocol is ultimately about respecting social relationships and obligations to family, clan, or community. This is quite a different approach to filmmaking than the Western emphasis on the ownership, authorship, and personal vision of the individual auteur filmmaker.

Second, Western avant-garde film often emphasizes a break from tradition articulating a modernist vision of a split from the past. Film scholar William Verrone describes the style of avant-garde film as "standing in opposition to tradition" (Verrone 2011, 17). Instead of rejecting tradition, Aboriginal filmmakers seek to honor their past and often place their cultural traditions center stage by integrating cultural protocols and indigenous aesthetics into their films while contextualizing their work in a broader matrix of Aboriginal histories. Third, Western avant-garde film has been defined by its capacity to instigate active spectatorship and to invite audience members to rethink what the medium of film is capable of doing and achieving. "The avant-garde filmmaker radically re-examines the creative process, asking questions of the medium itself. What can film do? What can film accomplish?" (10). Aboriginal experimental filmmakers fundamentally reimagine the possibilities of film by placing media technologies in the service of Aboriginal cultural protocols, aesthetic traditions, stories, and politics, thus expressing Aboriginal visual sovereignty. Likewise, Aboriginal experimental media demand interactive spectatorship and can place the viewer in a position to witness filmic explorations of Aboriginal social, political, and cultural issues to recognize Aboriginal rights and cinematic expression on Aboriginal terms. Aboriginal experimental media disrupts the notion of a unilineal trajectory for Aboriginal media production and reflects the diversity of practice within Aboriginal media. Aboriginal experimental media makers not only innovate within the field of Aboriginal media, but they also make unique contributions to the broader genre of avant-garde film.

As discussed in chapter 1, Vancouver's Aboriginal media world is intricately connected with the larger art scene in Vancouver that has long been a center for avant-garde video art and performance art. The presence of artist-run centers in Vancouver such as the grunt gallery, the Western Front, and Video In provide invaluable venues for Aboriginal filmmakers and artists to show their media.[3] The Emily Carr University of Art and Design in Vancouver with its cutting-edge media arts program has trained several of Vancouver's Aboriginal experimental video artists and

Fig. 17. The grunt gallery, Vancouver, British Columbia. September 2003. The grunt gallery's mandate includes showing contemporary First Nations art, such as performance art, new media, video installations, and experimental film. The grunt gallery was a collaborator of IMAG and is a key "hub" for avant-garde art in Vancouver. Photo by author.

performance artists, including Zachery Longboy, Cease Wyss, and Thirza Cuthand. The presence of prominent performance artists Dana Claxton, Rebecca Belmore, Archer Pechawis, Aiyanna Maracle, and Lawrence Paul Yuxweluptun has contributed to Vancouver's strong Aboriginal performance art and experimental video scene. Performance art, given its embodiment, is a vital artistic medium through which Aboriginal artists explore spiritual traditions, question sacred/secular boundaries, interrogate colonial histories, and incorporate cultural protocol into their artistic practice. Aboriginal performance art can also transform the mainstream art gallery institution, the "white cube" as Dana Claxton calls the Western art gallery, into a space that is responsive to and reflective of Aboriginal voices, stories, and experiences. Archer Pechawis contends that in Aboriginal performance art

> Indians stand up and claim space. In that space the stories are re-told, re-interpreting what was assumed understood. The performance space becomes part of the moccasin telegraph: a gathering space, a communal council fire. Grievances are aired. Relations are shown. News of the community is examined, the larger community of Indianness is considered (Pechawis 2000, 137).

Pechawis emphasizes the embeddedness of Aboriginal performance art within Aboriginal social relationships and identifies this practice as significant to community building. Aboriginal performance art is a highly variable practice, often encompassing many media from theater and song to dance, film, video, and new media.

It is no accident that Vancouver's Aboriginal media world has developed a strong experimental scene given the funding for experimental media available through the Canada Council for the Arts, the history of the Vancouver's avant-garde video arts world, and the presence of artist-run centers providing a venue for Aboriginal performance artists and experimental filmmakers to show their work, an art school that trains artists in experimental media, and established artists who serve as mentors to emerging artists. These are all critical institutional frameworks that have helped Aboriginal experimental media flourish in Vancouver.

Lakota History and Cosmology in the Experimental Media of Dana Claxton

Dana Claxton is an interdisciplinary artist who is a central figure to the avant-garde and experimental media scene in Vancouver.

She has mentored numerous Aboriginal artists, has served as a founding board member of IMAG, has been deeply involved with the grunt gallery, Western Front, and Video In, has taught as a faculty member at Emily Carr University of Art and Design, and is currently an assistant professor of visual art at the University of British Columbia. She has lived and worked in Vancouver for over two decades, and her critically acclaimed and award-winning art practice extends from experimental video to installation art to performance art. She grew up primarily in Moose Jaw, Saskatchewan, and her family reserve is the Lakota First Nations Wood Mountain Reserve. Her family is descended from Sitting Bull's followers, who fled persecution from the U.S. Army in 1877 following the fallout from the Battle of Little Bighorn, escaping across the border into Canada. Her media work confronts Canadian and U.S. colonial histories, interrogating the devastating impact of these policies within Aboriginal communities. Her media work also examines Aboriginal relationships to the land and reflects Lakota spirituality and cosmology.[4]

Claxton's powerfully intense black-and-white experimental video *I Want to Know Why* (1994) is an excellent example of the political dimension of Aboriginal experimental video. This video critically examines the intergenerational legacy of colonization through the life histories of Claxton's great-grandmother, who escaped into Canada with Sitting Bull's followers, and her grandmother and mother, both of whom died at a young age as the result of living under colonial oppression and in conditions of poverty. Relying on repetition, split screen, and audio manipulation, the film juxtaposes images of icons such as the Statue of Liberty with archival photographs of Claxton's ancestors while her voiceover implores, "Mastincala, my great-grandmother, walked to Canada with Sitting Bull. Mastincala, my great-grandmother, walked to Canada starving. And I want to know why!" followed by "Pearl Goodtrack, my grandmother, died of alcohol poisoning in a Skid Row hotel room. And I want to know why!" and then "Eli Goodtrack, my mother, o.d.-ed at

Fig. 18. Film still from *I Want to Know Why* (1994). Courtesy of filmmaker and Vtape.

the age of 37. And I want to know why." Repeating this refrain of questions regarding her family's history four times throughout the film the voiceover grows from "a whisper to a scream" (Bell 2010) as Claxton's anguished voice shouts, "And I want to know why!!" Claxton is literally screaming back against this painful history and legacy of settler colonialism while generating a unique cinematic vision utilizing experimentation in the visual track with split screen, repetition, and reverse imaging while experimenting with electronic music composed by Russell Wallace (Stl'atl'imx) that provides an electronic dance beat under the voiceover.

This powerful video confronts the horrific traumas faced by Aboriginal women as the result of policies of American and Canadian settler colonialism. Discussing this intergenerational impact on her own family in an interview, Claxton explained: "For my mother's generation the life expectancy for Aboriginal people was 38. That wasn't because people just happened to die young. It was because of the brutalities of Canadian government-sanctioned oppression. It was all part of a system that harmed people." From her political and activist work that links her own family history to the broader set of shared Aboriginal experiences in Canada to *Waterspeak* (2002), a two-channel video installation about the sacredness of water, to *Rattle* (2003), a four-channel video installation that Claxton describes as a visual prayer, it is evident that Claxton's work draws on Lakota cosmology and cultural protocols. In *Ablakela* (1999), a performance artwork about *wakan,* the Lakota concept of the sacred, Claxton transformed the art gallery space into a sacred space through peyote songs and the performance of ritual to invoke healing and a sense of calm, imbuing the gallery space with elements of Lakota cosmology. In addition to reflecting Lakota cultural protocol and cosmology through her art, she simultaneously critiques settler colonialism, redefining history from an Aboriginal perspective and all the while creating inventive, experimental forms of Aboriginal media art.

The playfulness of form and freedom from convention associated with avant-garde art forms and experimental media lend themselves well to invention and creativity within Aboriginal media. Although experimental media is not the predominant genre within Aboriginal media overall in Canada, it is a strong feature of Vancouver's Aboriginal media world and seems to appeal to some filmmakers as a genre better suited to the efforts to integrate Aboriginal aesthetic traditions and cultural protocols into the tools of media production. These media technologies are, as Aboriginal film critic Jesse Wente reminds us, "not born of our people." In a panel discussion about Aboriginal media at the 2009 imagineNATIVE Film and Media Arts Festival Wente exclaimed:

We have to understand that cinema was not born of our people. It's a European and largely American art form which means that its conventions are not of us, they're outside of us and embedded in some of those are colonial attitudes. Breaking free of the conventions of cinema and taking ownership of the art form has been a very long and involved process and it's far from over. I think we're at a point now where we're actually seeing an Indian cinema, which is a dramatically different thing. Where you actually see our stories being told in non-cinematic conventional ways and that will ultimately be the true key to our development. So this is a very exciting time and it took us a long period to get to this moment where we can truly own filmmaking in a way that we couldn't have before. And I think that's where we are now and the really great stuff starts from here and will go forward.

Aboriginal experimental filmmakers are deeply engaged with reimagining the possibilities of media technology, putting it in the service of Aboriginal visual sovereignty. Experimental film and videos can be subversive, as experimental media maker Victor Masayesva Jr. (Hopi) acknowledged in an essay on indigenous aesthetics and experimental media: "The gun/camera/computer are all aspects of the complete domination of indigenous cultures. From this perspective experimental films and videos can be defined by the degree to which they subvert the colonizer's indoctrination and champion indigenous expression in the political landscape. This act of protest and declaration of sovereignty is at the heart of experimental mediamaking in the indigenous communities" (Masayesva 1995, 174). In describing her attraction to the experimental genre Dana Claxton explained: "What I like about it is there's no boundaries, there's no conventions, there's no rules. And you can engage in the unconsciousness and it doesn't have to make sense. It doesn't have to have your traditional beginning, middle, and end, that kind of plot. The non-linear lends itself so well to experimental. And thinking about Lakota traditions about the dream world and dream state, experimental and non-linear lends itself well to those stories."

Cultural Protocol in Aboriginal Media

One way in which media technologies are "indigenized" is through the incorporation of Aboriginal cultural protocols on- and off-screen in Aboriginal media production. For many Vancouver filmmakers the use of these protocols reflects a desire to create their films and videos "in a good way" that demonstrates that they are respectful of and knowledgeable about their local traditions and cultural ways.

Cultural protocol is evident off-screen in such activities as offering tobacco to elders being interviewed for a film or video project, ensuring traditional foods are on set, burning sage or sweetgrass before or after filming, and following West Coast cultural protocol by acknowledging the Coast Salish peoples on whose territory Vancouver sits. Cultural protocol is reflected on-screen by not interrupting elders in the editing process, often resulting in longer "talking head" shots than would be acceptable in mainstream media, including honor songs to open or close a film or video, the centrality of images of the land, slower pacing in editing, using culturally specific iconography, and the way in which kinship and family lineage is acknowledged throughout the video, whether through archival photographs or interviewing relatives on camera.[5] Writing about the importance of protocol in Native film, scholar Carol Kalafatic asserts that "*as* a referent to history, and as a sign of respect for a code or form, protocol works as a cultural grid that allows the work of these filmmakers to be relevant to their peoples' lives" (Kalafatic 1999, 115). The use of cultural protocol in Aboriginal filmmaking not only connects Aboriginal filmmakers to a historical continuum of cultural traditions, but it also establishes a framework for maintaining and nurturing Aboriginal social and kinship relationships off camera.

The incorporation of cultural protocol into the process of media production highlights the way in which Aboriginal traditions influence the off-screen production practices of Aboriginal filmmakers. This also reflects the specific cultural worldviews or cosmologies of the numerous Aboriginal nations of filmmakers in Vancouver. Filmmakers with whom I worked emphasized the importance of Aboriginal media in articulating the perspectives, viewpoints, and cultural worlds of Aboriginal people. Cleo Reece succinctly stated: "I think Aboriginal media is how we look at things. It's our own unique viewpoint coming from the backgrounds that we have as Aboriginal people." In other words, Aboriginal media is inevitably affected by the cultural worldviews of filmmakers.

Dana Claxton highlights the importance of tribal iconography within Aboriginal aesthetics, arguing that there are culturally specific ways in which iconography is used to express Aboriginal aesthetics. She explains: "I think that there is [an Aboriginal aesthetic] in terms of iconography. We see how people incorporate different tribal iconography into their work and that's an aesthetic that nobody else has." Claxton contends that Aboriginal aesthetics stem from Aboriginal cultural worlds and cosmologies. She draws heavily upon Lakota cosmology throughout her work and consequently feels that her work reflects a Lakota aesthetic. Loretta Todd raises similar questions about Aboriginal film aesthetics when she asks: "Imagine how my philosophy as a Cree and Métis woman filmmaker influences how I make images and meaning. How have Aboriginal filmmakers reflected meaning and their relationship to knowledge and even our state of being in our work? How do we imagine ourselves? From what stories do our aesthetics flow?" (Todd 2005, 117). Dorothy Christian emphasizes the role of tribal iconography in Aboriginal aesthetics, arguing that certain iconography (i.e., the sun, moon, or eagles) will carry different meanings from Aboriginal nation to nation. In an interview one spring afternoon she reflected:

> You get culturally specific to each nation and depending on their cosmologies, on their creation stories it's different. Raven means a whole different thing to me than it does to a Haida person. The ocean means a whole different thing to

coastal peoples, than it does to me who's from the Interior. And cactus means a whole different thing to me than it does to people up north. I don't think again that it can be generalized because our archetypes are dependent upon the areas which we come from. Our songs, our stories, our colors and our designs come from the land that we live on so yes, we have our own aesthetic.

Christian cautions against a generalization into a single Aboriginal aesthetic, emphasizing the culturally specific ways in which Aboriginal filmmakers draw upon their cultural backgrounds and traditions in their work. Christian also expresses concern that younger Aboriginal filmmakers, many of whom are urban raised, risk falling into a generalized Aboriginal stereotype in their work because of their lack of connection to their communities. She explained:

I get kind of afraid that this venue of storytelling could promote a pan-Indianism. That's one of the things that I've attempted to do in all of my stories is to honor and respect the people who the story is about and use their songs and images. I get afraid sometimes when I see the young people who come to the media production programs and maybe they're third generation in the city and they have no clue about where they're from. They have no clue about who they are and they just start slapping things together and haven't taken the time for those deeper examinations which I think is necessary.

Claxton, Todd, and Christian emphasize the intricate ways in which cultural traditions, ideology and cosmology influence Aboriginal film aesthetics, anchoring the uniqueness of Aboriginal media aesthetics in local cultural worlds.

Cultural Protocols On-Screen: The Films of Loretta Todd

Loretta Todd's award-winning career has spanned an impressive range, from documentary videos for Native organizations to experimental art installations to feature documentaries for the National Film Board of Canada and feature film production. Her films address Aboriginal social memory, history, resistance, and cultural continuity in spite of colonization. Her earliest feature documentary, *The Learning Path* (1991), examined the devastating impact of the residential school system on Native children, while *Forgotten Warriors* (1996) tells the story of Aboriginal soldiers who served in the Canadian Army in World War II—during a time when Aboriginal people were not granted Canadian citizenship—and who returned home to face discrimination and a lack of recognition for their service to Canada. In *Hands of History* (1994) Todd creatively explored the unique artistic practice and cultural contributions of four Aboriginal women artists, while her documentary *Today Is a Good Day: Remembering the Legacy of Chief Dan George* (1999) honored the tremendous impact of actor and activist Chief Dan George (Tsleil-Waututh), who opened many doors for Aboriginal actors and filmmakers. Throughout her filmography it is evident that Loretta Todd has dedicated her career to providing voice and visibility for Aboriginal stories in a way that honors Aboriginal aesthetics and cultural traditions.

Todd's work reflects Aboriginal protocol and aesthetics, creating a rich media landscape expressing Aboriginal cultural memory, responsibility to the land, and spiritual traditions. Todd is drawn to the dynamic of shadow and light in the craft of filmmaking and attributes much of her film aesthetic to her experiences growing up as a child on the prairies of Alberta. In an interview with film critic Jason Silverman, Todd explained: "A sense of light has always informed my relationship to the image. I can't say I lived in the traplines and the bush, but I grew up close enough that I spent a lot of time under the [prairie] sun, in the winter and the summer, and under the moon. I spent a lot of time studying the way the land was lit. I looked at the shadows, and the spaces the light created" (Todd qtd. in Silverman 2002, 381). Todd's careful crafting of her film imagery reflects this interest in light and shadow.

Todd has described filmmaking as a "space of storytelling," explaining that this space is defined by "light, space, and protocol" (Todd qtd. in Kalafatic 1996). She continues: "We use cultural protocols and cultural codes to also enable the audience to participate in the story and exchange in the story." This dynamic use of protocol enacts connections not only between Todd and the people in her films but also between audience members and the people in film, opening up a filmic space for dialogue around Aboriginal stories and concerns. Todd often uses cultural protocol as a narrative structure throughout her films by including an honor song to open and close a film, such as in *Forgotten Warriors* (1996), or using the circle as an organizing framework to allow for seamless movement between the women's stories about their role as artists and community leaders in *Hands of History* (1994). In another interview she linked her use of protocol to her efforts to decolonize the documentary, noting:

> If we're trying to decolonize the documentary then we can bring in our own forms of how we talk and how we do business and how we deal with one another, and one of the ways we deal with one another is that we honor one another, and that often comes through song. That honor song hopefully creates a respectful space to start the film off so that the people who are there will listen and open their minds to the stories they are about to hear. It's also my way of honoring the people who have shared their stories with me to make the film. I am trying to bring those ways of how we do business into the practice of filmmaking. (Todd qtd. in L. Abbott 1998:339).

Todd uses Aboriginal cultural protocol as a guiding framework not only for her film aesthetic choices but also in her relationships with the people in her films.

As discussed in chapter 4, Todd was the first Aboriginal person to attend the film school at Simon Fraser University, and she has been an inspiration to many Aboriginal filmmakers in Vancouver's Aboriginal media world, which now spans several generations and decades. Her films honor Aboriginal cultural traditions and protocol while expressing her artistic voice as she uses filmmaking to tell the often-marginalized stories of Aboriginal people. Her contributions to the emergence of Vancouver as a center for Aboriginal media are innumerable, and she remains a strong leader in Vancouver's Aboriginal media world. Committed to her vision and to Aboriginal visual sovereignty, she has created a unique body of films that are credited by other Aboriginal filmmakers as helping build a cinematic Aboriginal aesthetic. This commitment is palpable throughout her work, and as she has eloquently articulated, her filmmaking begins "from my love of my people, my love of the land, for all my relations" (Todd qtd. in L. Abbott 1998, 341).

Kainayssini Imanistaisiwa: The People Go On (2003) vividly illuminates Todd's unique film aesthetic, visual sensibility, and articulation of visual sovereignty. This experimental documentary explores the issue of repatriation within the Kainai Blood community of southern Alberta. It is an impressionistic film that lyrically evokes a sense of home, land, ancestors, and memory. The film begins and ends with wide shots of the windswept open prairies that are home to the Kainai. Her innovative use of split screen for these wide shots of the prairie landscape has a panoramic effect that envelops the viewer in the lush rolling hills of the prairie and seemingly endless expanse of blue sky stretching across Kainai territory. She also intercuts shots of the film crew in the back of the pickup truck rolling along the highway, adding a layer of reflexivity to the film by acknowledging the production process in the film text. It is a striking documentary in many ways, not the least of which because it moves away from conventional documentary aesthetics, structure, and framing and focuses on the way in which the objects are connected to memory, Kainai ancestors, the land, a sense of home, and the Kainai way of life.

Todd stylistically blends sound, color, light, and language in order to convey a sense of Kainai cultural memory. During the scenes in which the objects are filmed inside glass museum cases, the Kainai language can be heard in soft whispers so that it seems as if the ancestors who created the objects are given voice on-screen. The Kainai language is used throughout the film, and Todd hired a local Kainai youth to film the B-roll on a second camera during the interviews with elders. She emphasized that she wanted to hire local people for the crew to provide opportunities for people on reserve to learn media production skills, and because fluent Kainai speakers would be able to anticipate culturally appropriate ways to film interviews with elders who primarily speak Kainai as their first language. Talking-head interviews are interspersed with extreme close-up shots of the elders speaking about the importance of these objects and their place in their cultural traditions. The interviews were also shot primarily outside with the landscape as a backdrop, further reinforcing the connection between the Kainai people and their homeland.

The People Go On seamlessly moves between past, present, and future; one powerful way in which Todd inserted the presence of the ancestors throughout the film was to film white flags on the prairie at dusk waving in the wind as archival photographs are projected onto them, inscribing the images of the ancestors onto the landscape. Through innovative on-screen aesthetics—interviewing people outside in the landscape, split screen, panoramic vistas, and inscribing the Kainai ancestral presence on-screen—*The People Go On* expresses visual sovereignty and experiments with the documentary genre, articulating a new vision for Aboriginal documentary practice. Todd continues to be a key leader in Aboriginal media, and her more recent media work has involved producing and directing three seasons of the APTN children's television show *Tansi! Nehiyawetan: Let's Speak Cree!*, and she is in the preproduction stage of a feature film that is an adaptation of the award-winning Eden Robinson (Haisla) novel *Monkey Beach* (2000).

Dana Claxton and Loretta Todd are key figures within

Vancouver's Aboriginal media world who work across genre — from television to documentary to experimental media — and whose filmmaking and scholarship have provided an instrumental foundation for Vancouver's Aboriginal media world. They serve as teachers and mentors to countless emerging Aboriginal filmmakers and see their art and film practice as deeply rooted in social connections to their respective Aboriginal nations, the urban Aboriginal community in Vancouver, and their families. They continue to innovate across genres of media, and their work is illustrative of Aboriginal visual sovereignty through their emphasis on cultural protocol, cosmology, land, sociality, and forceful critiques of Canadian settler colonialism.

Conclusion

This chapter has explored the ways in which Aboriginal filmmakers draw on cultural protocol and Aboriginal aesthetic traditions to indigenize the technologies of media production. Filmmakers often contrast Aboriginal media to mainstream media by highlighting differences regarding aesthetics, cultural protocol, and responsibility to community. For Aboriginal filmmakers, their media work circulates within a social world where relationships to the community, intergenerational connections, and kinship ties are the web that encompasses and nurtures Aboriginal media and ultimately where Aboriginal filmmakers are held accountable. The use of cultural protocols is merely one aspect of the way that practices of media production are used to negotiate social relationships and community interactions off-screen. Aboriginal media express and enact Aboriginality in myriad ways because they are firmly rooted in the social life of local Aboriginal cultural worlds. Throughout this book I have argued that Aboriginal media move beyond merely on-screen interventions in the Canadian mediascape and simultaneously provide a powerful practice through which Aboriginal sociality and community are transformed off-screen. The impact of the integration of cultural protocols into Aboriginal media practice is evident on- and off-screen and is a vital component to the expression of Aboriginal visual sovereignty, as we will see in the next chapter, which focuses on the work of two rising Aboriginal filmmakers, Kevin Lee Burton and Helen Haig-Brown, whose films articulate visual sovereignty and unique cinematic aesthetics.

CHAPTER SIX

Visual Sovereignty in Aboriginal Experimental Media

It is one of the hottest days on record in the interior of British Columbia as the caravan of cars ambles through Tsilhqot'in territory en route to the location for the first day of production on *ʔEʔAnx: The Cave*. The site where we are filming is located high on a rugged mountaintop overlooking the small community of the Stone Reserve, one of six villages that are members of the Tsilhqot'in Nation. There is an excited energy running through the production crew of approximately forty people, some of whom traveled a nine-hour road trip from Vancouver to participate in this shoot, and others for whom the Stone Reserve is home. The knowledge and expertise gathered for this shoot ranges from the familiarity with the high-end RED digital cinema camera to laying tracks for dolly shots to traditional ecological knowledge to Tsilhqot'in stories connected with the locations where we are filming. The filmmaker, Helen Haig-Brown, on whose traditional territory this film is being shot, spent days with elders and community members scouting the perfect locations for the storyboards and shot list associated with *The Cave*, her first short dramatic film. I sit with Helen and her sister Linda in a red pickup truck as we amble slowly back and forth up gravel switchbacks to the top of the mountain to reach the location site. One and a half

Fig. 19. Production crew on set of *ʔEʔAnx: The Cave* (2009). Photo by Sandlanee Gid Raven Ann Potschka. Courtesy of Rugged Media and Sandlanee Gid Raven Ann Potschka.

hours from Williams Lake, the nearest town, we are filming where there is no electricity, no cell phone coverage, and no way to communicate with the producer coordinating the production back in Williams Lake. Amid the bustle of production assistants setting up equipment, the assistant director of photography assembling the lens on the RED camera, horse wrangling, and prop preparation, Helen asks everyone to stop while she asks an elder to say a prayer over the production. She is concerned that filming be done "in a good way"[1] and that the production crew—Aboriginal and non-Aboriginal—follow Tsilhqot'in cultural protocols in this production process. After this brief interlude, the filming of *ʔEʔAnx: The Cave*, the first sci-fi film shot in the Tsilhqot'in language on Tsilhqot'in territory, resumes.

Visual Sovereignty in Aboriginal Media 155

Introduction

I began this book with a question: "What does Aboriginal sovereignty look like on- and off-screen?" Throughout this book I have explored the concept of Aboriginal visual sovereignty to analyze the ways in which Aboriginal filmmakers stake a claim for Aboriginal stories in the dominant Canadian mediascape while simultaneously reimagining the screen by incorporating Aboriginal cultural protocols, languages, and aesthetics into the production process. In this chapter I highlight the work of two rising filmmakers in the Aboriginal media world—Kevin Lee Burton and Helen Haig-Brown—both of whom were mentored by Dana Claxton and Loretta Todd and whose films are breaking new cinematic ground. In their innovative vision and unconventional narratives these media artists are redefining Aboriginal media practice in Canada. The media practice of Burton and Haig-Brown reflects an artistic vision informed by their individual artistic perspectives yet is deeply rooted in their cultural ties to the Swampy Cree and Tsilhqot'in Nations, respectively. Utilizing two short films and production stories, I analyze the ways in which Burton and Haig-Brown articulate Aboriginal visual sovereignty through the lenses of language, land, and cosmology.

On- and Off-Screen: Breaking New Cinematic Ground

Kevin Lee Burton and Helen Haig-Brown were both students of Dana Claxton's and Loretta Todd's at IMAG and at Capilano College. Both Burton and Haig-Brown come out of Vancouver's avant-garde, experimental video tradition and define themselves as media artists as well as filmmakers. In describing Burton and Haig-Brown's media practice as "experimental," I am referring to the experimentation of both with on-screen aesthetics as well as to experimentation in their off-screen production practices. Aesthetically their films experiment with form—in the case of *Nikamowin* with split screen, audio distortion, and motion effects, and in the case of *The Cave* in the experimentation with the sci-fi genre. Their production practices also involve experimentation, as Burton and Haig-Brown work to find ways to incorporate Cree and Tsilhqot'in cultural protocols into the production process. That involves practices such as consulting with elders on location scouting, filming on their traditional territory, prayers and smudging on-set. Aboriginal experimental filmmakers, such as Burton and Haig-Brown, are subversive and noncompliant in decolonizing the screen through their media practice. One of the appeals of experimental forms of media making is in the ability to reimagine media practices to fit within cultural values, iconography, and aesthetic frames of Aboriginal communities— this is "sovereignty taking shape in visual form" (Rickard 1995).

Kevin Lee Burton and Helen Haig-Brown are award-winning filmmakers who have collaborated on several short film projects since they first met as students in Vancouver. Both have received funding and support from key institutions such as the National Film Board of Canada and the Canada Council for the Arts. Their media works circulate in the Aboriginal and mainstream film festival circuits while their films are primarily directed toward Aboriginal audiences.

Kevin Lee Burton is Swampy Cree and was raised on the Gods Lake Narrows reserve in northern Manitoba, where he grew up speaking Cree as his first language. He left his community as a teenager to attend high school in Winnipeg. He has spent much time in Vancouver and currently resides in Winnipeg, although he continues to maintain close ties with his reserve community where the majority of his family still live. He is a fluent Cree speaker who feels very strongly about the importance of maintaining indigenous languages. He identifies his primary goal as creating films in the Cree language for Cree and indigenous audiences. Helen Haig-Brown is a Tsilhqot'in woman who grew up on the Stone Reserve and in Vancouver. She currently resides on the Stone Reserve on her traditional territory. She has made several experimental documentaries and works as a cinematographer as well as director. She views her media practice as a form of ceremony and seeks to use media to tell Tsilhqot'in stories "in a good way."[2] The videos of Burton and Haig-Brown, like those of Claxton and Todd discussed in the previous chapter, represent Aboriginal visual sovereignty on- and off-screen, particularly through their emphasis on land, language, and cosmology.

Envisioning a Cree Mediascape

The connection between language, land, and identity emerges strongly in Burton's film *Nikamowin* (2007), which translates into English as "Song." The Cree language is an absolutely central component to Burton's work; all of his films—with the exception of *Writing the Land* (2007)—are in the Cree language. *Nikamowin* emerged out of his experiences living in Vancouver and the sense of isolation he felt in not having any Cree speakers with whom to talk while in Vancouver. He once recalled to me how profoundly disorienting this experience was for him. He remembered how he used to repeat Cree words to himself over and over just to keep his language in his mind and on his tongue. This film, which visually and aurally is quite unlike anything most viewers have seen, is in Burton's words "based on how I hear things as a Cree speaker. Those fundamental sounds that shape how I hear and view the world." Raw and altered Cree sounds form the primary soundtrack for the film, and Burton's traditional territory on Gods Lake Narrows was also his muse for the film. Burton explained that he is committed to filming on his land, and it is this relationship to his traditional territory juxtaposed against images of the urban setting of Vancouver that forms the visual track of the film.

The film opens with a wide shot taken from inside a boat that rocks back and forth across a lake. The opening audio track is a soft whooshing sound that imitates slow deep breaths and also the sounds of waves lapping against a shore. A text panel declares, "Cree Narration, altered and in raw form, is the only source of sound in this film."[3] The bare winter woods surrounding

Fig. 20. Film still from *Nikamowin (Song)* (2007). Courtesy of filmmaker and Vtape.

Gods Lake frame the top part of the screen, and there is a doubling aesthetic effect as the trees are reflected in the crisp water. The opening of the film includes a voiceover in Cree and repeated in English between Burton and a personified voice representing the Cree language. The verbal repartee between these two voices (both voiced by Burton) illuminates the stakes for the link between language and cultural identity.

The personified voice of the Cree language: "Are you an Indian? Can you speak Cree?"

Young man: "No, I don't know, never taught I guess."

Voice of the Cree language: "Who taught you how to open your eyes and blink?"

Young man in an irritated tone: "No one. What kind of sense does that make anyways?"

Cree language: "You had the ability and you did it anyways didn't ya? Your tongue's the same."

Emphatically the young man replies: "But I don't know anyone who *speaks*."

A brief pronunciation lesson follows as the voice of the Cree language responds: "Nina ma?"

Young man: "Nee-nah-what?"

Drawing out the syllables the voice of the Cree language teaches the young man: "Nee-nah-mah."

Young man: "Nee-nah-mah."

The voice of the Cree language laughs: "Nina ma? What about me? That's good!"

"Who are you?" queries the young man.

At this point the film picks up pace and switches entirely into Cree with English subtitles as the voice explains that it is "your Cree language." The image of the boat bounces up and down on the water, and the audio track begins a manipulation, repetition, and layering of Cree words, sounds, and syllables. The continuous whooshing sound of deep breaths becomes the sound that remains constant through the whole video, providing an underlying layer to the manipulation and distortion of Cree syllables. The visual effects of color shifts also amplify the strong bass and repetition of certain audio sounds, and the image jumps to bass beats as if in a hip-hop rhythm.

Experimenting with focus, the size of the visual track on screen, and the play of lines and space on the water, Burton seeks to visually replicate the audio track that itself includes the voice repeating Cree sounds and the constant sound of breath. When the voiceover declares, "My friends, I give you this. . . . I give you. . . . Love," the visual track shifts from the water to a winter landscape of Burton's reserve. Long tracking shots from a car driving through the landscape are juxtaposed with close-up shots of bare tree limbs as the sun glistens on bright snow. The voiceover continues, "Where do you come from?" and when the answer, "Gods Lake Narrows," is spoken, the film shifts suddenly to a wide shot of houses nestled in white snow with a deep cerulean sky above the landscape and the voice of the young man wistfully recalling, "everyone I know who speaks Cree lives there." The visual tracks shift once more to a double horizontal split screen where the top image of someone walking in front of a house on the reserve is reversed through motion effects so that it appears that the person walks backward through the top visual track and into the bottom visual track, where the figure is shown walking forward in motion. These movements are repeated, with the bottom track eventually being reversed and shown upside down while the audio track continues the repetition of the sounds of the Cree words for Gods Lake Narrows. "Where are you from" becomes a refrain throughout the film, and the bright blue winter skies and long panning shots of woods covered in snow illuminate the beauty of this Cree territory. When the voiceover asks, "Do you live there now?" the screen is filled with sped-up images of close-up shots of verdant lily pads filling a spring pond, beginning the visual shift not only in seasons but the journey from the Gods Lake Narrows reserve to the urban city of Vancouver.

During this liminal space and journey between reserve and city, the voiceover asks, "What happens when you start speaking Cree?" Through motion effects, not only is the image sped up, but the size of the visual track also gradually shrinks down until all the viewer sees are the train tracks leading along the landscape into the city as the many layers of audio effects and Cree syllables repeat in a hip-hop rhythm.[4] Gradually the landscape shifts from lush green, forested mountains to concrete urban spaces, and the color scheme of the film shifts to a decidedly more gray palette, made all the more disorienting for the viewer by extreme motion effects speeding up the image, camera movements making the image go out of focus, and an increase in volume when suddenly the viewer sees a black screen, and a deep, distorted audio voice that sounds as if it is speaking through a megaphone insistently asks, "Are you afraid?" and then commands, "Do not put down your language."

The film moves from this black screen to a double horizontal split screen with images of cars driving through Vancouver's city streets at night, where motion effects are used to show cars driving first in one direction and then in the opposite direction on the screen. The cars move in time with the sound of the Cree syllables, creating an interesting doubling effect of the audio and visual tracks. In the darkened night cityscape scenes Burton plays with multiple vertical split screens as the screen is black except for a small slice of the image of a portion of the cityscape or car as these visual cutouts skip across the screen from right to left in time with the audible Cree syllables, and once again the image jumps to the bass of the audio, replicating a hip-hop rhythmic aesthetic.

The film rushes toward its powerful conclusion as the images are gradually widened and shrunk both horizontally and verti-cally through split screen cutouts, and the music made from repeated Cree syllables rapidly increases pace to the frantic closing sequence where the voiceover asks, "What are you going to do to bring your language home?" The film quickly moves from the space of the city back to the reserve landscape with wild camera movements and a sped-up pace visually and aurally. The final sequence includes five horizontal split screens with various images from Burton's reserve landscape framing the top of the screen juxtaposed against the city shots from Vancouver. The images in each of these split screens moves at a frantic pace that replicates a sense of disorientation in trying to navigate between the space of the reserve and the city. In a reference to and a critique of the detrimental impact of the residential school system on Aboriginal languages, the film closes on a black screen with a quote from Secwepemec artist and activist Tania Willard, "You cut my tongue now only my heart speaks," while the sound of the soft whooshing of breaths in and out fades in the background.

There is no doubt that this is a complex, many-layered film that deconstructs the Cree language while speaking to the ways in which Aboriginal individuals navigate between traditional territory and urban space. If this film has disturbed or unsettled viewers, that is precisely Burton's intention. He sees his primary

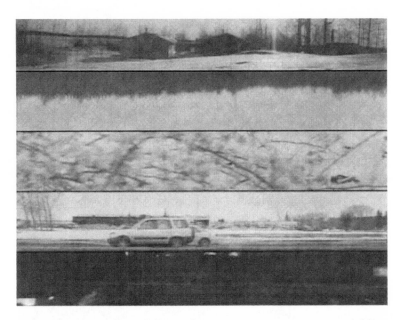

Fig. 21. Split-screen film still from *Nikamowin (Song)* (2007). Courtesy of film-maker and Vtape.

audience for this film as his peers—Aboriginal artists and film-makers of a younger generation living in urban areas. He wanted this film to haunt his peers and encourage them to start learning and speaking their languages. Through his experimentation with split screen, audio distortions, and motion effects, this powerful film, which was named one of Canada's Top Ten Short films of 2008 and was acquired in 2011 by the National Gallery of Canada, Burton creates a uniquely visual and aural Cree media landscape that meditates on the connection between land, language, iden-tity, and the implications of language loss for Aboriginal people and communities. This is made most apparent when the voiceover as a personified representation of the Cree language insistently asks, "What are you going to do to bring your language home?" and demands, "Do not put down your language."

There is a direct appeal to a younger Aboriginal generation in this film. Through distortion and repetition the Cree sounds become a hip-hop remix that Burton describes as his "experimentation with making language 'cool' to a younger generation." In a 2009 radio interview with Isuma TV, Burton explained, "I'm really adamant about keeping the language. I'm really adamant about talking with all the old people about it, and I'm really adamant about exploring how the language works. I'm an urbanized, tech-savvy individual living in 2009. What I'm exploring is how to bring traditional ways into contemporary ways and utilize them every day in order to create relationships with my peers and with my elders. And I thought this is how I need to make sense of that within my filmmaking."[5]

Nikamowin is Kevin Lee Burton's artistic and cinematic vision of a Cree media landscape that articulates Aboriginal visual sovereignty on- and off-screen: on-screen through his experimentation with visual and aural forms in the film, and off-screen through decisions to film on his traditional territory. When asked if his work has a particular Cree aesthetic, Burton replied affirmatively, linking the Cree aesthetic in his films to language and land. He explained: "With *Nikamowin* I have a particular rhythm and it's definitely based on how I hear things. *Nikamowin* is the most literal translation of that. The rhythm of how those syllables fall together is a translation of a Cree aesthetic. And visually my commitment to filming on my land absolutely creates a Cree aesthetic." In *Nikamowin* we see the importance of land and territory as the film examined the urban/reserve experience, emphasizing the importance of knowing where one is from. The work of Helen Haig-Brown also visually anchors her film in shots of her home territory of the Stone First Nation in the interior of British Columbia.

From Story to Screen: *The Cave* and the Spirit World

Helen Haig-Brown's short film *?E?Anx: The Cave* (2009) was commissioned by the imagineNATIVE Film Festival as part of their Embargo film collective in honor of their tenth anniversary[6] and was named one of Canada's Top Ten Short films of

Fig. 22. *ʔEʔAnx: The Cave* (2009). Courtesy of Rugged Media.

2009. In this film Haig-Brown reimagines the sci-fi genre in her adaptation of a story told by her great-uncle and recorded by her mother in the 1970s about a Tsilhqot'in man out bear hunting who comes across a cave that unbeknownst to him is a portal to the spirit world.

Riding across the vast Tsilhqot'in landscape, the hunter, represented in the film as a Tsilhqot'in cowboy from the early 1960s, notices a bear off in the distance heading into the woods. He immediately takes off to follow the bear into the woods. He slows down his horse, curiously noting the markings left by bear claws outside of a cave. Dismounting, he ties his horse to the tree, softly calling to the horse in Tsilhqot'in, "Wait here for me," before heading into the cave. As the hunter crawls through the cave, he is blinded by a bright light and his nose begins to bleed.

The screen cuts to black and then shows the hunter crawling out of the cave and ambling over to the edge of a lake noticing the markedly different landscape. He is startled to see ancestral spirit figures walking around the lake, building fires, and fishing in the lake. The spirit figures' rich coppery-colored skin shimmers and is adorned with traditional tattoos. The figures appear to breathe through their mouths, and white tufts, as if from dandelions, float through the air. The sunlight streams in iridescent shafts, and the colors are highly saturated.

Suddenly a young Spirit World woman notices him and strides toward him delivering an unseen force that paralyzes the hunter as she exclaims, "This place is not for you. You're not ready yet. Wherever you have crawled from, crawl back." After he is released, the hunter scrambles back toward the cave, diving into it and crawling out the other side, only to discover that his horse, which he had tied to a tree, is now a pile of bones.

Working with the Embargo Collective, Helen Haig-Brown was assigned the sci-fi genre. All the filmmakers were asked to push their boundaries and work outside of the genres in which they typically work. Haig-Brown experiments with form in *The Cave* by redefining the sci-fi genre from a Tsilhqot'in perspective, taking advantage of the high-end digital cinema technology of the RED camera and postproduction editing techniques. What might an indigenous sci-fi film look like on-screen? In an interview she explained: "Instead of the typical science fiction storyline of expansionism or colonialism where you're going into these other worlds to conquer this other world—is there a different way of telling that story? I knew I wanted to find a way to do it differently and honor our own stories because a lot of our stories focus on these other worlds that are right here."

When setting out to make the film the story of *The Cave* did not immediately come to mind. Haig-Brown was visiting with her relatives one day, and her cousin suggested the story of *The Cave* to her, reminding her that Haig-Brown's great-uncle had told the story for an audio-recording in the 1970s. In an interview she elaborated, "Our great uncle, who was quite well known in our family as a storyteller, had recorded the story and my uncle had transcribed it and translated it into English already. So I went to visit him and got the translation and used that as the basis for the script." It was Haig-Brown's kinship ties and rootedness in the very local cultural world of the Tsilhqot'in community of the Stone Reserve that connected with high-end digital technology to translate this story to screen. A culturally specific narrative, deeply imbued with kinship ties for the filmmaker, ultimately circulated globally through the production of the film *The Cave*.

Indigenous stories do not automatically or seamlessly transition from story to screen—this is an *active* process full of choices made at every stage of preproduction, production, and postproduction that involves negotiating the interface of digital technology, filmic conventions, indigenous knowledge, and cultural poetics of storytelling. At every stage of this process the filmmaker, along with the production crew, makes decisions that leave marks on the film itself. For instance, although the story is set in ancestral times and is a very old story, Haig-Brown decided to alter the traditional story from a hunter with two dogs to a cowboy on a horse when she decided set *The Cave* in 1961 because of her interest in the aesthetic and style of the Tsilhqot'in cowboy from this era.

Once she settled on using this traditional story as the basis for her script, she tackled the cultural and cinematic challenges of representing the Spirit World. Unlike mainstream science fiction films about "space: the final frontier," where intrepid explorers seek to colonize and conquer alien worlds, Haig-Brown was adamant about using the Tsilhqot'in cosmology of the Spirit World as her basis from which to redefine the science fiction genre. In Tsilhqot'in cosmology the Spirit World is a world of deceased ancestral figures existing on the same plane and at the same time as the present world, although there is a temporal difference between the two. She explained Tsilhqot'in cosmology regarding the Spirit World to me this way: "what feels like only a few hours or minutes in the Spirit World is many years in this world," a feature that has implications for the hunter's horse upon his return to the present world.

There are many Tsilhqot'in cultural protocols regarding the Spirit World, and much of the narrative of the film revolves around the breach that occurs when the hunter enters the Spirit World when it is not his time to do so.[7] Following the advice of elders who served as consultants on the film and using her artistic vision as a guiding framework she utilized color correction, filters, and special effects in the postproduction process to create a visual shift once the cowboy enters the Spirit World. The colors are much more highly saturated, there are extensive makeup effects for the actors in the Spirit World, and special motion effects are applied in this scene. Haig-Brown had access to the RED camera—a high-end professional digital camera that has revolutionized digital cinematography as it combines the ease of use and flexible editing of digital cameras with the high resolution image quality associated with 35mm film at a lower cost.[8] Utilizing this camera and the latest digital video recording and editing techniques enabled Helen Haig-Brown to bring to the screen a vivid, cinematic rendering of a traditional Tsilhqot'in story and in the process reenvision the screen and the sci-fi genre in a way that articulates Tsilhqot'in sovereignty and language, while paying homage to Tsilhqot'in territory, cosmological understandings of the Spirit World, and the family and kinship ties that were the inspiration for this film.

A Tsilhqot'in Media Practice On and Off-Screen

Helen Haig-Brown articulated her priorities in the production process in the following way: "It was important to film in my territory, it was important to film in my language, and it was important to have as many Tsilhqot'in people involved in the process and acting in the film." She hired many youth from her community as production assistants, prop designers, horse wranglers, location scouts, and makeup and costume assistants who worked with the elders serving as consultants on set. Five youth worked with elders to create the traditional fish hooks that were used in the Spirit World scene, while others developed an interest in learning about the technical aspects of filmmaking. It is precisely these social interactions that occur during and around

Fig. 23. Spirit World woman film still from *ʔEʔAnx: The Cave* (2009). Courtesy of Rugged Media.

the production process that open up opportunities for intergenerational transmission of cultural knowledge. Similarly to the social impact of the Igloolik Isuma video collective and other indigenous media initiatives, the production process of *The Cave* demonstrates that "media practices are part of a broader project of constituting a cultural future in which their traditions and contemporary technologies are combined in ways that can give new vitality" to Tsilhqot'in life (Ginsburg 2002, 43). Indeed, as Haig-Brown proudly noted in my interview with her:

> For our communities, just the idea and the concept of film or production, it was so foreign, they didn't really know what to expect. But after seeing the end product and being involved in it for the week, there's an excitement and a pride and a huge interest in film that is really great. All these young people are now coming out of the woodwork that are super committed to media and expression and that's really exciting.

Helen Haig-Brown's film *The Cave* represents a form of Tsilhqot'in visual sovereignty that stakes a presence within the

Canadian and Aboriginal mediascapes while redefining the sci-fi genre from an indigenous and Tsilhqot'in perspective. I see four primary ways in which Haig-Brown articulates Tsilhqot'in visual sovereignty though this film: territory, cosmology, cultural protocols and language. First, Haig-Brown placed a strong priority on filming on Tsilhqot'in territory and conducted extensive location scouting with relatives, elders, and community members about the social and cultural significance of the places she chose for film locations. For example, the emphasis on situating the narrative at Gwetsilh registers for Tsilhqot'in audience members as a bear-hunting place within the broad expanse of Tsilhqot'in territory.[9] There is no doubt that Tsilhqot'in land is certainly a central character in this film. Here I refer to Tsilhqot'in land not just in a spiritual or cultural sense, but also to the political dimension of Aboriginal land, which is significant given the current and ongoing treaty and land claims process in British Columbia. Second, Haig-Brown's choice to place Tsilhqot'in cosmology and beliefs about the Spirit World center stage redefines the sci-fi genre away from narratives about colonial exploration of "alien worlds" and anchors this genre within a Tsilhqot'in cosmology. Third, her incorporation of cultural protocols into the production process— consulting with elders, location scouting, smudging on set, incorporating people from her community in the production process, honoring family at the screening in her community—emphasized Aboriginal sovereignty through media practice. Last, the use of the Tsilhqot'in language and the use of the original recording of the late Henry Solomon marks the film with an aural Tsilhqot'in presence and links this twenty-first-century high-tech digital cinematic rendering of this story to the Tsilhqot'in oral tradition from which the script was derived and to Haig-Brown's kin—her great-uncle, aunt, and mother, who were involved with recording the story in the 1970s. The visual sovereignty of this film is anchored in Tsilhqot'in territory, language, kinship, protocol, and cosmology.

Conclusion

Helen Haig-Brown's film *The Cave* and Kevin Lee Burton's *Nikamowin* provide two examples of Aboriginal filmmakers as social actors negotiating the interface between digital technologies and indigenous knowledge through the media production process. Shooting *The Cave* on her territory, in her language, and with the social labor of many community members enabled Haig-Brown to experiment with the sci-fi genre and rework it in a way that spoke to Tsilhqot'in cosmology and worldview, just as Burton created a Cree mediascape through his experimentation with visual and aural film aesthetics in *Nikamowin*. Haig-Brown continues to live and work in her Tsilhqot'in community, currently working on a feature-length experimental documentary, *Legacy*, about four generations of Tsilhqot'in women in her family. An interactive website for this documentary was recently funded so she is now venturing into a new digital realm, Web 2.0, expanding her media practice once more. Burton has recently formed a media arts collective, Itwé (which translates from Cree as "to say it" or "to give voice") with Algonquin filmmaker Caroline Monnet (Algonquin/French) and Cree graphic designer Sebastian Aubin (Opaskwayak Cree), and they won a digital media initiative grant from the imagineNATIVE film festival and the National Film Board of Canada to develop their online interactive web-based project *De Nort* "exploring the life and experiences of people living on a northern Manitoba reserve through the objects in their households."[10] Burton also recently completed an award-winning interactive website *Gods Lake Narrows* with the National Film Board of Canada, which is a fascinating and deeply engaging portrait of his home reserve community. Juxtaposing photographs of the exteriors of homes on his reserve with portraits of the people who live in those homes, Burton encourages viewers to virtually visit his reserve community to break down misconceptions about Native life on reserves.

This chapter has explored the ways in which Aboriginal film-makers express visual sovereignty on- and off-screen. Kevin Lee Burton and Helen Haig-Brown's attention to land, language, and identity are central to the ways in which their films articulate and enact visual sovereignty. Aboriginal media, such as *Nika-mowin* and *ʔEʔAnx: The Cave*, express and enact Aboriginality in myriad ways because they are firmly rooted in the social life of the local cultural worlds and respective First Nations in which the filmmakers are citizens. Throughout this book I have argued that Aboriginal media is powerful because it inserts Aboriginal presence and stories on-screen in the Canadian mediascape. Aboriginal media also provide a powerful practice through which Aboriginal sociality and community are transformed off-screen. The ability of Aboriginal media to alter, nurture, and shape Aboriginal social relationships enables this practice to expand the horizon for Aboriginal cultural futures.

Epilogue

It is a blistering hot Oklahoma summer evening, and I am on my way to see a movie when I check Facebook on my iPhone. To my delighted surprise I see the following post in my newsfeed: "Vancouver Indigenous Media Arts Festival Kickstarter Campaign!! June 21, 2011 W2 Community Center."

What? An Indigenous Media Arts Festival starting back up again in Vancouver? I excitedly click the "Like" button so that I can be added to their Facebook page. Sure enough, on the information page for the organization is an explanation that this event is a fundraiser to hold an Indigenous Media Arts Festival in November 2011. The June 21st event, in honor of Canada's National Aboriginal Day, will feature a mini–film festival and will showcase both Kevin Lee Burton's *Nikamowin* and Helen Haig-Brown's *ʔEʔAnx: The Cave*. I am envious that I cannot be in Vancouver for the fundraising event, but I am pleased beyond words that another Indigenous Film Festival will once again be held in Vancouver. I click on the link to see who is involved with organizing this event and see that several of the people who were involved in IMAG's media training programs and festival activities in 2003 and 2004 are now taking up the reins to begin a new Indigenous Media Arts Festival in Vancouver.

Facebook and Filmmakers

Facebook has become an incredibly vital link for me to stay connected with many of the Aboriginal filmmakers with whom I work in Vancouver. In fact, I initially joined Facebook as a way to connect with these filmmakers, and this social networking site provides an invaluable way for me to keep up with the latest developments in Vancouver's Aboriginal media world as well as the latest projects of the filmmakers with whom I work. Through Facebook I find out when films are in production, when a filmmaker receives a grant, when casting calls are announced, when production help or equipment is needed, and when films have their premieres. These connections and social networks with filmmakers have become especially important given that I now live and work in Oklahoma, and it is harder to return to Vancouver for extended periods of time. The connections maintained with filmmakers on Facebook are also important because, like many anthropologists' collaborators, they are my dear friends.

One challenge to maintaining my connection to the Aboriginal filmmaking community in Vancouver is that many of the filmmakers with whom I worked between 2002 and 2005 have moved away. In fact, about half of the filmmakers that I interviewed between 2003 and 2004 no longer live in Vancouver. There are many reasons for their departure from Vancouver. Some have returned to their traditional territories, some have taken jobs in other cities, some have had family obligations that drew them away from Vancouver, others have left to attend university, while some have been priced out of Vancouver.

The increasing cost of living and housing expenses in Vancouver have pushed many artists and filmmakers out of the city in search of more affordable housing. The gentrification of Vancouver as a result of the 2010 Winter Olympics also had a dramatic impact on the city and on the cost of living. One section of Second Avenue in False Creek, a main thoroughfare near where IMAG's office was located on Main Street, was developed into the Olympic Village to house athletes and then later sold as apartment units. The average cost of a detached house in Vancouver in 2000 was around $400,000, whereas by 2010 it had jumped to over $1,000,000.[1] As of 2011 Vancouver has the highest average rent in Canada, with the average rent at $1,181 per month.[2] Vancouver is the second most expensive city in Canada, behind Toronto, and is considered to have the most unaffordable housing in Canada.[3] The 2010 Winter Olympics cost approximately $6 billion for Vancouver, a city that paradoxically is voted as one of the most livable cities in the world and yet is also home to Canada's poorest postal code, the Downtown Eastside, a neighborhood with a high Aboriginal population. It is still unclear whether Vancouver will fully recover the costs of the Winter Olympics, but what is clear is that the cost of living in Vancouver, which had already been on the rise, has continued to increase in the wake of the Winter Olympics. For some Aboriginal filmmakers, Vancouver is now unaffordable for them. However, other filmmakers have left Vancouver because professional and artistic opportunities have taken them elsewhere.

Of the filmmakers with whom I worked closely at IMAG, Vera Wabegijig now lives in Ottawa, where she is working as a writer and filmmaker and teaching her daughters Storm and Grace to make their own films. Leena Minifie moved to Santa Fe, New Mexico, where she completed a bachelor's degree in media arts and indigenous liberal studies at the Institute for American Indian Arts in 2012. She recently moved back to Vancouver, where she remains active in media production and activism for Aboriginal rights. Cleo Reece returned to Fort McMurray, her traditional territory in northern Alberta, where she continues to make videos documenting environmental activism in her community. She was recently elected as band councilor for the Fort McMurray First Nation. Helen Haig-Brown lives on her traditional territory outside Williams Lake, British Columbia, but she continues to visit Vancouver often for filmmaking and postproduction work. Kevin Lee Burton lives in Winnipeg, where he worked as a curator at the Urban Shaman gallery until he began the indigenous arts collective Itwé. Ryan Mitchell-Morrison now resides in Brooklyn, where he continues to create electronic music and experimental media art. Duane Gastant' Aucoin moved back to his reserve in Teslin, Yukon, where he serves as an executive councilor for his Yanyedi Clan and is an active participant in Canada's Truth and Reconciliation Commission. Zoe Hopkins, once an IMAG board member, moved to her Mohawk community of the Six Nations reserve in Ontario, where she is involved with her son's Mohawk language immersion school. She continues to make media at Six Nations and in her Heiltsuk community of Bella Bella, British Columbia. Tania Willard, active with the Redwire Native Youth Media Society, guest curator at the grunt gallery, and a talented artist, moved back to her traditional territory on the Neskonlith reserve near Chase, British Columbia.

This flow of individuals out of Vancouver's urban Aboriginal community is part of the flux that is characteristic of urban Aboriginal communities. As Vera Wabegijig reminded me, this migration from Vancouver does not diminish the impact of Vancouver as an urban Aboriginal center. She views Vancouver as an important training ground for artists, writers, and filmmakers to learn the skills of art and media production, and then they take those skills back to their home communities and their traditional lands (personal communication 2011). There are certainly plenty of people who have stayed in Vancouver and continue to be key figures in Vancouver's Aboriginal media world, including Loretta Todd and Kamala Todd, Dana Claxton, Jackson Crick, Odessa Shuquaya, Dorothy Christian, and Lisa Jackson.

Future Directions in Aboriginal Media

When I began my fieldwork in 2002, many filmmakers articulated a sense that Vancouver's Aboriginal media world was just on the cusp of coming into its own. They expressed satisfaction that they had been part of building Vancouver's Aboriginal media world and conveyed numerous hopes to me regarding future directions for Aboriginal media. Overall, Aboriginal filmmakers in Vancouver want to see the Aboriginal media industry continue to grow and expand over the next decade. They hope that it will build capacity and that a strong production community will continue to emerge in which Aboriginal filmmakers produce work in dramatic genres as well as documentary and television production. Zoe Hopkins hopes that Aboriginal media training programs will continue to train Aboriginal people in all technical positions so that filmmakers can rely upon all-Aboriginal production crews. She elaborated:

> I'd like to see a whole production community where we can crew a bunch of shows no problem. I'd like that to not be a challenge anymore. I'd like to see some television series that cover the breadth of who we are as a people and that we don't always have to be focusing on struggle. Because we're not a people that are always struggling. I would like to see some feature films that do well in distribution — that would be awesome. I guess I just would like to see us have a stronger voice.

Several people articulated a desire to see an Aboriginal film institute or production center based in Vancouver in order to meet the training and resource needs of Aboriginal filmmakers but also to provide access to high-quality equipment. Cleo Reece declared, "I really want to see a production center where we've got a really good studio, good equipment and our own television studio. The other thing I'd like to see is using media as a tool for community organizing, that's my other focus which I believe in."

Leena Minifie wants to see an increase in fiction films, new media, and creative work. In an interview one evening at her home, she acknowledged the funding restrictions on Aboriginal media, noting, "I would like to see more emphasis on non-documentary and creative work. Because of the scarcity of funding and money, I think people are relying on small crews and they're making documentaries and that's 99% of the work you see on APTN right now. I think that our stories are not only factual, they are very dramatic, beautiful, glamorous, and surreal and I don't think you can tell that necessarily in documentaries all the time." She paused thoughtfully, her dark brown eyes flashing, before continuing, "I'd really like to see the bar being raised every year. I'd like to see the quality, the technical abilities of crews, the production qualities, the post production qualities, the editing, and the sound, I'd like to see everything just keep going up and up and up until we're on an even bar with everything else. I think that we do have stuff that reflects that right now but I think that still needs to continue." Dana Claxton emphasized a desire to see more Aboriginal feature films, exclaiming: "I'd like to see more and more feature films, lots of feature films because that's what people want. People don't want experimental cinema! They don't!" She laughed out loud because she is an experimental media maker, and she continued: "I'll just keep plugging along doing what I do, but people want feature films. In terms of seeing themselves on screen, that is powerful. I also want to see more powerful women's stories where women are not always victimized and of course I'd like to see more women directors."

Many filmmakers articulated a desire to see increased inclusion of Aboriginal media within mainstream media, as well as a desire for a self-sustaining Aboriginal media industry. Dorothy Christian echoed Cleo Reece's call for an Aboriginal production studio, stating that she would like to see the development of an Aboriginal film institute in Vancouver where Aboriginal filmmakers can learn the technical skills in a space that honors Aboriginal cultural values. She remarked:

> I would love to see our own film institute. I know that there are people who have been doing a lot of the groundwork for that. I would love to see that, a place that is Aboriginal friendly, where we could feel comfortable and where cultural knowledge is a given to a certain degree. My work has been primarily in documentary, but I've started to branch out and I've started doing different things. I would love to see a

place where feature films were being directed, produced, and written by Native people. I would like to see the spectrum, from feature films to media art installation and everything in between being produced and directed by Aboriginal people who have a voice and have important things to say — productions that can educate everyone, including stories where Aboriginal people learn about other Aboriginal people.

Several other filmmakers expressed a concern that Aboriginal media have been so focused on the struggles of Aboriginal people that the creativity, humor, and light-hearted aspects of Aboriginal life have not yet been explored within Aboriginal media. Jackson Crick expressed a hope that in the future Aboriginal media will have less emphasis on social issues within Aboriginal communities in order to open up space for light-hearted sitcoms, comedies, and dramatic series. He declared: "I'd really like to see it going in the direction of seeing things like an Aboriginal perspective on a *Friends* show or a *Seinfeld* or even the dramas you know because there's a lot of drama in Aboriginal life!" He laughed before continuing: "Just like in any life, but like a real one, not a *North of 60*, but real stuff that people can actually relate to."[4]

Ryan Mitchell-Morrison articulated the impact of Aboriginal media as an integral part of the "healing process" of Aboriginal communities. He explained that while he sees the importance of Aboriginal media that addresses the suffering and trauma within Aboriginal communities, in the future he would like to see Aboriginal media move into a space where filmmakers can celebrate Aboriginal stories. He poignantly explained: "I hope in the future people are able to kind of open up. I think there's been a lot of closed feelings and it is part of the healing process, people need to kind of protect themselves for a little while." He paused before softly remarking, "So hopefully there will be more room for celebration again and less tears." The desire to see "more celebration and less tears" was also articulated by Vera Wabegijig, who would like to see Aboriginal media reflect the humorous side of Aboriginal life. She explained: "I would like to see more stories, more feature length films, more narrative pieces, and more comedies. I think right now everything's really serious, but it has to be. I think it's happening for a reason." She took a sip of her coffee and then continued: "I think it'll help people to heal and that's what a lot of the documentaries are about, they're all about healing. So everything has a way to work itself out somehow. That's what they call Indian time! Everything has a place and a time for it. You know when the people are ready the stories will be ready. So I think when we're ready to laugh, we'll laugh, we'll make the comedies again." She laughed, exclaiming, "Because our people are so funny. Indians *are* funny!"

While Crick, Wabegijig, and Mitchell-Morrison articulated an interest in seeing Aboriginal comedies and sitcoms reflecting Aboriginal humor in Aboriginal media, Tania Willard expressed a desire for Aboriginal media to become part of multicultural and mainstream media. She views this as a way to educate dominant Canadian society about Aboriginal issues, while also using the technology to meet the concerns of Aboriginal audiences and communities. We spoke one afternoon during her lunch break near the Redwire office, and she explained: "I think there always needs to be Aboriginal media for Aboriginal people. I also think it would be really cool to see more multicultural media that has a lot of strong Aboriginal people involved in it." Speaking about the ability of Aboriginal media to educate the Canadian public, she remarked: "I don't think we can move forward as a democratic society without looking at Aboriginal issues and righting the wrongs, the really terrible wrongs that were committed against Aboriginal people. So I'd like to see more Canadians be aware of that and have it [Aboriginal media] be accessible to them and maybe that means more support for it." She then turned to the topic of the role of Aboriginal media within Aboriginal communities, noting: "I would also like to see us create our forms of media. Something we create that's new that keeps traditions of storytelling and puts them together in a new way that's a new form of media. So I'd like to see us be really innovative because I think we have a lot that we can incorporate from a cultural or traditional kind of place as well as these new tools that are out there that make creating media a lot more accessible." Willard's comments encapsulate the desire of Aboriginal filmmakers to see their work make interventions in the on-screen politics of representation in Canadian society while impacting the off-screen social life of Aboriginal communities. All of these discussions regarding content (i.e., whether to make documentaries, feature films, or comedies) and infrastructure (i.e., the hope for a production studio) locate Aboriginal media as acts of visual sovereignty on-and off-screen.

Aboriginal Cultural Futures

In filmmakers' discussions about their hopes for the future directions of Aboriginal media, they articulate aims and goals that seek to further enmesh practices of media production within Aboriginal social life while working toward increased inclusion of Aboriginal media within mainstream venues. Aboriginal people, whose lives have been heavily circumscribed by the legal and political regimes of the Canadian nation-state, have taken up the tools of media production to define Aboriginal identity, cultural traditions, and futures on their own terms. Speaking about the role of Indigenous media makers in Australia, scholars Faye Ginsburg and Fred Myers argue, "Through their cultural production, the indigenous artists and intellectuals whose work we study and support are creating—in a range of media, from dot paintings to feature films—an indigenous presence for themselves and a force with which others must reckon" (Ginsburg and Myers 2006, 29). Aboriginal filmmakers in Vancouver, likewise, use the tools of media production to provide voice and visibility for Aboriginal stories and experiences while asserting Aboriginal sovereignty and self-determination. The capacity of film and video to circulate to audiences within Canada and internationally extends their declarations of Aboriginal visual sovereignty while enabling this media to speak to local and global audiences. Ginsburg and Myers argue: "Indigenous films are themselves performative of a transformation in Australian public culture in which indigenous people are talking back and gaining acknowledgement of their realities, from a range of subject positions that render evident the complexity and vitality of contemporary indigenous lives" (Ginsburg and Myers 2006, 43). Likewise, Dana Claxton articulates the profound ways in which Aboriginal media, as part of a broader corpus of Aboriginal expressive culture, provides a link between ancestral traditions and contemporary practices. She declares, "Our creative expression sustains a connection to ancient ways, places our identities and concerns in the immediate, while linking us to the future" (Claxton 2005, 40).

I was fortunate to conduct fieldwork in Vancouver's Aboriginal media world as it was flourishing in production and gaining recognition for its work. In the years since I left the field, Vancouver's Aboriginal world has continued to expand and grow as filmmakers move in new creative directions and work to build stronger infrastructure to provide support for Aboriginal media production. The groundwork for realizing the goal of developing an Aboriginal film institute was strengthened with the development of new programs, such as the Aboriginal Media Lab created by Loretta Todd in collaboration first with the Chief Dan George Center at Simon Fraser University and now with the Museum of Anthropology at the University of British Columbia.[5] Despite the closing of IMAG, Aboriginal media production in Vancouver continues with numerous APTN series, feature film projects, short narratives, new media, and video art installations created in any given year. Aboriginal media in Vancouver reflect the diversity of Aboriginal cinematic visions while honoring connections to Aboriginal cultural traditions, constructing a space for the recognition of contemporary Aboriginal life, and opening up new possibilities for Aboriginal cultural futures. The Vancouver Indigenous Media Arts Festival (VIMAF), is just one example of a renewed space to showcase the work of Aboriginal filmmakers. I honor the remarkable work of the filmmakers with whom I worked in Vancouver and eagerly anticipate the new directions yet to come as the next generations of Aboriginal filmmakers transform the horizon for Aboriginal media with their own imaginative cinematic visions.

RENEWAL: VANCOUVER INDIGENOUS MEDIA ARTS FESTIVAL—NOVEMBER 2011

It feels as if everything has come full circle. I arrive in Vancouver for the first annual Vancouver Indigenous Media Arts Festival, and I am struck—as I always am upon returning to Vancouver—at how incredibly beautiful the landscape of this city is. I am reminded once again how truly fortunate I am to call this place my field site, and in many ways it has become a second home.

I am giddy with excitement over the return of an Indigenous Media Arts Festival to Vancouver. It has been a long five years without this crucial venue to showcase Aboriginal media and bring the community together. When I arrive downtown at the W2 Media Centre for the opening night of VIMAF, there is a palpable sense of renewed energy pulsating among the crowd. At the screening venue there are old posters from the IMAGeNation film festivals adorning the walls. At the opening I reconnect with old friends, eat the traditional foods catered for the event, and have the pleasant opportunity to see my good friend Billy Luther's latest documentary, *Grab*, premiere on this opening night.

Over the course of the next couple of days I attend screenings, listen to filmmaker panel discussions, and catch up with dear friends over dinner and endless cups of coffee. VIMAF has partnered with W2, a community media space located in the refurbished Woodwards building on the Downtown Eastside.[6] There is a strong attendance at the screenings and panel discussions, and the festival has a decidedly grassroots, community feel, which carries a strong echo of the community orientation of the IMAGeNation Aboriginal Film and Video Festival. The audience is predominantly Aboriginal, and the location of the screening venues in the Downtown Eastside means that it is an accessible location for many in the urban Aboriginal community. There are a few technical malfunctions, impromptu impassioned speeches about Aboriginal rights and the role of Aboriginal activists at the current Occupy Vancouver sit-in, and occasionally long delays as screenings and panel discussions run overtime. But no one minds that the schedule is behind by an hour or that there are a few technical glitches. What matters is that people are gathered together in this dark space in the basement of the W2 community media center, sitting on uncomfortable metal folding chairs for hours to watch and discuss the latest Aboriginal films and videos. There is a hunger to drink it all in—to be present, to recognize the work of Aboriginal filmmakers from Vancouver, across Canada, and from international locations.

Two of the VIMAF organizers—Ron Harris, a.k.a. Os12, and Marie James—are filmmakers and artists who were actively involved with IMAG. They honor the work of IMAG on the second night of the festival. Cleo Reece's youngest daughter, Skeena, has recently given birth to her son, and Cleo is unable to attend the festival. But the VIMAF organizers honor Cleo by asking her son Simon Reece to serve as a host for that night and to speak about the work that Cleo had done with IMAG. This acknowledgment was done in a good way that spoke to the legacy of IMAG while forging a new direction in the creation of VIMAF.

On the same night there is a late-night screening of Aboriginal music videos and a live performance by Os12—one of the VIMAF organizers and hosts—and a dance that lasts late into the night. Indeed, this is a lively, well-attended celebration that everyone is still talking about the next day. The eagerness to gather together to celebrate this media is palpable. When was the last time so many Aboriginal artists, dancers, musicians, and filmmakers gathered in the same space in Vancouver?

Over three days I watch numerous documentaries, short films, experimental media, and feature films that tell inventive Aboriginal stories with unique aesthetics. I listen to a panel of young, up-and-coming Aboriginal filmmakers, actors, and producers—many of whom I don't know and whom I meet for the first time at VIMAF—speak about their hopes for the future of Aboriginal media. I am inspired by the spark of this new talent emerging within Vancouver's Aboriginal media world.

Attending VIMAF reminds me how resilient Vancouver's Aboriginal media world is. That IMAG no longer exists as an organization does not mean that Aboriginal media production isn't happening in Vancouver. No, indeed, the success of VIMAF demonstrates it feels more vibrant than ever. At the close of the first annual Vancouver Indigenous Media Arts Festival—there is already talk about next year's VIMAF festival—there are plans to ensure that this remains an ongoing showcase for Aboriginal media in Vancouver.

I cannot wait to see what the future has in store for VIMAF and for Vancouver's Aboriginal media world.

Appendix

Filmmakers and Films

Filmmaker Biographies

DUANE ĢASTANT' AUCOIN

Duane Ģastant' Aucoin is a Wolf/Yanyedi member of the Teslin Tlingit Council and recently returned home from Vancouver, BC. Aucoin produced, directed, wrote, and starred in *Children of the Rainbow (Kichx Anagaat Yatx'i)*. He received an international award by being named the "International Two-Spirit Male Warrior" at the 19th International Two-Spirit Gathering held in Saskatchewan in 2007. As part of his duties he publicly speaks on issues pertaining to two-spirited people, their history, duties, and rights in First Nations Society. He recently completed his latest documentary entitled *My Own Private Lower Post*, which explores the intergenerational impact of residential school in his family. He promised his mother Vicky before she passed away in 2011 that he would continue telling "our story." Aucoin continues to perform and make videos, but his most important work continues to be supporting his elders in his community of Teslin to help bring back his Inland Tlingit language and culture. He is currently his Yanyedi Clans representative on the Teslin Tlingit Executive Council. Aucoin can be reached at dga@northwestel.net, or check out his website at www.myspace.com/dgaproductions.

Kevin Lee Burton is a Winnipeg-based filmmaker and artist who is originally from Gods Lake Narrows in northern Manitoba. Burton's work often deals with concepts of place and identity. He is a graduate of Capilano University's Aboriginal Film and Television Production Diploma (with distinction), and he has trained with the Indigenous Media Arts Groups' Professional Media Art Development. Past projects include directorial work for *S.E.C.K.*, a video installation assembled for the Western Front Society in Vancouver with artist-curator Peter Morin (2009), and for *Writing the Land,* a short experimental documentary produced by the National Film Board (2007). His films have screened at festivals in Toronto (imagineNATIVE, 2007), New York (National Museum of the American Indian, Smithsonian, 2008), and Park City (Sundance, 2008), among others. In 2010 Burton collaborated with artist Caroline Monnet on the exhibition RESERVE(d) at Urban Shaman Gallery: Contemporary Aboriginal Art in Winnipeg. Burton was the 2011 recipient of the New Media prize at imagineNATIVE in Toronto for the interactive online piece *Gods Lake Narrows* presented with the National Film Board. Beyond his individual artistic and film-based practice, Burton is a member of the three-person Indigenous art collective ITWÉ, which means "to say it" or "to give voice" in Cree.

DOROTHY CHRISTIAN

Dorothy Christian is a writer, a visual storyteller, a director of documentaries, and a scholar. She is a member of the Splats'in Community, one of seventeen communities of the Secwepemc Nation. Dorothy has over a hundred professional production credits from her work with VISION TV's *Skylight Newsmagazine,* APTN *National News* program, *ArtZone, Creative Native,* and *Venturing Forth.* She freelanced for CTV's *First Story* and the Minerva Foundation for BC women. Christian's works have screened at regional, national, and international film festivals. Two of her productions, *Memorial Rodeo: Okanagan Cowboys* (1998) and *Visual Essay: Horses* (1998), launched in a national exhibit, *Legends of Our Times,* at the Canadian Museum of Civilization in Ottawa and traveled to the National Cowboy Hall of Fame in Oklahoma City, the Museum of Arts and Sciences in Macon, Georgia, and the National Museum of the American Indian in New York from 2000 to 2004. In June 2007

Dreamspeakers Aboriginal Film and Television Festival bestowed her with the Best Experimental Award for her first independent film, *a spiritual land claim.*

Christian's master's thesis, "A 'Cinema of Sovereignty': Working in the Cultural Interface to Create a Model for Fourth World Film Pre-production and Aesthetics," was successfully defended in the School of Communications at Simon Fraser University in May 2010. She is currently in the second year of her PhD program at UBC's Department of Educational Studies researching Fourth World cinema as public pedagogy. Indigenous self-representation and visual sovereignty in film and media are central to her doctoral research while she explores how indigenous epistemologies and knowledge systems influence the construct of the visual narrative.

DANA CLAXTON

Dana Claxton works in film, video, photography, single and multichannel video installation, and performance art. Her practice investigates beauty, the body, the sociopolitical, and the spiritual. Her work has been shown internationally at the Museum of Modern Art (New York City), Walker Art Centre, Sundance Film Festival, Eiteljorg Museum, and the Museum of Contemporary Art (Sydney, Australia) and is held in public collections including the Vancouver Art Gallery, National Gallery of Canada, Art Bank of Canada, and the Winnipeg Art Gallery. She has received numerous awards including the VIVA Award and the Eiteljorg Fellowship.

Claxton's work was selected for the 17th Biennale of Sydney (2010), de Biennale Montréal (2007), Biennale d'art contemporain du Havre, France (2006), Micro Wave, Hong Kong (2005) Art Star Biennale, Ottawa (2005), and Wro 03 Media Arts Biennale, Wroclaw, Poland (2003). She has created commissioned works for the University of Lethbridge Gallery, Alternator Gallery, Winnipeg Art Gallery, Urban Shaman, Moose Jaw Museum and Art Gallery, and Tribe (Saskatoon). She has presented talks at the Getty Institute (Los Angeles), the College Art Association (U.S.), and the Opening Week Forum of the Biennale of Sydney.

Claxton was born in Yorkton, Saskatchewan, and her family reserve is Lakota First Nations–Wood Mountain located in beautiful southwest Saskatchewan. Her paternal Euro-Canadian grandmother taught her how to harvest and preserve food, and her maternal Lakota grandmother taught her to seek justice. Claxton, the youngest of four siblings, is an auntie, niece, cousin, and daughter.

BARB CRANMER

Barb Cranmer is an award-winning director who is a member of the 'Naṃgis First Nation of Alert Bay, British Columbia, part of the Kwakwaḵa'wakw Nation. Her credits include *Laxwesa Wa: Strength of the River*, *Tlina: The Rendering of Wealth*, and *Gwishalaayt: The Spirit Wraps around You*, among many other films. She has coproduced *My Big Fat Diet*, *We Are One with the Land*, and *Potlatch: To Give*. Her films have been recognized with awards at many film festivals and have been broadcast across Canada, the United States, and Europe. She currently lives in Alert Bay, making films, sitting on the 'Naṃgis First Nation Council, and working as the business owner of Culture Shock Interactive Gallery.

JACKSON CRICK

Jackson Crick is an actor and filmmaker who is a member of the Xeni Gwet'in Tsilhqot'in Nation. He is the former director of the Capilano College Aboriginal Film and Television Program and has lived and worked actively in Vancouver's Aboriginal media world for many years.

HELEN HAIG-BROWN

Helen Haig-Brown is an award-winning director, director of photography and teacher, and a leading talent in producing experimental documentary shorts. Her work is broad ranging, from experiences within her own family to explorations of land and language that are of significance to many First Nations people. Her first fictional work, *ʔEʔAnx: The Cave*, is an official selection of the 2011 Sundance Film Festival and of Berlinale 2010, and in 2009 it was named one of Canada's Top Ten (Short Films) by the Toronto International Film Festival.

Haig-Brown's recent works include *Pelq'ilc*, about the Secwepemc Nation's language revitalization efforts, and works in the television series *Our First Voices*, which focuses on indigenous language. As a cinematographer Haig-Brown has worked with other outstanding experimental documentary directors, including Kevin Lee Burton and Kamala Todd, and for CBC, Knowledge (British Columbia's state-of-the-art educational television network) and the National Film Board of Canada. Haig-Brown is a graduate of the Aboriginal Film and Television Production Program at Capilano College in North Vancouver and now resides in Williams Lake, in her traditional lands in the interior of British Columbia. She is in postproduction of her first feature documentary *Legacy*, which explores love, intimacy, and strength through four generations of women in her family.

ZOE HOPKINS

Award-winning filmmaker and Sundance Feature Film Program alumna. Heiltsuk from Bella Bella, British Columbia, and Mohawk from Six Nations, Ontario. Zoe Hopkins's films have shown at Sundance and Berlin. As writer and director of a new short film, *Mohawk Midnight Runners*, Hopkins is also in development with her first feature, entitled *Running Home*. Hopkins now lives in Six Nations, where she is raising her young son and studying the Mohawk language.

LISA JACKSON

With a background in documentary, including the acclaimed short *Suckerfish* and the CTV one-hour *Reservation Soldiers*, award-winning Canadian filmmaker Lisa Jackson expanded into fiction with *Savage*, which won a 2010 Genie award for Best Short Film. As part of the Canadian Film Centre's Directors' Lab she completed the 35mm short *Parkdale* (2011) and is working on fiction and documentary projects, including writing her first fiction feature. Her work has played at festivals internationally, has been broadcast on CBC, CTV, Bravo!, Knowledge, SCN, and APTN, and is used extensively in educational settings. She is Anishinaabe, has a BFA in film production from Simon Fraser University, and lives in Vancouver.

TODD LAMIRANDE

Todd is a proud member of the Métis Nation. He began his journalism career as a freelance writer for the *First Perspective* in 1997, eventually becoming editor of the newspaper. After working as communications officer for the Manitoba Métis Federation, he joined APTN's news department in 2000. He started as a video-journalist in Vancouver, a position he held for four years, and then moved on to cohosting APTN *National News*. He is now part of APTN's investigative news unit.

Leena Minifie is a member of the Gitxaala Nation of Tsimshian and of British decent. She is a video, performance, and interactive artist. As a trained dancer and choreographer, movement greatly informs her practice and life. She grew up in a small industrial company town on the Douglas Channel near her traditional home territory of the Pacific Northwest Coast. Minifie graduated from the Aboriginal Film and Television Program at Capilano University and studied at the Indigenous Media Arts Group working with some of Canada's influential Native media artists such as Dana Claxton and Archer Pechawis. In 2009 Minifie relocated to Santa Fe, where she completed a BFA in new media and a BA in indigenous liberal studies in 2012. In 2012 she left Santa Fe and returned to Vancouver, where she continues to be involved in media and social activism. Minifie has completed two single-channel video installations including Beatnation.org and an interactive dance piece for New Forms Festival 2004. She produced three short films that have screened at film festivals internationally and premiered at the imagineNATIVE film festival in Toronto. Most recently the film *?E?Anx: The Cave* played at the prestigious Sundance Film Festival in 2011.

RYAN MITCHELL-MORRISON

Ryan Mitchell-Morrison hails from a Miig'mac reserve called Listiguj. He has lived in several cities making art, video, and music. He currently lives in Brooklyn, New York, still getting into mischief and building handmade axes.

ARCHER PECHAWIS

Performance artist, new media artist, filmmaker, writer, curator, and educator, Archer Pechawis was born in Alert Bay, British Columbia, in 1963. He has been a practicing artist since 1984 with particular interest in the intersection of Plains Cree culture and digital technology, merging "traditional" objects such as hand drums with video and audio sampling. His work has been exhibited across Canada and in Paris and featured in publications such as *Fuse Magazine* and *Canadian Theatre Review*. Pechawis has been the recipient of many Canada Council, British Columbia, and Ontario Arts Council awards, and he won the Best New Media Award at the 2007 imagineNATIVE Film +

Media Arts Festival and Best Experimental Short at imagineNATIVE in 2009. Pechawis also works extensively with Native youth as part of his art practice, teaching performance and digital media for various First Nations organizations and in the public school system. Of Cree and European ancestry, he is a member of Mistawasis First Nation, Saskatchewan.

CLEO REECE

Cleo Reece is a founder and former director of the Indigenous Media Arts Group. She was the festival director of the IMAGeNation Aboriginal Film and Video Festival from 1998 to 2004. She is a long-time activist for Aboriginal rights and environmental issues, and her film credits include *Land Use: Mother Earth* and *Red Power Women*. She currently resides on her traditional Cree territory in Fort McMurray, Alberta, where she serves as a tribal councilor for the Fort McMurray no. 468 First Nation.

ODESSA SHUQUAYA

Odessa Shuquaya is a member of the Kluane First Nation in Yukon Territory, Canada. Although raised in the interior of British Columbia and currently making Vancouver her home, she still has strong ties to her family and community up north. She is an actor and filmmaker who has worked in many capacities within the media industry, including as a location scout for commercials, television series (*LWord, Supernatural*), and a feature film (*The Butterfly*). She has also worked on several APTN shows, as a second assistant director on *Tansi! Nehiyawetan: Let's Speak Cree!*, a production assistant on *Venturing Forth*, and as a postproduction assistant on *Ravens and Eagles*. Her video *People of the River* documented Sto:lo fishing rights and screened at several film festivals. She also worked as a videographer for *Vancouver 125* to represent Aboriginal stories about Vancouver for the 125th anniversary of the founding of city of Vancouver. She was awarded a Canada Council for the Arts grant to research her traditional territory and stories to develop a script based on a Southern Tutchone story that she hopes to film in the Yukon. She has been active in Vancouver's theater scene for many years and recently acted in the play *Egnie's Eye*, a new work by Theatre Terrific.

KAMALA TODD

Kamala Todd was born and raised in the Coast Salish territory of Vancouver. She is Cree, Irish, and German. Kamala has a master's degree in urban geography from the University of British Columbia. Her work as a community planner, filmmaker, and writer is focused on facilitating and making space for Aboriginal stories and perspectives. She is creator of such projects as Storyscapes and Indigenous City. Her film credits include *Sharing Our Stories: The Vancouver Dialogues Project*, *Indigenous Plant Diva*, and *Cedar and Bamboo*. She also worked as a writer and director on the children's Cree language series *Tansi! Nehiyawetan: Let's Speak Cree!* Most recently, Kamala worked as a consultant and facilitator with the city of Vancouver Dialogues Project. She lives with her husband and two young sons in New Westminster, British Columbia.

LORETTA TODD

See Todd's biography at www.tansi.tv/corporate/crew_loretta.html.

VERA WABEGIJIG

Vera Wabegijig's roots come from the Mississauga First Nation and Wikwemikong Unceded Reserve. She is a member of the Bear Clan and Tricksters' Fireball Society and also is a board member at SAW Video Co-op.

"Life is good. Writing makes me happy-er. Taking photos gives me perspective. Walking brings me closer to what's real. Talking with my kids always results in good storytelling and laughter. Cycling makes me appreciate my body even more. Reading provides me great escape. Getting up in front of people helps me exercise my voice, my stage presence, and brings me face to face with a fear that is now subsiding each time. Breathing in and exhaling out clears my mind so that I can imagine and dream a new reality."

And there's a longer version for those who want to know about her credentials on her blog: http://verawaabegeeshig.wordpress.com.

TANIA WILLARD

Tania Willard, Secwepemc Nation, works within the shifting ideas about contemporary and traditional, often working with bodies of knowledge and skills that are conceptually linked to her interest in intersections between Aboriginal and other cultures. Willard's creative practice includes art, graphic design, and curatorial projects. She has worked as an artist in residence with Stanley Park, gallery gachet in Vancouver's Downtown Eastside, and in the Banff Centre's visual arts residency, and as a curator in residence with grunt gallery. Collections of Willard's work can be found at the Department of Foreign Affairs and International Trade, Thompson Rivers University, and Kamloops Art Gallery. Willard's recent curatorial work includes *Beat Nation: Art, Hip Hop and Aboriginal Culture*, featuring twenty-seven contemporary Aboriginal artists at the Vancouver Art Gallery in 2012 and touring to multiple venues until 2014.

Films and Television Programs Cited

?E?Anx: The Cave. 2009. Directed by Helen Haig-Brown. Toronto: Vtape. DVD.

APTN National News. Produced by Paul Barnsley and Francine Compton. Winnipeg: Aboriginal Peoples Television Network.

ArtZone. Produced by Dana Claxton and Kim Goodtrack. Winnipeg: Aboriginal Peoples Television Network.

Atanarjuat: The Fast Runner. 2001. Directed by Zacharias Kunuk. Los Angeles: Sony Pictures Home Entertainment. DVD.

Backbone of the World. 1997. Directed by George Burdeau. Berkeley CA: Berkeley Media. DVD.

The Ballad of Crowfoot. 1968. Directed by Willie Dunn. Montreal: National Film Board of Canada. DVD.

Bearwalker. 2000. Directed by Shirley Cheechoo. Thunder Bay ON: Thunder Girls from the Backroads Productions.

Before Tomorrow. 2009. Directed by Marie-Hélène Cousineau and Madeline Ivalu. Igloolik NU: Isuma Distribution International.

Beyond Words. Winnipeg: Aboriginal Peoples Television Network.

Blackstone. Produced by Ron E. Scott. Winnipeg: Aboriginal Peoples Television Network.

Boxed In. 2009. Directed by Shane Belcourt. Montreal: National Film Board of Canada. DVD.

Brain Plus World. 2001. Directed by James Diamond. Toronto: Vtape. DVD.

Buffalo Bone China. 1997. Directed by Dana Claxton. Toronto: Vtape. DVD.

Buffalo Tracks. Produced by Gary Farmer. Winnipeg: Aboriginal Peoples Television Network.

Cedar and Bamboo. 2010. Directed by Kamala Todd and Diana Leung. Vancouver: Moving Images.

A Century of Genocide in the Americas: The Residential School Experience. 2002. Directed by Rosemary Gibbons. Seattle: Native Voices Program, University of Washington. DVD.

Children of the Rainbow (Kichx Anagaat Yatx'i). 2003. Directed by Duane Gastant' Aucoin. Teslin YT.

Club Native. 2008. Directed by Tracey Deer. Montreal: National Film Board of Canada. DVD.

Connected by Innate Rhythm. 2003. Directed by Leena Minifie. Santa Fe: Stories First Productions.

Contact. Produced by Madeleine Allakariallak. Winnipeg: Aboriginal Peoples Television Network.

Creative Native. Produced by Tamara Bell. Winnipeg: Aboriginal Peoples Television Network.

Deep inside Clint Star. 1999. Directed by Clint Alberta. Montreal: National Film Board of Canada.

Encounter at Kwacha House. 1967. Directed by Rex Tasker. Montreal: National Film Board of Canada. DVD.

Finding Our Talk. Produced by Paul Rickard. Winnipeg: Aboriginal Peoples Television Network.

First Story. Produced by Pieter Romer. Vancouver: CTV BC.

Fogo Island Community Films. 1967–1969. Directed by Colin Low. Montreal: National Film Board of Canada. DVD.

Forgotten Warriors. 1997. Directed by Loretta Todd. Montreal: National Film Board of Canada. DVD.

Geeka. 2007. Directed by Leena Minifie. Santa Fe: Stories First Productions.

God Help the Man Who Would Part with His Land. 1971. Directed by George Stoney. Montreal: National Film Board of Canada.

Grab. 2011. Directed by Billy Luther. Hollywood: World of Wonder Productions.

Gwishalaayt: The Spirit Wraps around You. 2002. Directed by Barb Cranmer. Vancouver: Moving Images Distribution. DVD.

Hands of History. 1994. Directed by Loretta Todd. Montreal: National Film Board of Canada. DVD.

The Heist. 2010. Directed by Andrew Jack; produced by Leena Minifie and Kelly Balon. Santa Fe: Stories First Productions. DVD.

Helpless Maiden Makes an "I" Statement. 2000. Directed by Thirza Cuthand. Winnipeg: Video Pool. DVD.

Her Sugar Is? 2009. Directed by Dana Claxton. Toronto: Vtape. DVD.

The Hill. 2004. Directed by Dana Claxton. Toronto: Vtape. DVD.

Honey Moccasin. 1998. Directed by Shelley Niro. New York: Women Make Movies. DVD.

How the Fiddle Flows. 2002. Directed by Gregory Coyes. Montreal: National Film Board of Canada. DVD.

Incident at Restigouche. 1984. Directed by Alanis Obomsawin. Montreal: National Film Board of Canada. DVD.

Indigenous Plant Diva. 2008. Directed by Kamala Todd. Montreal: National Film Board of Canada. DVD.

Is the Crown at War with Us? 2002. Directed by Alanis Obomsawin. Montreal: National Film Board of Canada. DVD.

It Starts with a Whisper. 1993. Directed by Shelley Niro. Toronto: Canadian Filmmakers Distribution Centre. DVD.

I Want to Know Why. 1994. Directed by Dana Claxton. Toronto: Vtape. DVD.

Journals of Knud Rasmussen. 2006. Directed by Zacharias Kunuk and Norman Cohn. Igloolik NU: Isuma Distribution International.

Kainayssini Imanistaisiwa: The People Go On. 2003. Directed by Loretta Todd. Montreal: National Film Board of Canada. DVD.

Kanehsatake: 270 Years of Resistance. 1993. Directed by Alanis Obomsawin. Montreal: National Film Board of Canada. DVD.

Keepers of the Fire. 1994. Directed by Christine Welsh. Montreal: National Film Board of Canada.

Kinaaldá: Navajo Rite of Passage. 2000. Directed by Lena Carr. Albuquerque: Indian Summer Films. DVD.

The Land Is the Culture. 1975. Produced by the Union of B.C. Indian Chiefs. Vancouver.

Land Use: Mother Earth. 1993. Directed by Cleo Reece. Fort McMurray AB.

Laxwesa Wa: The Strength of the River. 1995. Directed by Barb Cranmer. Montreal: National Film Board of Canada. DVD.

The Learning Path. 1991. Directed by Loretta Todd. Montreal: National Film Board of Canada. DVD.

Legends/Sxwexwxwiy'am': The Story of Siwash Rock. 1999. Directed by Annie Frazier Henry. Montreal: National Film Board of Canada. DVD.

Little Big Man. 1970. Directed by Arthur Penn. Hollywood: Paramount Studios. DVD.

Mémère Métisse/My Métis Grandmother. 2009. Directed by Janelle Wookey. Winnipeg: Winnipeg Film Group. DVD.

Meskanahk (My Path). 2005. Directed by Kevin Lee Burton. Toronto: Vtape. DVD.

Migmaeoi Otjiosog/Mi'kmaq Family. 1994. Directed by Catherine Martin. Montreal: National Film Board of Canada. DVD.

My Life in the Gay Mafia. 2003. Directed by Dusty Hagerüd. Vancouver: Capilano College Aboriginal Film and Television Program.

My Name Is Kahentiiosta. 1995. Directed by Alanis Obomsawin. Montreal: National Film Board of Canada. DVD.

My Own Private Lower Post. 2008. Directed by Duane Gastant' Aucoin. Kelowna BC: Filmwest Associates. DVD.

Navajo Talking Picture. 1986. Directed by Arlene Bowman. New York: Women Make Movies. DVD.

Nikamowin (Song). 2007. Directed by Kevin Lee Burton. Toronto: Vtape. DVD.

No Turning Back. 1996. Directed by Gregory Coyes. Montreal: National Film Board of Canada. DVD.

Okimah. 1998. Directed by Paul Rickard. Montreal: National Film Board of Canada. DVD.

One Hundred Aboriginal Women. 1981. Produced by Amelia Productions. Vancouver: Video Out Distribution. DVD.

Our City, Our Voices: Follow the Eagle and Slo-Pitch. 2005. Directed by Lorraine Fox, David Moosetail, Vera Wabegijig, Louise Lagimodiere, and Mary Suchell. Montreal: National Film Board of Canada. DVD.

The People Dance. 2001. Directed by Dana Claxton. Toronto: Vtape. DVD.

People of the River. 2002. Directed by Odessa Shuquaya. Vancouver: Capilano College Aboriginal Film and Television Program.

Picturing a People: George Johnston, Tlingit Photographer. 1997. Directed by Carol Geddes. Montreal: National Film Board of Canada. DVD.

Prayer for a Good Day. 2003. Directed by Zoe Leigh Hopkins. Six Nations ON: Blanket Dance Productions.

Qatuwas: People Gathering Together. 1997. Directed by Barb Cranmer. Montreal: National Film Board of Canada. DVD.

Ravens and Eagles. Produced by Jeff Bear and Marianne Jones. Winnipeg: Aboriginal Peoples Television Network.

Raven Tales. Produced by Chris Kientz. Winnipeg: Aboriginal Peoples Television Network.

The Red Paper. 1996. Directed by Dana Claxton. Toronto: Vtape. DVD.

Red Power Women. 2000. Directed by Cleo Reece. Fort McMurray AB.

Reel Injun. 2009. Directed by Neil Diamond. Montreal: National Film Board of Canada. DVD.

Richard Cardinal: Cry from the Diary of a Métis Child. 1986. Directed by Alanis Obomsawin. Montreal: National Film Board of Canada. DVD.

Rocks at Whiskey Trench. 2000. Directed by Alanis Obomsawin. Montreal: National Film Board of Canada. DVD.

Savage. 2009. Directed by Lisa Jackson. Vancouver: Moving Images Distribution. DVD.

The Seventh Generation. Produced by Jennifer Podemski and Laura Milliken for Big Soul Productions. Winnipeg: Aboriginal Peoples Television Network.

Silent Tears. 1997. Directed by Shirley Cheechoo. Montreal: National Film Board of Canada. DVD

Singing Our Stories. 1998. Directed by Annie Frazier Henry. Montreal: National Film Board of Canada. DVD.

Smoke Signals. 1998. Directed by Chris Eyre. Santa Monica: Miramax. DVD.

Spudwrench: Kahnawake Man. 1997. Directed by Alanis Obomsawin. Montreal: National Film Board of Canada. DVD.

Stolen Spirits. 2004. Directed by Judy Manuel-Wilson. Vancouver.

Stories from the Seventh Fire. 2002. Directed by Gregory Coyes. Montreal: National Film Board of Canada. DVD.

Storytellers in Motion. 2005. Produced by Jeff Bear and Marianne Jones. Vancouver: Moving Images Distribution. DVD.

Suckerfish. 2004. Directed by Lisa Jackson. Montreal: National Film Board of Canada. DVD.

Tansi! Nehiyawetan: Let's Speak Cree! Produced by Loretta Todd. Winnipeg: Aboriginal Peoples Television Network.

The Things I Cannot Change. 1967. Directed by Tanya Ballantyne. Montreal: National Film Board of Canada.

Thorn Grass. 2002. Directed by D. Robin Hammer. Boulder CO: Light Circle Films.

Thriller. 1983. Directed by John Landis. Michael Jackson music video. New York: Epic Records.

Tkaronto. 2009. Directed by Shane Belcourt. Toronto: Kinosmith. DVD.

T'Lina: The Rendering of Wealth. 1999. Directed by Barb Cranmer. Montreal: National Film Board of Canada. DVD.

Today Is a Good Day: Remembering the Legacy of Chief Dan George. 1998. Directed by Loretta Todd. Montreal: National Film Board of Canada. DVD.

To Return: The John Walkus Story. 2000. Directed by Annie Frazier Henry. Vancouver: AM Productions. DVD.

Tree of Consumption. 1994. Directed by Dana Claxton. Toronto: Vtape. DVD.

Tsi tkahéhtayen (The Garden). 2009. Directed by Zoe Leigh Hopkins. Toronto: Vtape. DVD.

Up Against the System. 1969. Directed by Terence MacCartney-Filgate. Montreal: National Film Board of Canada.

Vanishing Link. 2004. Directed by Donna Rowell. Campbell CA: Digiglyphs. DVD.

Venturing Forth. Produced by Brenda Chambers. Winnipeg: Aboriginal Peoples Television Network.

Wakanheja (Sacred One). 2000. Directed by Dana Claxton and Kim Soo Goodtrack. Vancouver: FilmWest Associates.

Water into Fire. 1994. Directed by Zachery Longboy. Vancouver: Video Out Distribution. DVD.

Waterspeak. 2002. Directed by Dana Claxton. Two channel video installation. Vancouver.

Women in the Shadows. 1991. Directed by Christine Welsh. Montreal: National Film Board of Canada. DVD.

Wonders of Canada. 1906. Montreal: Charles Urban Trading Company and Kleine Optical Company.

Working Baby Dyke Theory. 1997. Directed by Thirza Cuthand. Winnipeg: Video Pool. DVD.

Writing the Land. 2007. Directed by Kevin Lee Burton. Montreal: National Film Board of Canada. DVD.

You Are on Indian Land. 1969. Directed by George Stoney. Montreal: National Film Board of Canada. DVD.

Notes

1. Throughout this book I use the terms *Aboriginal, Native, First Nations, Indian*, and *indigenous* depending on the historical and contemporary context. Whenever possible I identify the person's tribal affiliation. I use the term *Aboriginal* as that was the term most frequently used by the filmmakers with whom I worked. Canada recognizes three legal categories of Aboriginal peoples: First Nations, Inuit, and Métis. I find the term *Aboriginal* to be the most inclusive term to represent the diverse identities of all the filmmakers with whom I worked.

2. All individuals whom I interviewed were given the option of having their real names used in my research and publications. The names that are used throughout this text are the real names of the filmmakers, artists, and activists who gave permission for their real names to be used. There were individuals who did not want their real names used, and in those instances I do not use their name or a pseudonym. The wishes of the filmmakers to remain anonymous or to have their real names used have been honored throughout this book.

3. In my experience with Aboriginal media makers in Vancouver, the terms *film* and *filmmaker* are used to refer to the finished media projects and people who make them regardless of the fact that the vast majority of them are working with digital video technology, not 16mm or 35mm film. I recognize that the term *media maker* may be more appropriate

for encompassing the wide range of media in which individuals are working; however, the term that people most often used in referring to themselves and others was *filmmaker* or occasionally *media artist*.

4. The first question that I am often asked when I tell people that I do research in Vancouver is, "Are you Canadian?" To situate my position vis-à-vis this community of filmmakers, it is important to acknowledge that I am not Canadian, nor am I a long-term resident of Vancouver. I am a non-Native woman from a working-class background, primarily of Irish American heritage, who grew up on the East Coast. The story of how I ended up doing research on Aboriginal media in Vancouver is connected to a long-term academic and personal interest in Native American art and cultural production, and to my graduate studies at New York University, where I had the opportunity to participate in the Culture and Media certificate program and to intern at the Smithsonian's National Museum of the American Indian Film and Video Center.

5. This is reflective of the technology available at the time. Most of the filmmakers did not have the capability to make DVDs of their videos and made duplicate VHS copies of their work to submit to festivals. Much of the video work that I collected in Vancouver from filmmakers and recorded on APTN is in the VHS format.

6. As part of the festival I organized a film series, "Voices of Repatriation," that screened four international indigenous documentaries about repatriation at the Museum of Anthropology. This film series included a panel discussion with museum staff and Aboriginal activists about repatriation; this event was the first time that MOA collaborated with IMAG.

7. I conducted fourteen interviews with men and twenty-one interviews with women. Of my interviews, 34 percent of the filmmakers self-identified as mixed-blood Aboriginal, indicating that they have both Aboriginal and non-Aboriginal ancestry, while 20 percent of participants identified as having multiple band affiliations, meaning that their parents were from different First Nations. Eleven percent of participants self-identified as Métis, and 14 percent self-identified as two-spirit, a term that is commonly used by Aboriginal people who identify as gay, lesbian, bisexual, or transgendered. These tape-recorded interviews were typically conducted in a coffee shop, although several interviews were conducted over the phone, and generally lasted between an hour and a half and two hours. I began setting up these formal interviews

after seven months of fieldwork. My interviews were built upon prior knowledge and relationships I had established with people after working together at IMAG. In many cases the informal conversations I had with people over coffee, at their homes during dinner, and in helping to care for their children provided a wealth of information that further enriched the formal interviews.

8. It is an American writing convention, particularly in the curation of Native American film festivals, to indicate the tribal affiliation of a filmmaker in parentheses after his or her last name. This is not a Canadian writing convention, however, which speaks to some of the national differences with regard to the indigenous identity politics, which are incredibly complex on both sides of the border. However, I do feel that it is important to recognize the identity of the Aboriginal nations in which the filmmakers are citizens. Therefore, I include the tribal affiliation of the filmmakers after their last names the first time each name is used in the book. There are also often several different spellings of tribal names. I have honored the requests of each filmmaker in the specific spelling they prefer for their tribal affiliation. There is also an appendix at the end of the book that contains short biographies of each of the filmmakers featured here. I encourage readers to refer to those biographies for additional information regarding the cultural identities of the filmmakers.

9. Many thanks to my colleague Daniel Swan for pointing this out in a conversation about his experience with indigenous arts organizations. It is a Western notion to think that because an organization exists for a short time span (around nine years in the case of IMAG) that this is a failure. On the contrary, because the individuals who are involved with indigenous arts organizations are also leaders in other capacities in their communities as well as being practicing artists, there are many competing obligations on their time. An organization can form to meet a particular need for a given time and then disband as folks move other to pursue other interests.

Introduction

1. My research is deeply indebted to the scholarship of Faye Ginsburg, whose research on indigenous media has demonstrated that media production can provide a tool with which indigenous communities organize for social action to reimagine cultural identities. Her research reveals

that filmmakers negotiate the cultural politics of national and alternative media practices in multiple contexts (Ginsburg 1991, 2002, 2003, 2005). My research builds on this framework by analyzing Aboriginal filmmaking as an expression of Aboriginal visual sovereignty and cultural autonomy and as a practice around which a diverse, intertribal urban Aboriginal "community" is formed.

2. The Indian Act was passed by the Canadian government in 1876 and is the overarching piece of legislation governing the relationship between status Indians and the federal government. The Indian Act is still in place today and has been amended many times since 1876. When passed, the Indian Act created a system whereby status Indians were considered wards of the state. Key Indian Act amendments were made at various points to create reserves, to institute federal control over band councils, to prohibit the practice of Indian spiritual practices such as the potlatch and Sun Dance, and to enable Indian agents to remove Indian children from their families and place them in residential schools. The Indian Act also legislated Indian identity in Canada, creating this concept of "status" that is a recognition of Aboriginality by the federal government. Unlike the American system, which began implementing blood quantum as a measurement of Indian identity in 1887 with the passage of the Dawes Act, "status" as determined by the Indian Act was defined patrilineally. It was also possible to lose or acquire "status" through marriage. Between 1876 and 1985 status Indian women who married nonstatus (i.e., non-Aboriginal, American Indians from the United States, or Métis) men lost their status and were no longer legally recognized as Indian by the federal government. These women also lost the ability to pass on status to their children. Once they lost status, they were no longer able to live on reserve, access education on reserve, access social services, or receive treaty payments owed to them. This was a major influence on the movement of Indian women from reserves to urban areas. The Indian Act was insidious in undermining the ability of Aboriginal nations to determine their own membership criteria. For additional scholarship on these political issues see Green (2001), Lawrence (2004), and Simpson (2008).

3. The political enactment of Aboriginal sovereignty may come in the form of casino gaming or smoke shops on reservations (Cattelino 2008), activism and legal disputes about mobility across the U.S.-Canadian border (Simpson 2008), land claims and the treaty negotiation process

(C. Roth 2002), or the maintenance of Aboriginal fisheries and resource rights (Coates 2000; Menzies 1994).

4. The development of Aboriginal media production emerged out of a response to the misrepresentation of Aboriginal people within mainstream media. The "Noble Savage/Savage Savage" stereotype dichotomy within Hollywood movies has left a profound impact on the imaging of American Indians within the popular imaginary (Berkhofer 1978; Friar and Friar 1972; Rollins and O'Connor 1998). Scholars have addressed the construction of images of Native Americans through the impact of museum visuality and early ethnographic film (Griffiths 2002; R. Morris 1994), world's fairs (Rydell 1984), and photographic practices (Cohen-Scherer 1979; Edwards 1992; Lippard 1992). All of these practices—as well as dime store novels, captivity narratives, and narratives about "Manifest Destiny" and westward expansion—contributed to the development of a visual iconography of "Indianness." These images reduced Native people to stereotypical caricatures while contributing to ideologies of the "vanishing race" prevalent during the nineteenth and early twentieth centuries. The legacy of visual imagery of "Indianness" was perpetuated through Hollywood films, particularly in the Western genre, and remains a visual landscape against which Native filmmakers struggle in their own cinematic representations (Aleiss 2005; Loft 2005; Kilpatrick 1999; Raheja 2011; Singer 2001; Vail 1997).

5. According to the Statistics Canada 2006 Census, Vancouver's total Aboriginal population is 40,125. Many people in the Aboriginal community estimate that it may be closer to 50,000 because many Aboriginal people do not participate in government census records, and it is widely recognized that the statistics on the Aboriginal population are largely underreported. The total population of Vancouver in the 2006 census is approximately 2 million people, so the Aboriginal population is approximately 2 percent of the total population in Vancouver. The census information gathered in the Statistics Canada 2011 Census was not available at the time that this book went to press. The 2006 census data from the Aboriginal Peoples Survey is available online at http://www.statcan.gc.ca/bsolc/olc-cel/olc-cel?catno=89-637-X&lang=eng (accessed June 18, 2012).

6. Aboriginal Friendship Centres in Canada were established in the late 1950s and early 1960s as a way to provide social services, cultural

programming, and community outreach to urban Aboriginal populations. There are currently over 120 Friendship Centres throughout all provinces and territories across Canada. Aboriginal Friendship Centres receive most of their funding through the Department of the Secretary of State, although many Friendship Centres also receive funds through provincial and municipal governments. Vancouver's Aboriginal Friendship Centre has offered programs and services for Aboriginal families, children, and elders in the Vancouver and Lower Mainland area for over fifty years.

7. For further statistical information see the Statistics Canada 2006 Census and Statistics Canada 2001 Census, Aboriginal Peoples Survey, accessed June 18, 2012, http://www12.statcan.ca/english/profil01/ AP01/Index.cfm?Lang=E. The total Aboriginal population in Canada (approximately 1.2 million or 4 percent of the total Canadian population of approximately 31 million in 2006), as well as the urban Aboriginal population (approximately 765,000), may be larger than these numbers reflect because of low Aboriginal participation in the census and underreporting. The census information regarding data on Aboriginal peoples gathered in the Statistics Canada 2011 Census (accessed June 18, 2012, http://www.statcan.gc.ca/daily-quotidien/120208/dq120208a-eng.htm) was not available at the time that this book went to press.

8. This project involved collaboration between a number of organizations including the Vancouver Agreement and City of Vancouver, the Chief Dan George Center for Advanced Education, the Knowledgeable Youth Association (KAYA), City of Vancouver Social Planning, and Office of Cultural Affairs (K. Todd 2011b).

9. Vancouver Storyscapes, "Multi-Media Art," accessed June 18, 2012, http://www.storyscapes.ca/multimedia.htm. (The longevity of websites can be ephemeral, and the Storyscapes website is no longer active. I have left this reference in the event that the website becomes active again in the future. Throughout this book where I have drawn information from websites I provide the website information; however, these websites may not be working after this book is in press.)

10. This history of Vancouver's Aboriginal media world is drawn from conversations with many founding members of this community including Loretta Todd, Archer Pechawis, Dana Claxton, Aiyanna Maracle, Cleo Reece, Donald Morin, and Dorothy Christian. Any inaccuracies regarding this history are solely my own.

11. The White Paper policy was influenced by the Termination and Relocation policies enacted by the U.S. government in 1953, which sought to terminate the nation-to-nation relationship between the U.S. government and Native American tribal governments. The Relocation program relocated Native Americans from their reservation communities to urban areas (Burt 1986). The White Paper policy and the Termination and Relocation policies were designed with the intent of assimilating Native Americans and Aboriginal Canadians into mainstream society.

12. The UBCIC participated in the 1981 occupation of the Vancouver Department of Indian Affairs office by Aboriginal women who protested DIA policies, particularly the socioeconomic conditions of poverty and violence facing Aboriginal women as well as the removal of Aboriginal children from Aboriginal homes and the placement of them into non-Aboriginal foster homes. This occupation was documented in the video *One Hundred Aboriginal Women* (1981) produced by Amelia Productions and distributed by Video Out in Vancouver.

13. This program was named for actor and Vancouver resident Chief Dan George (Tsleil-Waututh)—nominated for an Oscar for his role as Old Lodge Skins in *Little Big Man* (1970)—who encouraged Aboriginal people to become filmmakers and begin producing their own media. In a 1967 speech to a crowd of thirty-five thousand people gathered in Vancouver's Empire Stadium to celebrate the city's centennial anniversary, George emphasized the injustices suffered by Aboriginal people and proclaimed, "I shall grab the instruments of the white man's success—his education, his skills, and with these new tools I shall build my race into the proudest segment of your society." Chief Dan George, "A Lament for Confederation," 1967, Centennial Speech, Empire Stadium, Vancouver, posted 2009, accessed June 18, 2012, http://www.empowermentweekly. com/2009/09/our-ancestors-lament-for-confederation.html.

14. Capilano College is now known as Capilano University; however, because it was Capilano College while I did fieldwork, and the filmmakers with whom I worked refer to it as Capilano College, I use Capilano College most frequently throughout the book.

15. For an excellent documentary chronicling the events of Mohawk activism during Oka see Alanis Obomsawin's critically acclaimed and award-winning documentary *Kanehsatake: 270 Years of Resistance*; see also Lewis 2006.

16. Larry Grant is Musqueam on his mother's side and Cantonese on his father's side. There is a long history of interaction and intermarriage between First Nations and Chinese people in Vancouver. Grant grew up on the Musqueam reserve and in Vancouver's Downtown Eastside and Strathcona, urban neighborhoods with large First Nations and Chinese populations. The complex histories and connections between these two cultural groups are explored in the film *Cedar and Bamboo* (2010) directed by Kamala Todd and Diana Leung.

1.The Indigenous Media Arts Group

1. *Kookum* is a Cree word for "grandmother."

2. Artist-run centers receive government funding and typically have status as nonprofit, and often charitable, organizations, generally managed by one or more staff and a board of directors made up of practicing artists. Their underlying philosophy is that artists are given creative control of their work rather than being constrained by the demands of the market (Douglas 1991).

3. Several of these long-standing artist-run centers include the grunt gallery, the Western Front, Artspeak, Or Gallery, and Video In, now known as VIVO Media Arts Centre.

4. Built on a commitment to social activism that challenges institutional art, Vivo is a Canadian artist-run center that has forged new territory in media arts since its inception in 1973. Vivo has consistently worked to push the boundaries of media art by exploring the latest technologies and has maintained a commitment to making the means of media production accessible to as many people as possible. Many of the projects produced under the auspices of Vivo have focused on using media technology in the service of social activism. For a detailed history of Vivo and its impact on Vancouver's art world see J. Abbott (2000).

5. Staff members for FNAP included Cease Wyss, Dana Claxton, Zachery Longboy, and Cleo Reece, all of whom were founding members of the Indigenous Media Arts Group.

6. Approximately 70 percent of Vancouver's Aboriginal population lives in the Downtown Eastside (DTES), one of Canada's poorest neighborhoods. Aboriginal people make up approximately 40 percent of the Downtown Eastside population and face the difficult social conditions of life in this neighborhood. The DTES has a disproportionately high

number of residents living below the poverty line (nearly 75 percent), with an annual income of only one-third of that of other Vancouver residents. For more information see Benoit and Carroll (2001) and Joseph (1999). The Vancouver Native Housing Society operates apartments in thirteen buildings designed to provide affordable housing for low-income Aboriginal individuals and families in Vancouver. These residences are located on Vancouver's Eastside around Commercial Drive, in Mount Pleasant, and in the Downtown Eastside. Rent is subsidized by the Canada Mortgage and Housing Corporation and BC Housing Management Commission and is adjusted depending on the tenant's income. Vancouver has some of the highest housing costs in Canada, and Native housing is highly sought after. Several Aboriginal community members told me that in 2003–2004 there was a two-year waiting list to get into Native housing. For more information on the Vancouver Native Housing Society see their website at http://www.vnhs.ca, accessed June 18, 2012.

7. Just after I finished my fieldwork in late August 2004, IMAG staff decided not to renew their lease in the building on Main Street and 4th Avenue and moved to a new building where they had substantially more space, including several office rooms and a large classroom for their training programs. This office facility was located in the Downtown Eastside on Pender and Abbott Streets across from a Native housing complex. IMAG staff wanted a new office site in a location more accessible to the Aboriginal community. This new office space firmly positioned IMAG within the urban Aboriginal landscape as the Downtown Eastside is marked, by Aboriginal and non-Aboriginal people, as an Aboriginal neighborhood. This new office dramatically improved office conditions, reducing the hectic nature that characterized the daily IMAG office activities during my fieldwork. IMAG stayed at this location for almost two years before relocating back to their office on Main Street when they were unable to make the higher rent payments on the lease in the building on the Downtown Eastside.

8. The mobilization of community members to help create Aboriginal productions has been discussed extensively in regard to the Igloolik Isuma videos and feature films. Within the Igloolik productions the community is mobilized to collectively create the props, costumes, and backdrop as well as serve as actors in videos that re-create traditional stories and cultural practices. Video production there serves as

vital form of enacting and remembering cultural memory and Inuit cultural practices. For more information on Igloolik Isuma see Berger (1995); Evans (2008); Fleming (1996); Ginsburg (2002); and the Igloolik Isuma Productions website at http://www.isuma.tv/isuma-productions, accessed June 18, 2012.

9. The Canada Council for the Arts, the primary source of government funding for artists in Canada, defines *media arts* as "works in film, video, audio or new media. Film and video productions in all styles, including documentary, experimental, drama and animation, are accepted. 'Audio' refers to sound recording to create sound-scapes, sound installations and sound sculptures. Audio also refers to documentary, narrative, conceptual and live works for radio." Canada Council for the Arts, "Media Arts," accessed June 18, 2012, http://www.canadacouncil.ca.

10. The Canada Council for the Arts defines *new media* as "works that use multimedia, computers, or communications or information technologies for creative expression."

11. The ability to make do with limited material conditions is also characteristic of reservation life, a key symbol of which is the "rez car," notorious for functioning with missing parts, duct tape holding doors together, brakes that might not work, or, as in a scene from *Smoke Signals* (1998), a car that only drives in reverse. "Rez cars" are the source of much laughter, joking, and shared cultural experience between Native people.

12. The term *community* is used to discuss a wide range of social and identity formations, from analyzing the way in which media such as newspapers have affected national identity and "imagined communities" (Anderson 1991) to the impact of transnational processes on the formation of diaspora communities (Clifford 1997; Gilroy 1993; Glick-Schiller, Blanc and Basch 1993; Hall 1990; J. Roth 2002; Siu 2005) to the use of shared social identity for claims to cultural citizenship (Flores and Benmayor 1997; Ong 1996; Rosaldo 1994; Torruellas et al. 1991) and the impact of language in developing speech communities (Gumperz 1968; Hymes 1962; Morgan 1992; Zentella 1997). The category *community* has also been critiqued for glossing over the debates, dissension, and difference within a community leading to a romanticized image of a harmonious, homogenous social group. I acknowledge that this is an imperfect term; however, it is a term that is used frequently

in the discourse of Aboriginal filmmakers in Vancouver to mark their media practice as one that is firmly grounded in Aboriginal social life.

13. The approximate total Métis population in Canada in 2006 was 389,000 (Statistics Canada 2006). Métis was the category of Aboriginal peoples with the largest percentage of increase between 1996 and 2001 with a 43 percent increase (Statistics Canada 2001). This has been attributed to the increasing willingness of people to self-identify as Métis. Statisticians and scholars have also noted similar increases in Native ethnic identification across the United States and Canada (Nagel 1997).

14. Métis people sometimes bear the brunt of joking from members of the Aboriginal community, as somehow not "authentic" or as "wannabes" who don't fit easily within the category *Aboriginal*. In many informal contexts within and outside IMAG I heard people joke about how anyone can obtain a Métis card—identity cards issues by the provincial Métis Councils, which are part of the Métis National Council—and joke about how light-skinned Métis people are. This is not to say that all Métis people visibly appear light-skinned; just as there is a tremendous range of appearances among Aboriginal people, there is also a range of "looks" among Métis people. However, the joking that I heard was directed toward light-skinned Métis people. It is notable that the conversations in which this discussion around Métis identity came up was raised in a joking register. This isn't to say that there isn't any serious commentary underlying these jokes, and indeed, as scholars have observed, in many Native communities it is a common practice to use humor as a way to deflect moments of internal tension, in addition to a means of entertainment and a tactic of survival in the face of difficult times (Basso 1979; Lincoln 1993; Ryan 1999). When I later asked individuals to reflect on these joking practices about the Métis, some said that it stemmed from resentment that Métis people don't acknowledge the privilege that comes with being lighter-skinned and that they don't fully embrace their Aboriginal heritage by identifying as Métis instead of Aboriginal.

15. Scholars have also addressed similar issues in the United States by examining internal debates around blood quantum, skin color, and enrollment in the Cherokee Nation in Oklahoma (Sturm 2002) and in discussion of how individuals with American Indian and African American ancestry have "confounded the color line" by contesting

racial boundaries while creating unique hybrid cultural identities and communities (Brooks 2002).

16. This concern about how to make art galleries and museums comfortable spaces for Native people was a prominent topic of discussion at a conference at the Banff Centre for the Arts in November 2003 entitled "Making a Noise! Aboriginal Perspectives on Art, Art History, Critical Writing and Community." This conference brought together international indigenous artists and curators for a three-day symposium to discuss the challenges, obstacles, and achievements in curating Aboriginal art within mainstream and community contexts. Much of the discussion centered on how to create Aboriginal spaces within the "white cube" (Claxton 2007) of the Western art gallery and museum space as well as how to draw Aboriginal audience members to art exhibits and exhibit openings. There seemed to be a theme among the discussion by conference participants that food, music, and following cultural protocol (e.g., inviting local singers to sing an honor song or inviting local traditional leaders or spiritual leaders to welcome guests) were key components to making the gallery space an Aboriginal space and creating a welcoming environment for Aboriginal audiences. For more information on this conference see Martin (2005).

17. The concern about art galleries and museums being off-putting, and even overtly racist, to Aboriginal people was echoed in my interviews with Aboriginal artists who exhibit their work in these spaces and who want to see community members feel comfortable enough to go to a gallery opening to see their exhibit. There was a consensus among the Aboriginal artists whom I interviewed that the grunt gallery has maintained strong relationships with Aboriginal community members and through its consistent exhibition of Aboriginal art is one of the few art gallery spaces in Vancouver in which Aboriginal people regularly attend exhibits and opening events and, more importantly, feel welcome and comfortable there.

18. The Chief Simon Baker Room is a smaller room adjacent to the Friendship Centre gymnasium that is often used for cultural and ceremonial events.

19. There is a growing circuit of Native film festivals in the United States and Canada as well as around the world that showcase indigenous media works. Festivals such as the Dreamspeakers Festival in Edmonton, the imagineNATIVE Film and Media Arts Festival in Toronto, the Terres

en Vue/Land InSights First Peoples Festival in Montreal, the Native American Film and Video Festival in New York City, the American Indian Film Festival in San Francisco, the Sundance Institute's Native and Indigenous Institute at the Sundance Film Festival, the Message Sticks Festival in Australia, National Geographic's All Roads Festival, and the Wairoa Maori Film Festival in New Zealand are a few examples of international indigenous film festivals that showcase the work of indigenous filmmakers and are key "hubs" where indigenous filmmakers can network and collaborate.

20. This filmmaker asked to remain anonymous, and this wish has been honored throughout the book.

2. Cultural Policy and Aboriginal Media

1. Early films, such as *Wonders of Canada* (1906), cinematically constructed the Canadian landscape as a resource over which white Canadians exert mastery while Aboriginal people were visually represented as "entertaining spectacles, exotica, that must be traversed, denigrated and manipulated to further the ends of empire" (Gittings 2002, 8). Early ethnographic films of Canada's Aboriginal communities also worked to support the idea of Aboriginal people as "vanishing," thus sustaining the dominant narrative of Canadian expansion and colonization (R. Morris 1994).

2. In 1918 Canada became the first federal government in the world to create a state-sponsored film production unit with the creation of the Canadian Government Motion Picture Bureau (CGMPB). The CGMPB was not in the feature film entertainment industry but primarily produced short films to promote Canadian trade (Gittings 2002).

3. It is important to acknowledge that the development of the National Film Board of Canada with the aim to use film to strengthen a sense of Canadian national identity was occurring during the seminal years of World War II and presumably was also intended to help solidify a sense of nationalism during the war. Many thanks to Karen Blu for pointing out this observation to me.

4. Studio D was critiqued for creating essentialist constructions of gender that subsumed diversity of sexuality, race, ethnicity, and class under monolithic representations of gender. In response to critiques by women of color the NFB created the New Initiatives in Film Programme that restructured Studio D by making representations of the ethnic and

racial diversity of women's culture in Canada a major component of the studio's production. Many Aboriginal women were trained through this initiative, and films highlighting the contributions of Aboriginal women such as *Women in the Shadows* (1991) and *Keepers of the Fire* (1994) were produced through this Studio D initiative. Unfortunately the NFB suffered budget cuts that contributed to the closing of Studio D in 1996 (Gittings 2002).

5. The height of Canadian collusion with American film interests came in 1948 when the Canadian government agreed to the Motion Picture Association of America's "Canadian Cooperation Project," pledging to do nothing to interfere with the dominance of American features on Canadian screens, including a guarantee that it would provide no federal support for a feature film industry (Feldman 1996). The Canadian Cooperation Project lasted until 1958 and further entrenched the dominance of American film within Canada. During this time the Canadian government did not implement legislation protecting the development of a Canadian feature film industry and instead chose to support film production for the purposes of education and the promotion of trade and immigration (P. Morris 1978). While many theorists argue that American film dominance amounted to media imperialism by working to limit the development of a Canadian feature film industry (Dorland 1998; Pendakur 1990), other scholars have argued that the Canadian government was complicit in creating legislation that further encouraged American film domination in Canada as it served Canadian business interests (Magder 1993).

6. In the 1970s Canada implemented tax shelters and Canadian content requirements to help create distribution venues for Canadian features, which by the 1970s and 1980s increasingly came in the form of television production. In 1984 the CFDC was renamed Telefilm Canada in response to the emergence of television production as a central venue for Canadian media production. In 1986 Telefilm created a Feature Film Fund that allocated $65 million to support the work of Canadian filmmakers, although limited distribution has continued to restrict the number of Canadian screens showing Canadian films (Feldman 1996).

7. Motion Picture Association of America, 2010, "Theatrical Market Statistics," accessed June 18, 2012, http://www.mpaa.org/policy/industry.

8. For more information on the specificities of CanCon legislation

see CRTC, "Canadian Content," 2012, accessed June 18, 2012, http://www.crtc.gc.ca/eng/cancon.htm.

9. Actors and activists supporting Canada's independent film and television industry note the difficulty of accessing Canadian media by Canadian audiences because of the dominance of American media on Canadian screens. The average Canadian feature film remains on screen in Canadian theaters for one week. Recognizing the importance of the first weekend box-office revenues in encouraging theater owners to extend a film's screening for longer than one week, organizations such as the First Weekend Club seek to get "bums in seats" by encouraging members to attend first weekend screenings of Canadian films. Writing about the First Weekend Club in Vancouver, writer Robert Alstead explains, "As the First Weekend Club's slogan, 'See it first, make it last' implies, the aim of the non-profit organization is to get as many people out to see Canadian films on the critical first weekend so the movies stay on theatre screens for a longer period of time" (Alstead 2004). Lobbying efforts by actors such as Sarah Polley and organizations such as the First Weekend Club seek to maintain Canadian content on Canadian screens and provide support for Canada's film and television industry. (CTV News Staff, "Sarah Polley Has Ideas to Save Canada's Film Industry," April 6, 2005, accessed June 18, 2012, http://www.ctv.ca/CTVNews/Entertainment/20050406/polley_films050406/.

10. National Museum of the American Indian, "Festival Bulletins: Canadian Films Shine in the 2011 Native American Film and Video Festival Lineup," 2011, accessed June 28, 2012, http://nativenetworks.si.edu/nafvf/press.aspx.

11. Challenge for Change quarterly newsletters distributed between 1968 and 1975 kept readers informed about the various film projects being produced under this program. For a thorough history of NFB support for Aboriginal media through the Challenge for Change program see the seminal scholarship of Michelle Stewart (2007) on the Indian Film Crews and the NFB's support for Aboriginal media under the Challenge for Change program, as well as her dissertation, "Sovereign Visions: Native North American Documentary" (2001).

12. Films such as *The Things I Cannot Change* (1967), the *Fogo Island Community Films* (1967–1969), *Up Against the System* (1969), *Encounter at Kwacha House* (1967), and *God Help the Man Who Would Part with His Land* (1971) examined the dynamics of communities experiencing

conflicts with government bureaucracy and the tremendous socioeconomic impact of unemployment and industrialization in rural areas. These films sought to use film to change mainstream Canadian society's attitudes toward disadvantaged communities as well as affect government services for these communities.

13. The Société Nouvelle was the French counterpart to the Challenge for Change program at the NFB. Société Nouvelle films explored social conditions and concerns among Quebecois communities and also played a role in helping to organize political action for Quebecois rights, which eventually culminated in the "Quiet Revolution" in Quebec in the late 1960s and early 1970s, leading to reform for French language rights in Canada.

14. I encourage readers to refer to *Challenge for Change: Activist Documentary at the National Film Board of Canada* (Waugh, Baker, and Winton 2010), the first book devoted exclusively to the history of the Challenge for Change program and its impact at the National Film Board of Canada as well as on Canadian filmmaking more generally. This innovative book combines archival materials, interviews with filmmakers and NFB staff, and scholarship about the Challenge for Change program and specific films produced as part of this extraordinary initiative.

15. The NFB has sought to stay ahead of the curve in new innovations in filmmaking and digital technologies and in 2004 created an online media project, CitizenShift, which was inspired by the spirit of the Challenge for Change program. "CitizenShift is a multimedia platform dedicated to media for social change." See the CitizenShift website at http://citizenshift.org/about, accessed June 18, 2012. This website makes use of the incredibly robust NFB archive of films related to social justice issues but also allows users to respond via blogging, commentary, and uploading of content.

16. In 2011 Prime Minister Stephen Harper, without consultation with First Nations political leaders, changed the name of the Department of Indian and Northern Affairs Canada to the Department of Aboriginal Affairs and Northern Development Canada. This name change was justified by Harper's administration as an effort to be more inclusive to all the Aboriginal peoples—First Nations, Métis, and Inuit. However, throughout the majority of my research and in these archival materials the name was the Department of Indian and Northern Affairs; therefore that is the name that appears throughout this book.

17. There seems to have been a misunderstanding between the Company of Young Canadians and the NFB in regard to the funding of the Indian Film Crew. Although the NFB was under the impression that the CYC would cover most of the expenses involved, the CYC thought that the NFB would be covering the living expenses of the filmmakers (Memo to NFB, November 14, 1968, from CYC, NFB archives, Indian Film Crew box, Montreal). This confusion over money and financial support for the members of the Indian Film Crew led one crew member, Noel Starblanket (Cree) to assert: "the most discouraging limitation to the Indian crew is our dissatisfaction about the present set-up—the CYC-NFB arrangement. There is discontent about the lack of funds for location expenses, though we are becoming semi-professional filmmakers we exist on the barest of living expenses" (Starblanket 1968, 11). Starblanket later quit the Indian Film Crew in 1970, citing his frustration at the financial limitations for the Indian Film Crew and the confused arrangement with the CYC. In his resignation letter he cited an inequity in funding for the Indian Film Crew, noting that they only received $3,000 per year while white counterparts at the NFB made $10,000, $15,000, and even $20,000 a year. He also asserted that the NFB "owed to the Indian people of this country a personal and moral obligation at least, if not, financial commitment so that they themselves can realize their ends in this field" (Noel Starblanket, letter to George Stoney, May 20, 1970, p. 2, NFB archives, Indian Film Crew box). This dissatisfaction with the often significantly less money allotted to Aboriginal filmmakers than their white counterparts remains a frustration and concern of Aboriginal filmmakers working with the NFB today.

18. The choice of who would participate in the Indian Film Crew was made by the Department of Indian and Northern Affairs. The individuals came from different regions, band affiliations, and community experiences, causing some tension among the group (G. Evans 1991).

19. Letter from J. B. Bergevin to NFB, November 23, 1970, NFB archives, Indian Film Crew box.

20. Other examples of government-sponsored initiatives to integrate Aboriginal people into the national economy and job market include government-sponsored art programs in Aboriginal communities in Australia (Myers 2002) and the Indian Arts and Crafts Board programs in the United States (Gritton 2000).

21. The Indian Film Crew and the Indian Film Training Program initiatives were firmly rooted in Aboriginal political activism, and all of the members of the IFC were members of an early Native rights organization, the Protest Alliance Against Native Extermination (PANE). Willie Dunn (Mi'kmaq), an IFC participant, was a founding member of the Native Alliance for Red Power (NARP). The members of the Indian Film Crew and Indian Film Training Program maintained their involvement in Aboriginal activism and politics, with several members becoming chiefs of their reserves and holding leadership positions within national Aboriginal organizations. Mike Mitchell (Mohawk) and Noel Starblanket (Cree) both went on to become chiefs of their reserves, and Starblanket served as National Chief for the Assembly of First Nations from 1976 to 1980 after becoming the youngest elected chief in Canada in 1971 at the age of twenty-four. Barbara Wilson (Haida) became a cultural leader in her community as well as a cultural resources manager where she continues to use video production in her cultural work. Willie Dunn won several international awards for *The Ballad of Crowfoot* (1971) and has spent the last thirty years using his career as a folk musician to raise awareness about Aboriginal history, languages, and contemporary issues.

22. Footage from the AIM standoff at Wounded Knee in 1973 also traveled across the border into Canada, where it was screened for local Aboriginal activists and filmmakers at the Video In artist-run center in Vancouver (Claxton 2005, 18).

23. Indian Film Studio Proposal by Mike Mitchell, 1973, NFB archives, Indian Film Training Program box.

24. Studio One was originally named Studio I for indigenous but was later renamed Studio One.

25. The Oka crisis was a seventy-eight-day standoff during the summer of 1990 when Mohawk activists created a blockade in an area of traditional Mohawk territory known as the Pines upon which the town of Oka sought to build a nine-hole golf course on a Mohawk burial ground and sacred territory. This was a seminal moment that revealed the racism and oppression facing Aboriginal communities and also instigated a strong show of Aboriginal solidarity for the Mohawk blockade across Canada and internationally. The images of tanks rolling into Mohawk territory and Canadian soldiers with guns in the faces of Mohawk activists, many of whom were women and children, had

an indelible impact in the minds of Canadians, ultimately forcing the government to reexamine its relationship with Aboriginal communities. Although this was not the first time the Canadian government had used armed force on Aboriginal protestors (see *Incident at Restigouche*, 1984 as an earlier example), it was a pivotal moment for Aboriginal people and especially for Aboriginal filmmakers, who saw the way in which this story was manipulated and misrepresented in the mainstream media, thereby reinforcing the importance of presenting Aboriginal news, stories, and events from Aboriginal perspectives. For more details on the events of Oka see the films of Alanis Obomsawin including: *Kanehsatake: 270 Years of Resistance* (1993), *Spudwrench: Kahnawake Man* (1997), *My Name is Kahentiiosta* (1995), and *Rocks at Whiskey Trench* (2000).

26. It's also important to note that the climate of the 1992 Quincentennial celebrations of the arrival of Christopher Columbus and Aboriginal protests over these celebrations influenced the NFB's creation of Studio One. "Throughout 1992, considerable attention will be brought to aboriginal issues as the year marks the 500th anniversary of Columbus' voyage to this continent . . . Studio I will undoubtedly contribute to a more balanced cinematic view of historical events than we have seen in the past" (NFB, Studio I report, 1991, p. 4, NFB archive, Studio One box). For other Aboriginal art and writing against the Quincentennial see McMaster and Martin (1992).

27. NFB, "Our People . . . Our Vision," Studio One Proposal, 1991, p. 1, NFB archive, Studio One box.

28. NFB, "Our People," pp. 2, 3.

29. A range of work was produced under Studio One, and many notable Aboriginal producers, including Loretta Todd, Gregory Coyes, Barb Cranmer, and Annie Frazier-Henry, gained experience there. Documentary films such as Barb Cranmer's *Laxwesa Wa: The Strength of the River* (1995), Loretta Todd's *Forgotten Warriors* (1996), Carol Geddes's *Picturing a People: George Johnston, Tlingit Photographer* (1997), and Gregory Coyes's *No Turning Back* (1996) were all produced in the first years of Studio One.

30. Anthropologist Faye Ginsburg has observed that the relatively small budgets for Aboriginal media production at organizations such as the National Film Board do not anticipate a feature film project from Aboriginal filmmakers, since the cost of a single feature film production

often far exceeds the total amount of money available in these funding streams. (Ginsburg 2003).

31. While Aboriginal filmmakers in the West expressed concern that a "virtual studio" would lessen the support or funding of Aboriginal media, filmmakers in the East had less direct engagement with the programs of Studio One because of its location in Edmonton. It was eastern filmmakers who advocated most strongly for the decentralization of Studio One. An Innu filmmaker from Montreal asserted: "Studio One needs regional offices. I don't see how you can produce a film from Edmonton if the director lives in this area" (Dudemaine qtd. in de Rosa 1995, 20). While Aboriginal filmmakers in the East pushed for decentralization of Studio One and the creation of a "virtual studio" under the rubric of various regional offices, filmmakers in the West saw the strong film industry in their region as one reason to keep the Studio in the West. One filmmaker even encouraged the NFB to move Studio One to Vancouver because there were so many Aboriginal producers working there (de Rosa 1995). It seems that perhaps the concerns of eastern filmmakers might have been privileged over others in the NFB's decision to dismantle Studio One. This East/West division may also be reflected more broadly in dominant Canadian society as well.

32. For instance, in 2002–2003 the NFB allocated $1 million for the Aboriginal Filmmaking Program out of a total production budget of $41 million, or approximately 2.5 percent of the total budget (Bear 2004, 29).

33. Although the AFP primarily supports documentary production, Aboriginal directors began to produce work in other genres including animation, narrative, and experimental shorts. Films produced under AFP have explored a wide array of issues and stories, including the revitalization of cultural practices in *Qatuwas: People Gathering Together* (1987), the importance of hunting to Native bush life in *Okimah* (1998), the stories of First Nations veterans in *Forgotten Warriors* (1997), a Mi'kmaq woman's exploration of her heritage in *Migmaeoi Otjiosog/ Mi'kmaq Family* (1994), First Nations women's singing traditions in *Singing Our Stories* (1998), Native sexuality in *Deep inside Clint Star* (1999), the distinctive Métis fiddling practice in *How the Fiddle Flows* (2002), and the role of First Nations women activists in *Keepers of the Fire* (1994). In 1997 the AFP produced its first drama, *Silent Tears* by Cree filmmaker and playwright Shirley Cheechoo. Annie Frazier Henry's

narrative short *Legends Sxwexwxiy'am': The Story of Siwash Rock* was produced in 1999, and the AFP supported the critically acclaimed Inuit feature film *Atanarjuat: The Fast Runner* directed by Inuk filmmaker Zacharias Kunuk in 2001.

34. As Guy Dixon noted in a *Globe and Mail* article on April 16, 2012, the National Film Board of Canada continues to face budget cuts. The 2012 Canadian federal budget resulted in another 10 percent budget cut for the NFB and for other cultural institutions such as the Canadian Broadcasting Corporation (CBC). The NFB lost $6.7 million dollars with this budget cut and planned to provide less money for filmmaker assistance programs, to produce three or four fewer large budget films per year, and to eliminate seventy-three jobs.

35. My understanding regarding funding and budgets as it relates to Canadian cultural policy and the role of Canadian cultural institutions in funding Aboriginal media is indebted to conversations with Loretta Todd and Jeff Bear, who have been instrumental in pushing for greater access to funding and resources as well as helping to change cultural policy to support Aboriginal media. I am very grateful for the time that they shared talking with me about this topic and for helping put the funding of Aboriginal media in Canada in a broader perspective. Any inaccuracies or mistakes regarding figures, budgets, or policies here are strictly my own.

36. The diversity of this work is illustrated in Shelley Niro's innovative narrative films (*Honey Moccasin*, 1998, and *It Starts with a Whisper*, 1993), Dana Claxton's powerful experimental videos (*Buffalo Bone China*, 1997, and *I Want to Know Why*, 1994) and the numerous films of renowned Abenaki filmmaker Alanis Obomsawin documenting generations of Aboriginal political activism (*Is the Crown at War with Us?*, 2002, *Rocks at Whiskey Trench*, 2000, *Kanehsatake: 270 Years of Resistance*, 1993, and *Incident at Restigouche*, 1984). The range is apparent from Gregory Coyes's unique animations for Native children's television (*Stories from the Seventh Fire*, 2002) to Barb Cranmer's documentary portraits of West Coast culture (*Gwishalaayt: The Spirit Wraps around You*, 2002, and *T'Lina: The Rendering of Wealth*, 1999) to Loretta Todd's powerful explorations of Native historical experiences erased in Canadian national narratives (*Forgotten Warriors*, 1997, and *The Learning Path*, 1991) to Aboriginal feature films by Shirley Cheechoo (*Bearwalker*, 2000) and Zacharias Kunuk (*Atanarjuat: The Fast Runner*, 2001) and

the Native programming produced for APTN (*Buffalo Tracks*, *Contact*, *The Seventh Generation*, *Finding Our Talk*, *Tansi! Nehiyawetan: Let's Speak Cree!*, and *Blackstone*).

37. The Communications Department of the Union of B.C. Indian Chiefs has an extensive archival collection that includes photographs, newsletters, audio and video recordings of meetings, negotiations, and testimonies as well as videos such as *The Land Is the Culture* (1975) produced by the UBCIC to support Aboriginal land claims in British Columbia.

38. When British Columbia joined Canada under confederation in 1871, there were only fourteen treaties signed between First Nations on Vancouver Island and the British Crown, while the rest of the province was left unresolved.

39. Many thanks to Amanda Minks for pointing out this clarification in an earlier draft of this chapter.

3. Aboriginal Diversity On-Screen

1. For an excellent film that explores the impact of the "Hollywood Indian" see Neil Diamond's (Cree) film *Reel Injun* (2009).

2. *Two-spirit* is a term that has come into use by Native activists in the last twenty-five years to refer to gay, lesbian, bisexual, and transgendered identity. It is an alternative term to *berdache*, an anthropological term referencing the third gender category traditionally found in some Native societies. Many two-spirit people articulate a narrative of acceptance of gay and lesbian individuals within Native communities prior to colonization and attribute homophobia in Native communities today to the legacy of colonization. However, some individuals with whom I worked in Vancouver reject the term *two-spirit* because they feel that this is a romanticized rewriting of history. Those individuals prefer to use the term *queer* in their self-identification. For more information on two-spirit, berdache, and alternative gender categories in Native communities see Gilley (2006); Jacobs, Thomas, and Lang (2007); and Roscoe (1992).

3. The Canadian Broadcasting Corporation, Canada's premier national news network, employs only a handful of Aboriginal reporters and researchers and only one Aboriginal journalist for *The National*, CBC's nightly national news program. These examples indicate that diversity initiatives and panels addressing diversity needs within the

media industry have yet to make an impact on media institutional structures.

4. CTV is one of the main Canadian television broadcasters operating nationally throughout Canada. Through local channels throughout Canada CTV broadcasts news, sports, and entertainment programming. CTV Inc. is owned by Bell Media, a prominent Canadian multimedia company (www.ctv.ca).

5. For an in-depth discussion of APTN and it impact on Aboriginal media production in Canada see Hafsteinsson and Bredin (2010).

6. APTN has collaborated with other indigenous broadcasting efforts, most recently supporting Maori filmmakers and activists successfully launching Maori TV in New Zealand in spring 2004 (Ginsburg and Strickland 2004). For information on international indigenous broadcasting see Auferheide (1995); Batty (1993); Ginsburg (1993, 1994); Himpele (2004, 2008); Molnar and Meadows (2001); Wilson and Stewart (2008); and Wortham (2004).

7. The terms *northern* and *southern* are used in Canada to distinguish the Canadian Arctic and northern territories from the southern provinces. People living in northern areas use the term *southern* in reference to dominant Canadian society. There have been some tensions between northern and southern Aboriginal producers largely as a result of competition over broadcasting resources as well as perceived cultural differences. Much of the early history of Aboriginal broadcasting was produced in the North among Inuit and northern Aboriginal producers, and this remains reflected in the large amount of northern programming on the Aboriginal Peoples Television Network. For an excellent history of the development of Aboriginal broadcasting in Canada see L. Roth (2005) and Alia (1999).

8. Aboriginal Peoples Television Network, "Audience," 2011, accessed June 18, 2012, http://www.aptn.ca/corporate/producers/audience.php.

9. *Contact* was an hour-long current affairs program that was broadcast on APTN for several seasons. It included Aboriginal leaders and experts talking about key, and often controversial, current events and issues. The show also featured a call-in portion during which Aboriginal members from around Canada could phone in and express their opinions and perspectives on a topic. The setup was similar to the popular radio program *Native America Calling*, formerly hosted by Harlan McKosato (Sac and Fox) in the United States.

10. I am using the term *Métis* here to refer specifically to descendants of primarily Cree, Anishinaabe, or Saulteaux and French, Scottish, or Irish fur traders. The term *Métis* historically referred to people of these heritages residing in the Red River area of Manitoba. It is important to note that not all people who have mixed-blood Native ancestry are Métis, but that Métis refers to a distinctive group descended from the intermarriage between primarily Native women and European fur traders and that the Métis maintain a distinctive language, heritage, and cultural practices. The following is the legal definition of Métis used by the Métis National Council: "Métis means a person who self-identifies as Métis, is of historic Métis Nation Ancestry, is distinct from other Aboriginal Peoples and is accepted by the Métis Nation." Métis National Council, "Who Are the Métis?" accessed January 21, 2013, http://www.metisnation.ca.

11. For an in-depth ethnography of the impact of Canadian policy—particularly the gendered discrimination within the Indian Act—on the disenfranchisement and dispossession of mixed-blood Native people and Métis people, see Lawrence (2004).

12. For films that address family silence about Native and Métis heritage, the politics of skin color, and reclamations of this heritage by the filmmaker see *Women in the Shadows* (1991) by Christine Welsh (Métis), *Mémère Métisse/My Métis Grandmother* (2009) by Janelle Wookey (Métis), and *Tkaronto* (2009) and *Boxed In* (2009) by Shane Belcourt (Métis).

13. This is particular not only to mixed-blood Aboriginal and Métis individuals but also to other multiracial people who discuss their experiences. For more information on mixed-race identity see Brooks (2002); Ifekwunigwe (1999); Mahtani (2002); Parker and Song (2001); Root (1992); and Thompson and Tyagi (1996).

14. For an excellent anthropological analysis of the racial and ethnic casting politics in the fashion industry see Sadre-Orafai (2008, 2010).

15. The feature film *Tkaronto* (2009) by Shane Belcourt (Métis) and the film *Mémère Métisse/My Métis Grandmother* (2009) by Janelle Wookey (Métis) are more recent examples.

16. There is a sizeable body of anthropological literature on two-spirit traditions in Native communities including berdache, the "Zuni man-woman," and winkte traditions. For more information see Jacobs, Thomas, and Lang (1997) and Roscoe (1992).

17. For an in-depth ethnographic analysis of two-spirit activism in Oklahoma and Colorado see Gilley (2006).

18. There is a relatively large number of Aboriginal experimental videos that address two-spirit identity, particularly the work of Thirza Cuthand (Cree) and Zachery Longboy (Dene). Cuthand's film *Helpless Maiden Makes an "I" Statement* (2000) examines bondage, domination, and subordination between lesbian partners, while her film *Working Baby Dyke Theory* (1997) explores the intergenerational aspects of lesbian relationships and the disempowerment of dyke youth in lesbian culture. In Longboy's film *Water into Fire* (1994) the filmmaker "outs himself" as a "First Nations fag" and explores his identity and HIV status.

4. Building Community Off-Screen

1. For key scholarship examining the impact of identity legislation see Lawrence (2004) and Sturm (2002). Some Native communities have also internalized these systems of identity legislation. See Tracey Deer's insightful film *Club Native* (2008) for an extensive discussion about the individual, family, and community impacts of the identity legislation in the Kahnawake Mohawk Nation.

2. CBC News, "A History of Residential Schools in Canada," 2011, accessed June 18, 2012, http://www.cbc.ca/news/canada/story/2008/05/16/f-faqs-residential-schools.html

3. There was considerable activism around reparations for residential school survivors as well as numerous healing organizations for survivors. One filmmaker remarked how there's a "healing industry" now, with some individuals feeling that these healing organizations are making money off the trauma of residential school survivors.

4. For Aboriginal videos addressing the sensitive issue of residential schools see *A Century of Genocide in the Americas: The Residential School Experience* (2002), which chronicles the impact of sexual and physical abuse that children faced in residential schools; *Stolen Spirits* (2005), a half-hour documentary that also addresses the lasting legacy of residential schools in Aboriginal communities; and *The Learning Path* (1991), a documentary that addresses the impact of residential schools on Aboriginal learning and education.

5. CTV News, "Text of Stephen Harper's Residential Schools Apology," June 11, 2008, accessed June 18, 2012, http://www.ctvnews.ca/text-of-stephen-harper-s-residential-schools-apology-1.301820.

6. Truth and Reconciliation Commission of Canada, "FAQs," 2011, accessed June 18, 2012, http://www.trc.ca/websites/trcinstitution/index.php?p=10.

7. Under this financial settlement individual residential school survivors are eligible to seek compensation funds called "common experience payments" for $10,000 for the first year they attended school, plus $3,000 for each subsequent year (CBC News, "History of Residential Schools").

8. CBC News, "History of Residential Schools."

9. The Genie Awards are awarded annually by the Academy of Canadian Cinema and Television to recognize outstanding work in Canadian cinema and are analogous to the Oscars awarded by the Academy of Motion Pictures Arts and Sciences in the United States.

10. Another disruption in Aboriginal family structure was the adoption of Aboriginal children into non-Aboriginal families. The Child Welfare Department often removed Aboriginal children from their homes, placing them in the foster care system and disconnecting them from their families and communities of origin. In what was known colloquially as the "Sixties Scoop," thousands of children were removed from their Native homes and placed up for adoption or put into the foster care system from the 1960s until the early 1980s. Today legislation regarding Aboriginal child welfare varies from province to province, with a priority on keeping Aboriginal children within Aboriginal communities. If children have to be removed from their homes, efforts are made to keep the children in homes of extended family members or community members. For a thorough discussion of the impact of Native adoption into non-Native families see Fournier and Crey (1998). For Aboriginal media representations of this issue see *Richard Cardinal: Cry from the Diary of a Métis Child* (1986) by Alanis Obomsawin, which profiled Richard Cardinal, a young Métis teenager who committed suicide after being moved to twenty-eight different foster care homes over the course of fifteen years. This video initiated changes in the child welfare system's policy regarding Aboriginal cases, as the Alberta provincial government enacted legislation to improve this system. Another documentary about the effects of adoption is Annie Frazier Henry's *To Return: The John Walkus Story* (2000), which follows a young man as he returns to his home community years after his adoption. He reconnects with his community and begins to learn

the Kwak'wala language and cultural practices while becoming an apprentice carver.

11. Prior to participating in this training program Shuquaya worked primarily in mainstream theater and independent film in Vancouver, but since completing the Capilano College program she has worked predominantly in Aboriginal media. She directed *People of the River* (2002), an award-winning short documentary about Sto:lo fishing rights, worked as an editor's assistant on the APTN program *Ravens and Eagles*, worked as a scriptwriter for APTN's *ArtZone*, and served as the festival coordinator for the 2004 IMAGeNation Film Festival. Shuquaya has recently become more involved with her home community and is in the process of developing a short narrative script in collaboration with her father based on a traditional Tutchone story that she plans to film in the Yukon.

12. Minifie is a media artist, dancer, filmmaker, and curator and has created several video installation pieces. She produced *Connected by Innate Rhythm* (2003), a video installation piece exploring connections between traditional Aboriginal dance and contemporary forms of Aboriginal dance, hip-hop dance in particular. A 2004 untitled live performance/experimental video piece addressed the residential school experience, combining archival footage from residential schools with a live electronic soundtrack created by Ryan Mitchell-Morrison. Minifie directed an experimental dance film, *Geeka* (2007), about water loss and environmental damage on Aboriginal lands, and was the producer for the sci-fi short *ʔEʔAnx: The Cave* (2009) and the short dance caper *The Heist* (2010). In 2005 Minifie left Vancouver and returned to live in Prince Rupert to be closer to her traditional territory, where she worked as a radio journalist for two years. She then moved to Santa Fe, New Mexico, where she was a student at the Institute for American Indian Arts.

13. The strong role of family in Aboriginal media is illustrated by Zoe Hopkins (Heiltsuk/Mohawk), whose production company is named Blanket Dance Productions in honor of her mother, who held blanket dances in Bella Bella to raise money for her production company. In describing the way in which her family has supported her filmmaking career, Hopkins remarked: "My mom was constantly raising money for my production company so I could start my business. I named my production company Blanket Dance Productions because my mom arranged to have two blanket dances for me in Bella Bella in which we raised almost $2000 for my business costs and start-up."

14. This is not to say that these social relationships or kin ties are always positive. While it is inappropriate to reveal details here, there are examples of the bonds of kinship forged through media production that do not last or that last for awhile and then are severed, which is very painful for all those involved. Additionally, instead of functioning as a form of inclusion, sometimes these social networks or kin ties can be perceived as excluding certain individuals, in which case these ties may be perceived by those on the outside as cliques. The bonds of kinship in Aboriginal communities, as in all communities, are complex and complicated. As anthropologist Elizabeth Chin astutely points out—kinship ties can bind social worlds together, but they can also cut and chafe (Chin 2001, 5–6).

15. There is a common narrative of "being on a journey" that generally means talking about the process of reconnecting with Aboriginal cultural traditions or spiritual knowledge. It is also used to talk about the "healing process" that can encompass addressing traumatic events in one's family or personal history and coming to terms with the grief and trauma of being disconnected from a cultural heritage and Aboriginal community as a result of colonial practices such as residential schools, the foster care system, or adoption of Native children into non-Native families. This is also linked to the intertribal spiritual discourse of being "on the Red Road," which is connected to the Native American Church.

16. Other films made in the United States with this theme include *Kinaaldá: Navajo Rite of Passage* (2000), a documentary that traces the filmmaker's journey back to her Navajo community by following her daughter's *kinaaldá*, a woman's rite of passage ceremony that the filmmaker never had; *Backbone of the World* (1997), in which the filmmaker returns to his Blackfeet reserve in Montana to reconnect with his community by teaching video production to community members to document Blackfeet language and cultural practices; *Navajo Talking Picture* (1986), in which the filmmaker painfully struggles to establish a connection with her grandmother by returning to the Navajo reservation to make a film about her grandmother, but the older woman vehemently refuses to participate in the film; and *Vanishing Link* (2004), in which the urban filmmaker returns to her Kiowa reservation community to help document elders' life histories and Kiowa oral history on video.

17. ImagineNATIVE, Facebook post on Northern Ontario Film and Video Tour, January 2010, accessed June 18, 2012, https://www.facebook.com/imagineNATIVE?ref=ts.

18. Wapikoni Mobile, "The Universe Wapikoni," 2011, accessed June 18, 2012, http://wapikoni.tv/.

5. Cultural Protocol in Aboriginal Media

1. One measure of the prominence of experimental media in Vancouver's Aboriginal media world is the representation of experimental films in the IMAGeNation Aboriginal Film and Video Festival. Between 1998 and 2006 experimental media counted for at least 11 percent in some years and as much as 30 percent in other years of the work screened—much of it produced locally by Aboriginal filmmakers in Vancouver.

2. The term *seven generations* refers to an Aboriginal philosophy that teaches individuals to think about how their actions will impact people seven generations into the future.

3. For a detailed history of Vancouver's art scene see J. Abbott (2000) and Douglas (1991).

4. Some of Claxton's most prominent videos include *I Want to Know Why* (1994), an experimental video that explores her great-grandmother's journey into Canada; *The People Dance* (2001), examining the importance of dance within Lakota cultural life; *The Red Paper* (1996), a critique of Canadian colonization and relationships with Aboriginal peoples; *Tree of Consumption* (1994), a look at the environmental impacts of consumerism; *Buffalo Bone China* (1997), an interrogation of the colonial practice of hunting buffalo, sacred to the Lakota way of life, to make bone china; *The Hill* (2004), an exploration of the tricky entanglements between Aboriginal people and the Canadian government; and *Her Sugar Is?* (2009), a quirky look at the racial and sexual politics of the appropriation of Indian iconography by burlesque dancers in the 1930s and 1940s.

5. Cultural protocol often enters the filmmaking process at the earliest stage as a filmmaker decides which stories are appropriate or inappropriate to be told. Leena Minifie articulated this in regard to her discomfort making a documentary about her reserve because she was not raised there, and she wants to ensure that she follows protocol by not filming stories that she doesn't have rights to tell. In an interview one evening at her home she explained: "A lot of times I don't feel like

I have the authority to talk about my community because I'm not from there officially so politically I can't really say stuff that's happening back there. I feel like I really need to pay respect and honor and get to know the community before I'm able to tell those stories or to choose somebody else who's already in the communities to tell those stories." Minifie's concern to respect her community's protocol of restrictions around ownership and authority over stories is a common concern across many artistic and cultural domains in Aboriginal communities on the West Coast resulting from the cultural system of ownership rights over stories, designs, ritual knowledge, and art based on family lineage, cultural standing, and inheritance. Minifie follows this protocol by being careful not to overstep any boundaries by telling stories through media that she might not have the authority to tell.

6. Visual Sovereignty in Aboriginal Media

1. In my work with Aboriginal filmmakers in Vancouver I heard the phrase "in a good way" used colloquially, particularly by younger filmmakers, to reference the process of following spiritual teachings and being respectful of cultural traditions and the complex processes through which indigenous cultural protocols are integrated into their filmmaking practice. Helen Haig-Brown articulates her philosophy behind her media practice as being integrated with cultural protocols, explaining, "One of the things I usually do with actors and people I'm working with in general is that we usually start off with a prayer, and smudging and ask for guidance and support and help and for us to remain open, for us to work in a good way, with the stories, with the land and with each other."

2. While I cannot go into great length here about the intercultural on-set production experience, it is important to recognize that cultural differences between the filmmaker and the non-Native camera crew and producers were navigated throughout the production process on *The Cave*. This sometimes raised tensions on set, but at other times resulted in a rich dialogue and cultural exchange during social interactions on set. Helen Haig-Brown describes her practice as beginning with ceremony, noting: "Ceremony is a big part of my process. When things are blocked or aren't well I know when they're not good, I know when something's wrong and six months will go by, I don't care about deadlines. It's important that you're doing it in a good way and respectfully and

that you do ceremony around that stuff." This emphasis on ceremony was evident throughout the production process from the presence of elders and spiritual leaders on set to smudging the equipment and production crew to protocols of honoring the land as the production crew and actors camped out on set in the Nemiah Valley. Haig-Brown recalled: "Where we had camped out we were by two old, old graves, so that made me a little concerned. And we have beliefs and certain omens, there were dead birds at different parts of our set and so we had those removed and we had everybody smudged. It was a hilarious process to see because some people were not Native and are from the fast, busy world of the city and the busy world of the film world. They (members of the non-Native film world) use their stress in those times to machine through things. For me in those moments, I'm trying to practice ways that we don't machine through, we stop for a moment and do some caretaking. So one of the women who was on set who had quite a bit of spiritual teaching, I just had her go and smudge people down, one on one in the middle of their job. With a couple of people she had to be like, "No stop, take your sunglasses off, breathe, close your eyes," because they were in the zone of getting this done. So it was neat to watch her almost forcibly make people slow down and take this time."

3. This is an interesting text panel because the opening two minutes of the film include a voiceover that is in both Cree and English. The refusal to recognize English as a language in the text panel may be a political statement in which Burton critiques the historical legacy of the Canadian government's attempt to eradicate Aboriginal languages while overturning the position of power that the English language typically holds. Many thanks to Eleana Kim for making this observation to me.

4. I want to acknowledge the talented audio engineer D'Arcy O'Connor (Wiimpatja), who designed the audio for both *Nikamowin* and *ʔEʔAnx: The Cave*. O'Connor has worked on many Aboriginal productions in Vancouver and was involved with the Indigenous Media Arts Group Professional Development Training Program in 2005 and also with Loretta Todd's Aboriginal Media Lab. The sound design in both these films is extraordinary and deserves a much more in-depth discussion than I am able to focus on here.

5. Isuma TV, "Kevin Burton, Cree Filmmaker," 2009, accessed June 18, 2012, http://www.isuma.tv/hi/en/isumatv-interviews/kevin-burton -cree-filmmaker.

6. It is interesting to note that in many ways the Embargo film collective projects reproduced national differences in funding sources for the filmmakers. The three filmmakers from Canada—Zoe Hopkins (Heiltsuk/Mohawk), Lisa Jackson (Anishinaabe), and Helen Haig-Brown (Tsilhqot'in)—had the opportunity to apply for and ultimately received additional funds from the NFB, Canada Council for the Arts, and, in one case, the British Columbia Arts Council. The filmmakers working in the United States, lacking analogous venues to which to apply for funding, utilized just the $7,000 grant from imagineNATIVE. For additional analysis of the political economy and cultural policy impacting indigenous media and the national contexts in which they are produced see Bear (2004); Dowell (2006a); Stewart (2007); Smith (2008); and Wilson and Stewart (2008).

7. While there are many variations of this story within the repertoire of Tsilhqot'in oral tradition, most of the versions center around a morality lesson about the consequences of violating the cosmological order and entering the Spirit World at an inappropriate time. This is a predominant audience reading of the film *The Cave*, by Tsilhqot'in and non-Tsilhqot'in audiences as well. However, Haig-Brown raises the possibility of an alternative interpretation of the story as a morality tale about the negative consequences of violating Tsilhqot'in cultural protocols around bear hunting. In an interview she observed: "Bears are a major protocol, so hunting bears is one of the most challenging arts in the Tsilhqot'in world. There's a gazillion rules of how to bear hunt properly, you really don't want to offend a bear. I've always been interested in why nobody has read the story as though he has gone and messed up with the bear. I'm interested in why people don't think that even in my own community."

8. Several advantages of the RED camera include the high resolution level ("4K," which refers to 4,096 lines of horizontal resolution by 2,304 of vertical resolution) and full-frame sensor that matches the detail and richness of 35mm film and enables cinematographers to have greater control over focus, compact Flash and RAID recording, which eases the digital editing workflow, and the ability to use interchangeable lenses (Behar 2008, 3).

9. This story of the hunter who crawls into the cave and enters the Spirit World is a common narrative in the repertoire of Tsilhqot'in oral tradition. Anthropologist David Dinwoodie includes a full transcript

of a version he recorded with William Abraham of the Nemiah Valley in 1991 (Dinwoodie 2002, 68–72). Dinwoodie does not analyze this narrative for its representation of Tsilhqot'in cosmological understandings of the Spirit World but instead focuses on a textual and contextual analysis of the particular performance of this mythical narrative by William Abraham. He is particularly focused on the interplay between the narrative of the myth and the interpretive commentary that William intersperses throughout the speech event. He speculates whether this commentary was added to provide further cultural context for him as the anthropologist recording the narrative, noting the variations of this story in his recording of it versus the original version he overheard in a conversation between William and Erving, another community member. Dinwoodie speculates about William's commentary, noting, "He then fills in background information regarding the nature of those times, perhaps for the benefit of the incompletely socialized anthropologist: "they ate only bear in this area, they hunted for bear with two dogs. . . . They brought them for chasing the bears" (Dinwoodie 2002, 72). However, in an interview Helen Haig-Brown provides an alternative interpretation of the inclusion of the detail about Gwetsilh in the audio recording with which she opens her film, noting the way in which this *situates* Tsilhqot'in viewers and listeners within a particular place, Gwetsilh, in Tsilhqot'in territory, a community that Tsilhqot'in viewers and listeners will immediately recognize as a place that traditionally relied on bear hunting for subsistence. She observed: "It set a great context because it talked about the love of bear hunting and that's what the people mostly ate at Gwetsilh, which is one of our areas in Tsilhqot'in territory. I just loved that it really set a location, probably not for people outside of the Chilcotin, but for people in the Tsilhqot'in Nation it really set a location of exactly where in our territory these people were from." A comparison of the transcript found in Dinwoodie's ethnography with Haig-Brown's film highlights the variation of versions of this traditional story as well as artistic choices that Haig-Brown takes in translating the story to the screen—for example, changing the presence of two dogs in the traditional story for a horse in the filmed version because of her choice to move the story from ancestral times to the 1960s to have a Tsilhqot'in cowboy as the protagonist.

10. ImagineNATIVE, "NFB/ImagineNATIVE Digital Media Project Winner Announced!" 2011, accessed June 18, 2012, http://www.imaginenative.org/newsdetails.php?id=145.

Epilogue

1. All figures listed are in Canadian dollars. Yatter Matters: Insight on Vancouver's Real Estate, "Vancouver's Average Price—Mythical," November 1, 2010, accessed June 18, 2012, http://www.yattermatters.com/2010/11/vancouver-averager-price-mythical/.

2. John Morrissy, "Sampling of Vancouver's Apartment Rentals, Canada's Most Expensive Market," *Times Colonist*, June 14, 2011, accessed June 18, 2012, summary available at http://www.immconsultant.net/Immigration-news/samplingofvancouverapartmentrentalscanadasmostexpensivemarket.

3. CBC News, "Toronto, Vancouver Most Expensive Cities in Canada," June 19, 2012, accessed January 21, 2013, http://www.cbc.ca/news/canada/story/2012/06/19/most-expensive-cities-living-costs.html; Trevor Melanson, "Canada's Most Expensive Real Estate Markets," "Blogs & Comment," *Canadian Business*, March 26, 2012, accessed January 21, 2013, http://www.canadianbusiness.com/blogs-and-comment/canadas-most-expensive-real-estate-markets/.

4. *North of 60* was a popular Canadian television show in the mid-1990s that depicted life in a predominantly Aboriginal town in the Northwest Territories. While the television show provided work for many Aboriginal actors, it was written and directed primarily by non-Aboriginal people and was critiqued by some for its emphasis on Aboriginal poverty and alcoholism.

5. The Aboriginal Media Lab is currently inactive but is still in existence. Loretta Todd has been busy with her work on *Tansi! Nehiyawetan: Let's Speak Cree!* for APTN and with preproduction on the feature film *Monkey Beach*. She has plans to have the Aboriginal Media Lab become more active at UBC in the future.

6. In many ways the creation of W2 Community Media Arts Society, a community media organization and production facility, is the embodiment of some Aboriginal filmmakers' dreams of a film institute, although W2 is not exclusively an Aboriginal media organization. It does collaborate extensively with Aboriginal filmmakers, artists, and activists, and in 2011–12 served as a home base for the Vancouver Indigenous

Media Arts Festival. W2 Media Café, where the majority of the VIMAF events were held, includes a state-of-the-art 10,000-square-foot facility that includes production space, screening venues, and café. For more information about W2 Community Media Arts Society visit their website: http://www.creativetechnology.org.

References

Abbott, Jennifer, ed. 2000. *Making Video "In": The Contested Ground of Alternative Video on the West Coast.* Vancouver: Hignell Printing.

Abbott, Lawrence. 1998. Interviews with Loretta Todd, Shelley Niro, and Patricia Deadman. *Canadian Journal of Native Studies* 18(2): 335–73.

Ablakela. 1999. CD-ROM of performance art piece by Dana Claxton. Vancouver: grunt gallery.

Abu-Lughod, Lila. 1991. "Writing Against Culture." In *Recapturing Anthropology: Working in the Present,* edited by Richard Fox, 137–62. Santa Fe: School for Advanced Research Press.

Aleiss, Angela. 2005. *Making the White Man's Indian: Native Americans and Hollywood Movies.* Santa Barbara CA: Praeger Press.

Alia, Valerie. 1999. *Un/Covering the North: News, Media, and Aboriginal People.* Vancouver: University of British Columbia Press.

———. 2010. *New Media Nation: Indigenous People and Global Communication.* New York: Berghahn Books.

Alstead, Robert. 2004. "Number One Fans." *Vancouver Courier,* December 13.

Anderson, Benedict. 1991. *Imagined Communities: Reflection on the Origins and Spread of Nationalism.* New York: New Left Books.

Appadurai, Arjun. 1991. "Global Ethnoscapes: Notes and Queries for a Transnational Anthropology." In *Recapturing Anthropology: Working in the Present,* edited by Richard Fox, 191–210. Santa Fe: School of American Research Press.

Armatage, Kay, Kass Banning, Brenda Longfellow, and Janine Marchessault, eds. 1999. *Gendering the Nation: Canadian Women's Cinema.* Toronto: University of Toronto Press.

Asch, Michael. 1984. *Home and Native Land: Aboriginal Rights and the Canadian Constitution.* Toronto: Methuen Press.

———, ed. 1997. *Aboriginal and Treaty Rights in Canada: Essays on Law, Equality and Respect for Difference.* Vancouver: University of British Columbia Press.

Auferheide, Patricia. 1995. "The Video in the Villages Project: Videomaking with and by Brazilian Indians." *Visual Anthropology Review* 11(2): 83–93.

Baltruschat, Doris. 2004. "Television and Canada's Aboriginal Communities." *Canadian Journal of Communications* 29(1): 47–59.

Basso, Keith. 1979. *Portraits of the "Whiteman": Linguistic Play and Cultural Symbols among the Western Apache.* Cambridge: Cambridge University Press.

Batty, Phillip. 1993. "Singing the Electric: Aboriginal Television in Australia." In *Channels of Resistance: Global Television and Local Empowerment,* edited by Tony Dowmunt, 106–25. London: British Film Institute.

Bear, Jeff. 2004. *At the Crossroads.* Prepared for Telefilm Canada, the Canadian Television Fund, the National Film Board of Canada, the Department of Canadian Heritage, and the Canadian Broadcasting Corporation.

Behar, Michael. 2008. "Analog Meets Its Match in Red Digital Cinema's Ultrahigh-Res Camera." *Wired Magazine* 16(9): 1–13.

Bell, Lynne. 2010. "Dana Claxton: From a Whisper to a Scream." *Canadian Art,* December, 102–7.

Benoit, Cecilia, and Dena Carroll. 2001. *Marginalized Voices from the Downtown Eastside: Aboriginal Women Speak about Their Health Experiences.* Prepared for the National Network on Environments and Women's Health, Centre of Excellence on Women's Health, York University. NNEWH Working Paper Series no. 12.

Berger, Sally. 1995. "Move Over Nanook." *Wide Angle* 17(1–4): 177–92.

Berkhofer, Robert. 1978. *The White Man's Indian: Images of the American Indian from Columbus to the Present.* New York: Alfred P. Knopf.

Bourdieu, Pierre. 1993. *The Field of Cultural Production.* New York: Columbia University Press.

Bredin, Marian. 2010. "APTN and Its Audiences." In *Indigenous Screen Cultures in Canada*, edited by Sigurjón Hafsteinsson and Marian Bredin, 69–87. Winnipeg: University of Manitoba Press.

Brooks, James, ed. 2002. *Confounding the Color Line: The Indian-Black Relations in North America*. Lincoln: University of Nebraska Press.

Burt, Larry. 1986. "Roots of the Native American Urban Experience: Relocation Policy in the 1950s." *American Indian Quarterly* 10(2): 85–99.

Cairns, Alan. 2000. *Citizens Plus: Aboriginal Peoples and the Canadian State*. Vancouver: University of British Columbia Press.

Campbell, Maria. 1973. *Halfbreed*. Toronto: McClelland and Stewart.

Cardinal, Harold. 1969. *The Unjust Society: The Tragedy of Canada's Indians*. Edmonton AB: New Press.

Carriere, Marcel. 1990. *Training at the National Film Board of Canada: Observations "50 Years of Filmmaking Experience,"* 5–9. NFB archives, Indian Film Crew box, Montreal.

Cattelino, Jessica. 2008. *High Stakes: Florida Seminole Gaming and Sovereignty*. Durham NC: Duke University Press.

Chaat Smith, Paul. 1994. "Land of a Thousand Dances." *Sundance Film Festival '94*: 48–52.

Chin, Elizabeth. 2001. *Purchasing Power: Black Kids and American Consumer Culture*. Minneapolis: University of Minnesota Press.

Claxton, Dana. 2005. "Re:wind." In *Transference, Tradition, Technology: Native New Media Exploring Visual and Digital Culture*, edited by Dana Claxton, Steven Loft, Melanie Townsend, and Candice Hopkins, 60–68. Banff AB: Walter Phillips Gallery Editions.

———. 2007. "Red Woman White Cube: First Nations Art and Racialized Space." Master's thesis, Simon Fraser University.

Claxton, Dana, Steven Loft, Melanie Townsend, and Candice Hopkins, eds. 2005. *Transference, Tradition, Technology: Native New Media Exploring Visual and Digital Culture*. Banff AB: Walter Phillips Gallery Editions.

Clifford, James. 1988. *The Predicament of Culture: Twentieth-Century Ethnography, Literature, and Art*. Cambridge MA: Harvard University Press.

———. 1997. "Diasporas." In *Routes: Travel and Translation in the Late 20th Century*, edited by James Clifford, 244–79. Cambridge MA: Harvard University Press.

Coates, Kenneth. 2000. *Marshall Decision and Native Rights: The Marshall Decision and Mi'kmaq Rights in the Maritimes*. Montreal: McGill-Queens University Press.

Coffey, Wallace, and Rebecca Tsosie. 2001. "Rethinking the Tribal Sovereignty Doctrine: Cultural Sovereignty and the Collective Future of Indian Nations." *Stanford Law and Policy Review* 12:191–221.

Cohen-Scherer, Joanna. 1979. "You Can't Believe Your Eyes: Inaccuracies in Photographs of North American Indians." Reprinted in *Exposure: The Journal of the Society for Photographic Education* 16(4). Originally published in *Studies in the Anthropology of Visual Communication* 2(2): 67–79, 1975.

Columpar, Corinn. 2010. *Unsettling Sights: The Fourth World on Film*. Carbondale: Southern Illinois Press.

Deloria, Philip. 1998. *Playing Indian*. New Haven CT: Yale University Press.

Deloria, Vine, Jr., and Clifford Lytle. 1984. *The Nations Within: The Past and Future of American Indian Sovereignty*. New York: Pantheon Books.

de Rosa, Maria. 1995. *The NFB's Studio One: Future Directions: An Evaluation Study for the National Film Board of Canada*. National Film Board of Canada archives. Montreal.

———. 2002. "Studio One: Of Storytellers and Stories." In *North of Everything: English-Canadian Cinema since 1980*, edited by William Beard and Jerry White, 328–42. Edmonton: University of Alberta Press.

Dinwoodie, David. 2002. *Reserve Memories: The Power of the Past in a Chilcotin Community*. Lincoln: University of Nebraska Press.

Dixon, Guy. 2012. "Budget Cuts? National Film Board Is Not Afraid." *Globe and Mail*, April 16.

Dorland, Michael, ed. 1996. *The Culture Industries in Canada*. Toronto: James Lorimer.

———. 1998. *So Close to the State/s: The Emergence of Canadian Feature Film Policy*. Toronto: University of Toronto Press.

Douglas, Stan, ed. 1991. *Vancouver Anthology: The Institutional Politics of Art: A Project of the Or Gallery*. Vancouver: Talonbooks.

Dowell, Kristin. 2006a. "Honoring Stories: Aboriginal Media, Art and Activism in Vancouver." PhD diss., New York University.

———. 2006b. "Indigenous Media Gone Global: Strengthening Indigenous Identity On- and Offscreen at the First Nations/First Features Film Showcase." *American Anthropologist* 108(2): 376–84.

Eckert, Penelope, and Sarah McConnell-Ginet. 1992. "Think Practically and Look Locally: Language and Gender as Community-Based Practice." *Annual Review of Anthropology* 21: 461–90.

Edwards, Elizabeth, ed. 1992. *Anthropology and Photography, 1860–1920*. New Haven CT: Yale University Press.

Evans, Gary. 1991. *In the National Interest: A Chronicle of the National Film Board of Canada, 1949–1989*. Toronto: University of Toronto Press.

Evans, Michael. 2008. *Isuma: Inuit Video Art*. Montreal: McGill-Queens University Press.

Feldman, Seth. 1996. "And Always Will Be: The Canadian Film Industry." In *Seeing Ourselves: Media Power and Policy in Canada*, edited by Helen Holmes, 99–115. Toronto: Harcourt Brace.

Fixico, Donald. 2000. *The Urban Indian Experience in America*. Albuquerque: University of New Mexico Press.

Fleming, Kathleen. 1996. "Igloolik Video: An Organic Response from a Culturally Sound Community." *Inuit Art Quarterly* 11(1): 26–34.

Flores, William, and Rina Benmayor, eds. 1997. *Latino Cultural Citizenship: Claiming Identity, Space, and Rights*. New York: Beacon Press.

Fournier, Suzanne, and Ernie Crey. 1998. *Stolen from Our Embrace: The Abduction of First Nations Children and the Restoration of Aboriginal Communities*. Vancouver: Roundhouse.

Friar, Natasha, and Ralph Friar. 1972. *The Only Good Indian: The Hollywood Gospel*. New York: Drama Book Specialists.

Gagnon, Monika Kin. 2000. "Worldviews in Collision: Dana Claxton's Video Installations." In *Other Conundrums: Race, Culture, and Canadian Art*, edited by Monika Kin Gagnon, 33–48. Vancouver: Arsenal Pulp Press.

Gasher, Mike. 2002. *Hollywood North: The Feature Film Industry in British Columbia*. Vancouver: University of British Columbia Press.

Gilley, Brian. 2006. *Becoming Two Spirit: Gay Identity and Social Acceptance in Indian Country*. Lincoln: University of Nebraska Press.

Gilroy, Paul. 1993. *The Black Atlantic: Modernity and Double Consciousness*. Cambridge MA: Harvard University Press.

Ginsburg, Faye. 1991. "Indigenous Media: Faustian Contract or Global Village?" *Cultural Anthropology* 6(1): 92–111.

———. 1993. "Aboriginal Media and the Australian Imaginary." *Public Culture* 5(3): 557–78.

———. 1994a. "Culture/Media: A (Mild) Polemic." *Anthropology Today* 10(2): 5–15.

———. 1994b. "Embedded Aesthetics: Creating a Discursive Space for Indigenous Media." *Cultural Anthropology* 9(3): 3565–82.

———. 1997. "'From Little Things Big Things Grow': Indigenous Media and Cultural Activism." In *Between Resistance and Revolution: Culture and Social Protest*, edited by Richard Fox and Orin Starn, 118–45. New Brunswick NJ: Rutgers University Press.

———. 1999. "The After-Life of Documentary: The Impact of *You Are on Indian Land*." *Wide Angle* 21(2): 60–70.

———. 2002. "Screen Memories: Resignifying the Traditional in Indigenous Media." In *Media Worlds: Anthropology on New Terrain*, edited by Faye Ginsburg, Lila Abu-Lughod, and Brian Larkin, 39–58. Berkeley: University of California Press.

———. 2003. "Atanarjuat Off-Screen: From "Media Reservations" to the World Stage." *American Anthropologist* 105(4): 827–31.

———. 2005. "Black Screens and Cultural Citizenship." *Visual Anthropology Review* 21(1/2): 80–97.

Ginsburg, Faye, and April Strickland. 2005. "The Latest in Reality TV?: Maori Television Stakes a Claim on the Worldstage." *Flow: A Critical Forum on Television and Media Culture*. July 22. Accessed June 18, 2012. http://flowtv.org/2005/07/maori-television-global-television-first-peoples-television/.

Ginsburg, Faye, and Fred Myers. 2006. "A History of Aboriginal Futures." *Critique of Anthropology* 26(1): 27–45.

Ginsburg, Faye, and Lorna Roth. 2002. "First Peoples Television." In *Television Studies*, edited by Toby Miller, 130–32. London: British Film Institute.

Ginsburg, Faye, Lila Abu-Lughod, and Brian Larkin, eds. 2002. *Media Worlds: Anthropology on New Terrain*. Berkeley: University of California Press.

Gittings, Christopher. 2002. *Canadian National Cinema*. London: Routledge Press.

Glick-Schiller, Nina, Christina Blanc, and Linda Basch, eds. 1993. *Nations Unbound: Transnational Projects, Postcolonial Predicaments, and Deterritorialized Nation-States*. New York: Taylor & Francis.

Government of Canada. 1996. *Report on the Royal Commission of Aboriginal Peoples*. Department of Indian and Northern Affairs Canada. Ottawa.

Green, Joyce. 2001. "Canaries in the Mines of Citizenship: Indian Women in Canada." *Canadian Journal of Political Science* 34(4): 715–38.

Griffiths, Alison. 2002. *Wondrous Difference: Cinema, Anthropology, and Turn-of-the-Century Visual Culture*. New York: Columbia University Press.

Gritton, Joy. 2000. *The Institute of American Indian Arts: Modernism and U.S. Policy*. Albuquerque: University of New Mexico Press.

Guillemin, Jean. 1973. *Urban Renegades: The Cultural Strategy of American Indians*. New York: Columbia University Press.

Gumperz, John. 1968. "The Speech Community." In *The International Encyclopedia of the Social Sciences*, vol. 9, edited by David L. Sills. New York: Macmillan Library Reference.

Hafsteinsson, Sigurjón, and Marian Bredin, eds. 2010. *Indigenous Screen Cultures in Canada*. Winnipeg: University of Manitoba Press.

Hall, Stuart. 1990. "Cultural Identity and Diaspora." In *Identity: Community, Culture, Difference*, edited by Jonathan Rutherford, 222–37. London: Lawrence and Wishart Press.

———. 1996. "New Ethnicities." In *Black British Cultural Studies: A Reader*, edited by Howard Baker, Manthia Diawara, and Ruth Lindeborg, 163–73. Chicago: University of Chicago Press.

Hénaut, Dorothy. 1970. "Editor's Response." *Challenge for Change Newsletter* 5: 2.

Hénaut, Dorothy, and Bonnie Klein. 1969. "In the Hands of Citizens: A Video Report". *Challenge for Change Newsletter* 4: 2–6.

Himpele, Jeffrey. 2004. "Packaging Indigenous Media: An Interview with Ivan Sanjines and Jesus Tapia." *American Anthropologist* 106(2): 354–63.

———. 2008. *Circuits of Culture: Media, Politics and Indigenous Identity in the Andes*. Minneapolis: University of Minnesota Press.

Holmes, Helen, ed. 1992. *Seeing Ourselves: Media Power and Policy in Canada*. Toronto: Harcourt Brace Jovanovich.

Hymes, Dell. 1962. "The Ethnography of Speaking." *Anthropology and Human Behavior*, 15–53. Washington DC: Anthropological Society of Washington.

Ifekwunigwe, Jayne. 1999. *Scattered Belongings: Cultural Paradoxes of "Race," Nation, and Gender.* London: Routledge Press.

Jacobs, Sue-Ellen, Wesley Thomas, and Sabine Lang, eds. 1997. *Two-Spirit People: Native American Identity, Sexuality and Spirituality.* Urbana: University of Illinois Press.

Johnson, Troy, Duane Champagne, and Joanne Nagel. 1999. "American Indian Activism and Transformation: Lessons from Alcatraz." In *Contemporary Native American Political Issues*, edited by Troy Johnson, 283–315. Walnut Creek CA: Altamira Press.

Joseph, Rhea. 1999. *Healing Ways: Aboriginal Health and Service Review.* Report for the Vancouver/Richmond Health Board.

Kalafatic, Carol. 1996. *Interview with Loretta Todd.* Center for Media, Culture, and History, New York University.

———. 1999. "Keepers of the Power: Story as Covenant in the Films of Loretta Todd, Shelley Niro, and Christine Welsh." In *Gendering the Nation: Canadian Women's Cinema*, edited by Kay Armatage, Kass Banning, Brenda Longfellow, and Janine Marchessault, 109–20. Toronto: University of Toronto Press.

Kilpatrick, Jacquelin. 1999. *Celluloid Indians: Native Americans and Film.* Lincoln: University of Nebraska Press.

Knopf, Kerstin. 2010. "Aboriginal Media on the Move: An Outside Perspective on APTN." In *Indigenous Screen Cultures of Canada*, edited by Sigurjón Hafsteinsson and Marian Bredin, 87–105. Winnipeg: University of Manitoba Press.

La Flamme, Michelle. 2003. "Unsettling the West: First Nations Films in British Columbia." In *Women Filmmakers: Refocusing*, edited by Jacqueline Levitin, Judith Plessis, and Valerie Raoul, 403–18. Vancouver: University of British Columbia Press.

Lave, Jean, and Etienne Wenger. 1991. *Situated Learning: Legitimate Peripheral Participation.* Cambridge: Cambridge University Press.

Lawrence, Bonita. 2004. *"Real" Indians and Others: Mixed-Blood Urban Native Peoples and Indigenous Nationhood.* Lincoln: University of Nebraska Press.

Leuthold, Steven. 1998. *Indigenous Aesthetics: Native American Art, Media, and Identity.* Austin: University of Texas Press.

Lewis, Randolph. 2003. "In Conversation: Canadian Filmmaker Alanis Obomsawin." *Brooklyn Rail*, June–July, 1–5.

———. 2006. *Alanis Obomsawin: The Vision of a Native Filmmaker.* Lincoln: University of Nebraska Press.

Lincoln, Kenneth. 1993. *Indi'n Humor: Bicultural Play in Native America.* Oxford: Oxford University Press.

Lippard, Lucy, ed. 1992. *Partial Recall: With Essays on Photographs of Native North Americans.* New York: New Press.

Lobo, Susan. 2003. "Urban Clan Mothers: Key Households in Cities." *American Indian Quarterly* 27(3&4): 505–23.

Lobo, Susan, and Kurt Peters, ed. 2001. *American Indians and the Urban Experience.* Walnut Creek CA: Altamira Press.

Loft, Steven. 2005. "Sovereignty, Subjectivity, and Social Action." In *Transference, Tradition, Technology: Native New Media Exploring Visual and Digital Culture,* edited by Dana Claxton, Steven Loft, Melanie Townsend, and Candice Hopkins. 60–68. Banff AB: Walter Phillips Gallery Editions.

Madden, Kate. 1992. "Video and Cultural Identity: The Inuit Broadcasting Corporation Experience." In *Mass Media Effects across Cultures,* edited by Felipe Korzenny, Stella Ting-Toomey, and Elizabeth Schiff, 130–49. Newbury Park CA: Sage.

Magder, Ted. 1993. *Canada's Hollywood: Feature Films and the Canadian State.* Toronto: University of Toronto Press.

Mahtani, Minelle. 2002. "Interrogating the Hyphen-Nation: Canadian Multicultural Policy and 'Mixed-Race' Identities." *Social Identities* 8(1): 67–90.

Mankiller, Wilma. 2002. Foreword to *Urban Voices: The Bay Area American Indian Community,* edited by Susan Lobo, Sharon Mitchell Bennett, Charlene Betsillie, Joyce Keoke, Geraldine Martinez Lira, and Marilyn LaPlante St. Germaine, xxv–xvii. Tucson: University of Arizona Press.

Martin, Lee-Ann, ed. 2005. *Making a Noise!: Aboriginal Perspectives on Art, Art History, Critical Writing, and Community.* Banff AB: Banff Centre for the Arts Press.

Masayesva, Victor. 1995. "The Emerging Native American Aesthetics in Film and Video." *Felix: A Journal of Media Arts and Communication* 2(1): 156–60.

McMaster, Gerald, and Lee-Ann Martin, eds. 1992. *Indigena: Contemporary Native Perspectives*. Vancouver: Douglas & McIntyre.

Menzies, Charles. 1994. "Stories from Home: First Nations, Land Claims, and Euro-Canadians." *American Ethnologist* 21(4): 776–91.

Minore, J. B., and M. E. Hill. 1990. "Native Language Broadcasting: An Experiment in Empowerment." *Canadian Journal of Native Studies* 10(1): 97–119.

Molnar, Helen, and Michael Meadows. 2001. *Songlines to Satellites—Indigenous Communication in Australia, South Pacific, and Canada*. Sydney: Pluto Press.

Morgan, Marcyliena. 1992. "Indirectness and Interpretation in African American Women's Discourse." *Pragmatics* 1: 421–50.

Morris, Peter. 1978. *Embattled Shadows: A History of Canadian Cinema, 1895–1939*. Montreal: McGill-Queen's University Press.

Morris, Rosalind. 1994. *New Worlds from Fragments: Film, Ethnography, and Representation on the Northwest Coast*. Boulder CO: Westview Press.

Murray, Catherine. 2002. *Silent on the Set: Cultural Diversity and Race in English Canadian TV Drama*. A Study Prepared for the Strategic and Research Analysis, Strategic Policy and Research, Department of Canadian Heritage. SRA-587. Hull QC.

Myers, Fred. 2002. *Painting Culture: The Making of an Aboriginal Fine Art*. Durham NC: Duke University Press.

Nagel, Joanne. 1997. *American Indian Ethnic Renewal: Red Power and the Resurgence of Identity and Culture*. Oxford: Oxford University Press.

Neizen, Ronald. 2000. *Spirit Wars: Native North American Religions in the Age of Nation Building*. Norman: University of Oklahoma Press.

Ong, Aihwa. 1996. "Cultural Citizenship as Subject Making: Immigrants Negotiate Racial and Cultural Boundaries in the United States." *Current Anthropology* 37(5): 737–62.

O'Pray, Michael. 2003. *Avant-Garde Film: Forms, Themes, and Passions*. London: Wallflower Press.

Parker, David, and Miri Song, eds. 2001. *Rethinking "Mixed Race."* London: Pluto Press.

Pechawis, Archer. 2000. "New Traditions: Post-Oka Aboriginal Performance Art in Vancouver." In *Live at the End of the Century: Aspects of Performance Art in Vancouver*, edited by Brice Canyon, 136–42. Vancouver: grunt gallery.

Pendakur, Manjunath. 1990. *Canadian Dreams and American Control: The Political Economy of the Canadian Film Industry*. Toronto: Garamond Press.

Peters, Evelyn. 1998. "Subversive Spaces: First Nations Women and the City." *Environment and Planning D: Society and Space* 16(6): 665–85.

Pick, Zuzana. 1999. "Storytelling and Resistance: The Documentary Practice of Alanis Obomsawin." In *Gendering the Nation: Canadian Women's Cinema*, edited by Kay Armatage, Kass Banning, Brenda Longfellow, and Janine Marchessault, 76–94. Toronto: University of Toronto Press.

Raboy, Marc. 1990. *Missed Opportunities: The Story of Canada's Broadcasting Policy*. Montreal: McGill-Queens University Press.

———. 1996. "Linguistic Duality in Broadcasting Policy: A Microcosm of Canada's Constitutional Policies." In *Seeing Ourselves: Media Power and Policy in Canada*, edited by Helen Holmes, 154–73. Toronto: Harcourt Brace.

Radz, Mark. 1998. "Hollywood North." *Montreal Gazette*, October 17, D3.

Raheja, Michelle. 2007. "Reading Nanook's Smile: Visual Sovereignty, Indigenous Revisions of Ethnography and *Atanarjuat* (The Fast Runner)." *American Quarterly* 59(4): 1159–85.

———. 2011. *Reservation Reelism: Redfacing, Visual Sovereignty, and Representations of Native Americans in Film*. Lincoln: University of Nebraska Press.

Ramirez, Renya. 2007. *Native Hubs: Culture, Community and Belonging in Silicon Valley and Beyond*. Durham NC: Duke University Press.

Reece, Cleo. 2004. "Festival Director's Welcome." *IMAGeNation Aboriginal Film and Video Festival Program*, 21–23.

Rickard, Jolene. 1995. "Sovereignty: A Line in the Sand." In *Strong Hearts: Native American Visions and Voices*, edited by Peggy Roalf, 51–61. New York: Aperture.

Robinson, Eden. 2000. *Monkey Beach*. Boston: Houghton Mifflin.

Rollins, Peter C., and John E. O'Connor, eds. 1998. *Hollywood's Indian: The Portrayal of the Native American in Film*. Lexington: University Press of Kentucky.

Root, Maria, ed. 1992. *Racially Mixed People in America*. Newbury Park CA: Sage.

Rosaldo, Renato. 1994. "Cultural Citizenship and Educational Democracy." *Cultural Anthropology* 9(3): 402–11.

Roscoe, Will. 1992. *The Zuni Man-Woman*. Albuquerque: University of New Mexico Press.

Roth, Christopher. 2002. "Without Treaty, Without Conquest: Indigenous Sovereignty in Post-Delgamuukw British Columbia." *Wicazo Sa Review* 17(2): 143–66.

Roth, Joshua. 2002. *Brokered Homeland: Japanese Brazilian Migrants in Japan*. Ithaca NY: Cornell University Press.

Roth, Lorna. 1996. "Northern Voices and Mediating Structures: First Peoples' Television Broadcasting North of 60." In *Seeing Ourselves: Media Power and Policy in Canada*, edited by Helen Holmes, 173–92. Toronto: Harcourt Brace.

———. 1998. "The Delicate Acts of 'Colour Balancing': Multiculturalism and Canadian Television Policies and Practices." *Canadian Journal of Communication* 23(4): 35–45.

———. 2005. *Something New in the Air: The Story of First Peoples Television Broadcasting in Canada*. Montreal: McGill-Queens University Press.

Ryan, Allan. 1999. *The Trickster Shift: Humour and Irony in Contemporary Native American Art*. Vancouver: University of British Columbia Press.

Rydell, Robert. 1984. *All the World's a Fair: Visions of Empire at American International Expositions, 1876–1916*. Chicago: University of Chicago Press.

Sadre-Orafai, Stephanie. 2008. "Developing Images: Race, Language, and Perception in Fashion-Model Casting." In *Fashion as Photograph: Viewing and Reviewing Images of Fashion*, edited by Eugenie Shinkle, 141–53. London: IB Tauris.

———. 2010. "Casting "Difference": Visual Anxiety and the New York Fashion Industry." PhD diss., New York University.

Sawchuck, Joe. 2001. "Negotiating an Identity: Metis Political Organizations, the Canadian Government, and Competing Concepts of Aboriginality." *American Indian Quarterly* 25(1): 73–92.

Scofield, Gregory A. 1999. *Thunder through My Veins: Memories of a Métis Childhood*. Toronto: HarperFlamingoCanada.

Silverman, Jason. 2002. "Uncommon Visions: The Films of Loretta Todd." In *North of Everything: English-Canadian Cinema since 1980*, edited by William Beard and Jerry White, 376–92. Edmonton: University of Alberta Press.

Simpson, Audra. 2000. "Paths toward a Mohawk Nation: Narratives of Citizenship and Nationhood in Kahnawake." In *Political Theory and the Rights of Indigenous Peoples,* edited by Duncan Ivison, Paul Patton, and Will Sanders, 113–37. Cambridge: Cambridge University Press.

———. 2007. "On Ethnographic Refusal: Indigeneity, 'Voice' and Colonial Citizenship." *Junctures: The Journal for Thematic Dialogue* 9 (December): 67–80.

———. 2008. "Subjects of Sovereignty: Indigeneity, the Revenue Rule and Juridics of Failed Consent." *Law and Contemporary Problems* 71: 191–215.

Singer, Beverly. 2001. *Wiping the War Paint off the Lens: Native American Film and Video.* Minneapolis: University of Minnesota Press.

Siu, Lok. 2005. *Memories of a Future Home: Diasporic Citizenship of Chinese in Panama.* Stanford: Stanford University Press.

Smith, Laurel. 2008. "The Search for Well-Being: Placing Development with Indigenous Identity." In *Global Indigenous Media: Culture, Poetics, and Politics,* edited by Pam Wilson and Michelle Stewart, 183–97. Durham NC: Duke University Press.

Spaner, David. 2003. *Dreaming in the Rain: How Vancouver Became Hollywood North by Northwest.* Vancouver: Arsenal Pulp Press.

Starblanket, Noel. 1968. "A Voice for Canadian Indians: An Indian Film Crew." *Challenge For Change Newsletter* 1(2): 11.

Stewart, Michelle. 2001. "Sovereign Visions: Native North American Documentary." PhD diss., University of Minnesota.

———. 2007. "The Indian Film Crews of Challenge for Change: Representation and the State." *Canadian Journal of Film Studies* 16(2): 49–81.

Sturm, Circe. 2002. *Blood Politics: Race, Culture and Identity in the Cherokee Nation of Oklahoma.* Berkeley: University of California Press.

Thompson, Becky, and Sangeeta Tyagi, eds. 1996. *Names We Call Home: Autobiography on Racial Identity.* New York: Routledge.

Todd, Kamala. 2011a. "Indigenous City: Getting to the Roots of Vancouver." Unpublished essay.

———. 2011b. "(Un)divided." Unpublished essay.

Todd, Loretta. 1992. "What More Do They Want?" In *Indigena: Contemporary Native Perspectives,* edited by Gerald McMaster and Lee-Ann Martin, 71–81. Vancouver: Douglas & McIntyre.

———. 2005. "Polemics, Philosophies, and a Story: Aboriginal Aesthetics and the Media of This Land." In *Transference, Tradition, Technology: Native New Media Exploring Visual and Digital Culture*, edited by Dana Claxton, Steven Loft, Candice Hopkins, and Melanie Townsend, 104–26. Banff AB: Walter Phillips Gallery Editions.

Torruellas, Rosa M., Rina Benmayor, Anneris Goris, and Ana Juarbe. 1991. *Affirming Cultural Citizenship in the Puerto Rican Community: Critical Literacy and the El Barrio Popular Education Program*. New York: Centro de Estudios Puertorriqueños, Hunter College.

Turner, Terence. 1992. "Defiant Images: The Kayapo Appropriation of Video." *Anthropology Today* 8(6): 5–16.

Union of BC Indian Chiefs. 2011. "Our History." Accessed June 18, 2012. http://www.ubcic.bc.ca/about/history.htm.

Vail, Pegi. 1997. "Producing America: The Native American Producer's Alliance." Master's thesis. New York University.

Valaskakis, Gail. 1992. "Communication, Culture, and Technology: Satellites and Northern Native Broadcasting in Canada." In *Ethnic Minority Media: An International Perspective*, edited by Stephen Riggins, 63–82. Newbury Park CA: Sage.

Verrone, William. 2011. *Avant-Garde Feature Film: A Critical History*. Jefferson NC: McFarland.

Vizenor, Gerald. 1987. "Crows Written on the Poplars." In *I Tell You Now: Autobiographical Essays by Native American Writers*, edited by Brian Swann and Arnold Krupat, 99–110. Lincoln: University of Nebraska Press.

———. 1994. *Manifest Manners: Narratives on Postindian Survivance*. Lincoln: University of Nebraska Press.

Warrior, Robert. 1994. *Tribal Secrets: Recovering American Indian Intellectual Traditions*. Minneapolis: University of Minnesota Press.

Waugh, Thomas, Michael Baker, and Ezra Winton, eds. 2010. *Challenge for Change: Activist Documentary at the National Film Board of Canada*. Montreal: McGill-Queen's University Press.

Weatherford, Elizabeth. 1996. "Native Media-Making: A Growing Potential." *Native Americas: Akwe:kon's Journal of Indigenous Issues* 13(1): 56–59.

Wilson, Pamela, and Michelle Stewart, eds. 2008. *Global Indigenous Media: Cultures, Poetics, and Politics*. Durham NC: Duke University Press.

Wortham, Erica Cusi. 2013. *Indigenous Media in Mexico: Culture, Community, and the State*. Durham NC: Duke University Press.

York, Geoffrey. 1989. *The Dispossessed: Life and Death in Native Canada*. Toronto: Lester & Orpen Dennys.

Zentella, Ana Celia. 1997. *Growing Up Bilingual: Puerto Rican Children in New York*. Malden MA: Blackwell.

Index

Ablakela (Claxton), 143

Aboriginal, definition of, 201n1

Aboriginal aesthetics, 2, 4, 94, 143, 146–47, 148, 164

Aboriginal Film and Video Makers Symposium, 61

Aboriginal film institute: need for, 177, 178–79, 182, 234n6

Aboriginal Filmmaking Program, 56, 64–65, 220n32, 220n33

Aboriginal media: access to, 88–89, 131; Canadian state support for, xii–xiii, 55–75, 76–105; community support for, 13, 45–46, 209n8; diversity of, 138; experimental, 135, 136–44, 150, 154–57, 178, 225n18, 227n12, 229n1; funding, 67–68, 217n17, 219–20n30, 220n32, 221n35; ghettoization of, 91–92; infrastructure for, 86, 87, 182; mainstream media and, 38, 79, 80–84, 85–86, 92, 178, 180; non-Native producers and, 56, 63, 74, 81–83, 230n2; screening venues for, 27, 46–47, 86, 91, 140; as "struggle"-focused, 177, 179–80

Aboriginal Media Lab, 182, 234n5

Aboriginal peoples: Canadian government and, 6, 39–40, 68–69, 70, 73, 107–8, 181, 204n2, 225n1; diversity of, 77–78, 80, 94, 145–47; domination of, 144; intermarriage with Chinese, 208n16; media exclusion of, 68; migration to cities by, 7–8; political status of, 71; rights of, 10, 61, 70–71, 86, 184, 204–5n3, 230n5. *See also* urban Aboriginal

Aboriginal Peoples Survey, 205n5, 206n7

Chief Simon Baker Room, 212n18
childcare, 47, 123
Children of the Rainbow (Aucoin), 101–3
Child Welfare Department, 226n10
Chin, Elizabeth, 228n14
Chrétien, Jean, 10
Christian, Dorothy, 45, 78, 82, 92, 131, 146–47, 176, 178–79
"cinema of sovereignty," 72
CitizenShift, 216n15
citizenship, overlapping, 70, 83, 104
"citizens plus," 70
Claxton, Dana, xvii, 11, 19, 27, 34, 47, 66, 86–87, 119, 120, 139, 140–44, 146, 151–52, 156, 176, 178, 182, 208n5
Claxton, Dana, works: *Ablakela*, 143; *Buffalo Bone China*, 221n36, 229n4; *Her Sugar Is?*, 229n4; *The Hill*, 229n4; *I Want to Know Why*, 130–31, 141–43, 221n36, 229n4; *The People Dance*, 229n4; *Rattle*, 143; *The Red Paper*, 229n4; *Tree of Consumption*, 229n4; *Waterspeak*, 143
Clearsky, Curtis, 134
Club Native (Deer), 225n1
Coast Salish people, 6, 8, 9, 14, 16, 145
Coffey, Wallace, 71–72
Cohn, Norman, 56
collaboration, 44–45, 122
colonialism, 12, 19–20, 40, 70, 84, 101, 141, 213n1; cultural, 50–51, 63; as destructive of community, 41, 97–98, 99, 107–8,

110–11, 115, 118, 132, 141–43; embedded in film genre, 143–44; in science fiction, 166, 167, 170
Columbus, Christopher, 219n26
comedy, 179, 180
coming out, 102
communication policy, 57, 75
communication rights, 86
communities of color, 12
community, 37–42; boundaries of, 38–40; defined, 36, 210–11n12; divisions within, 40; responsibility to, 38, 41–42, 87, 123, 124–25, 137, 152
community building, 22, 33–35, 41, 46–47; landlessness and, 35; in Vancouver, 25–26. *See also* "hub"; social ties
"community of practice," 40
community organizing, 26, 177
Company of Young Canadians (CYC), 58, 217n17
Connected by Innate Rhythm, 227n12
Constitution Act (1982), 70–71
Contact, 89, 222n36, 223n9
copyright ownership, 50, 63, 126
Coyes, Gregory: *No Turning Back*, 219n29; *Stories from the Seventh Fire*, 221n36
Cranmer, Barb, 38, 78, 89, 90, 122, 127, 219n29
Cranmer, Barb, works: *Gwishalaayt: The Spirit Wraps around You*, 221n36; *Laxwesa Wa: The Strength of the River*, 219n29; *T'Lina: The Rendering of Wealth*, 221n36
Cree language, 157, 158–64

Hagerüd, Dusty: *My Life in the Gay Mafia*, 103

Haig-Brown, Helen, 14, 122, 125, 154–55, 156, 157–58, 171–72, 175, 230n1, 230–31n2, 232n6

Haig-Brown, Helen, works: *The Cave*, 3, 154, 157, 164–71, 173, 230n2, 231n4, 232–33n9, 232n7; *Legacy*, 171

Hall, Stuart, 4

Hands of History (L. Todd), 148, 149

Harjo, Joy, 79

Harper, Stephen, 65, 110–11, 216n16

Harris, Ron, 184

healing, 143, 179, 180; as a journey, 228n15; from residential schools, 110, 114–15, 225n3

"Healing Hands: Voices of Resistance," 27

"healing industry," 225n3

Helpless Maiden Makes an "I" Statement (T. Cuthand), 225n18

Hénaut, Dorothy, 56, 57–58

Her Sugar Is? (Claxton), 229n4

High Stakes (Cattelino), 72

The Hill (Claxton), 229n4

Hollywood, 54, 55, 85, 205n4, 214n5

"Hollywood Indian," 79, 95, 205n4, 222n1

homophobia, 101

Honey Moccasin (Niro), 27, 221n36

honor songs, 145, 149

Hopkins, Zoe, 44, 89, 93, 176, 177, 227n13, 232n6

Hopkins, Zoe, works: *Prayer for a Good Day*, 129–30; *Tsi tkahéhtayen (The Garden)*, 130

How the Fiddle Flows, 220n33

"hub," 35–36, 37, 132; IMAG as, 42, 47

humor, Aboriginal, 179, 180

Hungry Wolf, Beverly, 135

hybrid identities, 211–12n15

iconography, tribal, 145, 146

identity, Aboriginal, 17, 38–40, 99–100, 107, 116, 159, 202n7, 203n8; Canadian legislation of, 39–40, 107–8, 181, 204n2, 225n1; community and, 47; family silence and, 95, 118, 224n12; and "going home" narrative, 130–31; strengthening, 116, 117–18, 122, 132. *See also* land; languages, Aboriginal

identity, Canadian, 52, 53

identity politics, 203n8

Igloolik Isuma Productions, 56, 67, 68, 70, 93, 169, 209n8

"image nation," xi–xii

IMAGeNation Aboriginal Film and Video Festival, xi, xiv, xv, xvii, 13, 23, 27, 39, 44–47, 103–4, 131, 183, 229n1

ImagineNATIVE Film and Media Arts Festival, 130, 131, 132, 143, 164, 171, 212n19, 232n6

"in a good way," 230n1

Incident at Restigouche (Obomsawin), 221n36

Indian Act, 7, 109, 115, 204n2

Indian Film Crew (IFC), 57, 58–61, 217n17, 217n18, 218n21; goals of, 59

Indian Film Training Program, 59, 218n21

aspects of, 228n14; performance art embedded in, 140; represented in media, 46. *See also* cultural protocol

Société Nouvelle, 216n13

soldiers, Aboriginal, 148

Solomon, Henry, 170

"southern," 223n7

sovereignty: Canadian cultural, 51, 54, 57, 69, 70, 75; cultural, 4, 71–74, 168; as interdependence, 73; political, 1–2, 70, 204n3. *See also* visual sovereignty

Spahan, Rose, 120

Sparrow case (1990), 71

Spirit Song Native Theatre School, 11

spirituality, Aboriginal, 204n2

Spirit World, 165, 167–68, 170, 232n7

split screen, 14, 15, 141, 142, 150, 151, 156, 161, 162, 163

Spudwrench: Kahnawake Man (Obomsawin), 219n25

Squamish relationship to land, 15–16

Stanley Park, 9

Starblanket, Noel, 217n17, 218n21

status, 39–40, 108, 115, 201n1, 204n2

stereotypes of Aboriginals, 78, 79, 95, 205n4

Stewart, Michelle, 4

Stolen Spirits, 225n4

Stoney, George, 56, 58; *You Are on Indian Land*, 60

Stories from the Seventh Fire (Coyes), 221n36

"Storykeepers," 125–26

Storyscapes (K. Todd), 9

Storytellers in Motion, 27, 97

storytelling, xiii, 2, 26, 56, 149; culturally specific, 145–47, 167; indigenous, 69, 81–83

structural inequality, 61

Studio D, 53, 213–14n4

Studio One, 61–64, 219n26, 219n29; as "virtual studio," 64, 220n31

Suckerfish (Jackson), 96–100, 110, 131

"Sunbox" (Aucoin), 102

Sundance Film Festival, 55

Swan, Daniel, 203n9

Tansi! Nehiyawetan: Let's Speak Cree! (K. and L. Todd), 120, 151, 222n36, 234n5

tar sands oil fields, 129

technology, 168, 201–2n3, 202n5, 232n8

Telefilm Canada, 65, 67, 214n6

television, 65

Termination and Relocation policies, 207n11

terra nullius, myth of, 8

text-on-screen, 14, 15, 18, 231n3

The Things I Cannot Change, 215n12

13 Minutes (Jones), 103

Thorn Grass, 103

Tkaronto (Belcourt), 224n12, 224n15

T'Lina: The Rendering of Wealth (Cranmer), 221n36

tobacco, 145

Today Is a Good Day (L. Todd), 148

Todd, Kamala, 5–6, 8–10, 81–82, 91, 92, 119, 120, 126, 176